THE
COMPLETE
IDIOT'S
GUIDE® TO

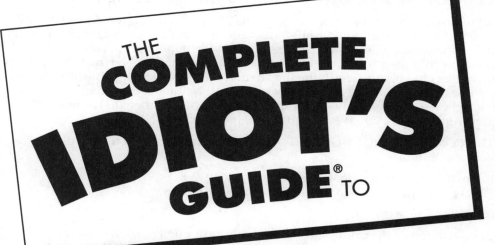

Retiring Early

by Dee Lee and Jim Flewelling

ALPHA
A Pearson Education Company

International Standard Book Number: 0-02-864012-8
Library of Congress Catalog Card Number: 2001091096

03   02   8   7   6   5   4   3

Interpretation of the printing code: The rightmost number of the first series of numbers is the year of the book's printing; the rightmost number of the second series of numbers is the number of the book's printing. For example, a printing code of 01-1 shows that the first printing occurred in 2001.

Printed in the United States of America

Note: This publication contains the opinions and ideas of its authors. It is intended to provide helpful and informative material on the subject matter covered. It is sold with the understanding that the authors and publisher are not engaged in rendering professional services in the book. If the reader requires personal assistance or advice, a competent professional should be consulted.

Publisher
Marie Butler-Knight

Product Manager
Phil Kitchel

Managing Editor
Jennifer Chisholm

Acquisitions Editor
Mike Sanders

Development Editor
Michael Thomas

Production Editor
Billy Fields

Copy Editor
Krista Hansing

Illustrator
Jody Schaeffer

Cover Designers
Mike Freeland
Kevin Spear

Book Designers
Scott Cook and Amy Adams of DesignLab

Indexer
Angie Bess

Layout/Proofreading
Angela Calvert
Mary Hunt
Daryl Kessler

Contents at a Glance

Contents

xi

Foreword

When I started at Morningstar in 1986, I had a pretty conventional view of the investing markets. The goal was to win—to get a higher return than the next person by knowing more, working harder, and acting faster. It was all part of the big game of finance being played out on many levels. Portfolio managers battle intensely to generate a higher return than their peers, analysts race for the latest quarterly earnings insight, and individuals choose which stocks or funds they think will generate the highest return. So long as you select the best investments, you're sure to win, right?

I thought that I was on the path to becoming a pretty sophisticated investor. Then I attended my first conference of Certified Financial Planners. Sure, these planners cared about identifying the best stocks and funds, but they also cared about a host of other issues. They spent 14-hour days discussing ways to help their clients define goals, understand risk, avoid taxes, plan for their estates, and maximize charitable contributions. To them, investing was much more than finding good stocks or funds. It was matching the right investment to the right investor for the right reasons.

I soon realized that these independent planners were carrying on a conversation that was infinitely more sophisticated than that of the personal finance magazines or investment best sellers of the time. While the rest of Wall Street was speaking in sound bites, these planners were talking in fully formed paragraphs. Moreover, they were reaching out to academia, to the best fund managers, to anyone who could help them in their quest to learn more and to better serve their clients. They were elevating the investment debate, and I wanted to be a part of the discussion.

In time, I became a regular on the financial planning conference circuit. I got to know professionals like Dee Lee and the other top planners who were leading this debate. I listened to them and looked for ways that Morningstar could contribute to their cause. We developed a host of new tools like the Morningstar style box that responded to the challenges these advisors faced in constructing portfolios. We took up the fight for better disclosure of the names of portfolio managers and the holdings within fund portfolios. As these advisors told us, it wasn't enough to know that a fund had done well; if you wanted to use a fund intelligently in a portfolio it was essential to know who won the record and what strategies they followed to do so.

What motivated these planners was to do what was right for their clients. While much of Wall Street continued to be dragged down by rampant conflicts of interest, these advisors had a remarkable clarity of purpose. They had flipped Wall Street's power structure. Rather than seeing themselves as employees of a big financial carrier whose job it was to maximize sales for the mother company, these advisors had broken from the pack (philosophically and in many cases physically) and saw their role as a fiduciary one to their client. They listened to their clients and they passed on their clients' concerns to us. We took those concerns and looked for ways to gather new data or reposition existing information to address them. It's been a wonderful partnership so far. These great planners have made us a better company, and we've given them tools that help them to better do their jobs.

Now the game has come full circle. These independent, renegade planners, the ones with the nerve to break from the traditional brokerage model and to put the needs of the client ahead of the desires of the carrier, have become the models for how to serve clients. Rather than fight against the get-rich-quick advice of the best seller list, these advisors are now writing the top investment books. And they've brought not only their conviction for serving the individual investor, but also all of their collective wisdom with them. You'll see that Dee Lee's advice is not only uncompromising in its philosophical commitment to helping the investor succeed, it's also peppered with practical tips and insights that only someone who's been in the trenches would know.

This book treats investing as a means to an end. It's not about easy answers; it's about the best path to smart answers. It's about defining what you want out of life and enlisting your money as an ally in that quest. There's nothing formulaic here. No two readers will come with the same goals or leave with the same answers. But all readers will have learned how to outline the problem, focus on the right issues, and ask intelligent questions. There's much to master: stocks, funds, insurance, and pensions. But when you've framed the questions correctly, as Dee Lee has done, you'll find that even a money idiot can take control of their finances and by extension their lives. As Dee says, it's about having options. You have more than you think, and this book shows you how to choose the path that's right for you.

Don Phillips
Managing Director
Morningstar, Inc.

Introduction

Will this great book tell you everything you need to know to retire early? In a way, yes. We'll tell you what you need to know, to do, to learn, and to practice, and how to get started. It's up to you to learn it, do it, and practice it until you know what you need to know. We'll give you lots of information and a few pearls of wisdom we've discovered. The rest is up to you.

As a practicing financial educator and certified financial planner, Dee is having too much fun to retire yet. Jim's having too much fun after retiring in 1995, at the age of 45, to want to work. He even thinks that writing a book is fun, not work! But both of us continually seek more knowledge about financial management and investing. Adding the knowledge shared by others to our own hard-won knowledge is an on-going quest that you can share, too.

Your desire to retire early is really a yearning for financial freedom. When you reach that point, you can decide to retire, to change careers, to devote more time to your hobbies, to volunteer in your community, or to keep working. Whatever you do, it will be because you choose to do it, not because you feel that you *have* to do it for the money.

Your decision to follow the path to financial freedom that we outline in this book will bring you personal knowledge on all the subjects that we present. True knowledge arises when information and experience interact in a human mind. It's a process of learning by doing. We're happy to assist by drawing a map of the path and putting up signs. The rest of the fun is yours.

What This Book Is About

The Complete Idiot's Guide to Retiring Early is designed to help you think about what you really want to do with your life. Retirement is not simply a matter of dollars and cents. We prefer to say that it's about dollars and *sense*. And the sense part really comes first.

Part 1, "Retirement": Our concept of retirement is the financial freedom to pursue what you really want to do in life. Retirement as we know it is a recent phenomenon, only about 50 years old. And it's past time to retire that definition of "work until age 62 or 65, get the gold watch, and settle into the rocker for a few remaining years." That didn't last very long. Americans are already busily reinventing retirement, and you will become part of that process. These chapters will put ideas in your head about how you can invent your own retirement. And we'll show you what you're up against when you do decide to retire early. You need to think it through all the way.

Part 2, "Planning the Path to Wealth": Early retirement isn't going to happen just because you want it to. You need a well-thought-out plan to follow. That means finding out exactly where you are today so that you know where your plan starts. Then you create your own map to follow, one that allows you to reach your financial goals. We provide the step-by-step process and all the necessary forms to generate your plan. Yep, there are numbers and arithmetic, but if you can balance a checkbook, you can do this. A $5 calculator will get you through this easily.

Part 3, "Investing for Your Retirement": Successful investing isn't about buying great stocks or hot mutual funds. It's really a way of thinking about and acting with your money. This doesn't come naturally to most people, but it can be learned. True knowledge comes from experience, including learning from the mistakes that you make. This knowledge will give you the confidence to become a successful long-term investor.

Part 4, "A Safari on Wall Street": Stocks, mutual funds, and bonds (and the markets that they all trade in) are confusing. We try to boil it down to what you really need to understand about what they are and how you can use them. The markets can look pretty wild and scary at times. That's because they are—at least, in the short term. But for you, a very long-term investor, there are much greater risks in *not* being in the market.

Part 5, "Tools You Should Use": Over the course of your working life, you'll have one or more opportunities to use a tax-sheltered retirement plan. These plans are crucial to your early retirement because you'll hopefully have a long, long retirement. Tax-deferred compounding can make that retirement financially comfortable to the very end, if you use it properly. Social Security and Medicare are, at least for those who retire early, just some icing on the cake that you bake yourself from the recipe in this book. But you're not finished with your plan when you reach financial freedom. Your plan continues for many years. Long before then, you need to protect your wealth with a will and an estate plan so that your money will continue working for your family after you die.

Appendix A, "Financial Worksheets," contains forms you will use to help you estimate your retirement costs and achieve your retirement goals.

In Appendix B, "Glossary," you'll find a helpful glossary of terms used in all the areas covered in the book. You'll use this as a handy reference along your journey.

Appendix C, "Web Sites," has a list of Web sites, organized by subject. You'll add your favorites to the list, too. Use these sites to explore and learn more about the topics that interest you. Your journey goes on.

Extras

Stay alert to helpful sidebars generously allocated throughout the pages of this book to help you along your path to early retirement. Here's what they look like:

From the Hammock

We're really not resting, and to prove it, these sidebars contain some special insights that we've gained on early retirement.

Potholes

Money, finance, and life in general have plenty of "gotchas" that we'll expose for you before they get you.

It's Been Said

Here you'll find quips and quotes on money, life, and investing that remind us that everyone treads this path for better or worse.

Say What?

The language of finance and investing can be enough to turn people off without the clear, useful explanations that you'll find in these boxes.

A Nugget of Gold

Bet you didn't know this: Everything is easier to understand when you have the advantage of the knowledge learned by others to guide you.

Acknowledgments

We certainly didn't invent all the information we present in this book; this is our expression of how it all washed through us and what we've filtered out through our experience over many years. So we're extremely grateful for the efforts of thousands of other writers who shared their experience in books and articles just as we have done. A financially successful life doesn't happen by accident for most of us, so it's an ongoing process of education to which we and others are happy to contribute small pieces.

A successful book owes much to the efforts of the editors who guide, question, correct, and occasionally rein in the authors. We are grateful to our editors at Alpha Books for their efforts to make this a better book. Our thanks to Michael Sanders, our acquisitions editor, for giving us the opportunity and his encouragement; to Michael Thomas, our development editor, for his precise guidance and editing; and to Krista Hansing, our copy editor, who cleaned up the presentation and expression of our thoughts.

Trademarks

All terms mentioned in this book that are known to be or are suspected of being trademarks or service marks have been appropriately capitalized. Alpha Books and Pearson Education, Inc., cannot attest to the accuracy of this information. Use of a term in this book should not be regarded as affecting the validity of any trademark or service mark.

Part 1

Retirement

The day you get your first paycheck, your employer deducts a Social Security and Medicare tax and sends that money to the federal government. Like it or not, a plan for your retirement is in place from that day forward.

If you want to retire early, you need to take control of your retirement plan as soon as possible. We'll show you how to get started on the road to financial freedom. It isn't going to happen by itself; you have to make it happen.

If you retire early, you may have as much as half your life ahead of you after you retire. Therefore, you need to spend time thinking and planning what you want to do, as well as how you're going to pay for it. Retirement can include work as well as play. It's your life, and we think that you should plan to do whatever you want to do when you're financially free.

Chapter 1

It's About Having Options

> **In This Chapter**
>
> ➤ How to think about retirement
>
> ➤ What you need to consider
>
> ➤ How to plan a creative retirement
>
> ➤ Why retirement keeps changing

What does retiring early mean to you? A month of Sundays stretched out as far as you can see? A life of fun, excitement, and travel to new places? Living a quiet life by the shore or in the mountains? Time to follow your muse wherever it may lead? All these and more are possible for you in retirement. Doing them sooner rather than later sure sounds attractive, doesn't it?

Whatever your dream is, if it no longer involves hitting the alarm clock and showing up for work day after day, it's retirement. What most of these dreams have in common is financial freedom. You're no longer driven by a paycheck because you can afford to do what you really want.

Successful early retirement isn't really a single goal, a point in time that you strive for. It's a way of living, of being, over a long time. It doesn't begin the day you retire. It begins right now.

Retirement, whether early or late, is a process of establishing a series of goals and objectives stretching years into your future, and then continuously working to reach

each of them. It's the plan of your life, and life is not just a financial plan. Life is a spiritual journey. If you think you want to enjoy the fruits of early retirement along your journey, the only thing stopping you is you. Let's begin the journey.

Why Retire?

Some people out there really like their jobs and careers. They get great satisfaction from what they do, and they can't imagine not doing it—retirement would be a penalty. In the previous generation, people like these were hustled out the door with a gold watch and spent the rest of their lives complaining about it. So we have laws now that enable them to work beyond age 65 or 70. This book is not for them. This book is for the rest of you.

If retirement means not working at all, who would want to retire? Practically no one does, if you believe several recent studies. A February 1999 study by the American Association of Retired Persons (AARP) found that 8 out of 10 baby boomers (you're one if you were born from 1946 through 1963) are planning to work at least part time during their retirement. Only 16 percent said they wouldn't work at some kind of job in retirement. I guess that means more retirement for the rest of us!

A Working Retirement

We'll bet that most of the two thirds of baby boomers who don't plan to fully retire have something else in mind. They hope to retire from the 40-hour (or 50- or 60-hour) weeks, year-'round/different-day/same-stuff jobs and work more creatively. They might do something like this:

➤ Work part-time for a previous employer or a new one

➤ Start a whole new career

➤ Go back to school for something they wished they'd done in the beginning

➤ Start a new business

These are all great ideas, and we're sure you can come up with your own. That's how this book and many others got written.

If you discover something you think you might want to do, look into it well before you're ready to jump into it in your retirement. It may not even pay what you're making now, and it may cost you money to get more education. But at 50 or 60, you'll be ready to make the move if you planned well. The name of this game is to get more satisfaction from your work later in life. The paycheck may be just a bonus.

Another study reports that a lot of people will need to work part-time in retirement to make ends meet. This book is designed to give you our best advice on making your ends meet in retirement, but it's just not going to happen for a lot of folks for a variety of reasons (including those who didn't read this book).

A Lot of Living Left

You're likely to have many years of living to go, no matter when you retire. Today, at age 65, healthy men can expect another 18 years or so (half will live longer); women can expect to live another 22 years. And the longer you live, the longer you can *expect* to live. Even a 90-year-old can still buy green bananas because life expectancy is then 95 according to the IRS life expectancy table for those who make it to age 90.

If your genes are inclined toward longevity and you're healthy, life goes on. Identify and track your standard issue of four grandparents if you can. See how long they live(d). Odds are, you'll beat them.

The Livin' May be Easy, But It's Not Cheap

You'll have to support yourself for all those years in retirement, and that will take money and good planning. Financial planners today advise married clients approaching retirement to plan on at least one of them living to age 90 or longer. For younger clients, age 95 is safer. That way, the worst that can happen (assuming that your plan works reasonably well) is that you die before the money runs out. It's not pretty the other way around.

Income from part-time work in retirement for several years may make a big difference in how comfortable your retirement will be. Add the satisfaction gained from your efforts and the companionship of co-workers, and it doesn't sound so bad.

> **From the Hammock**
>
> Another big advantage to working part-time in early retirement is that it helps get you accustomed to having time on your hands. A phased-in retirement after working full-time for 40 or more years allows for a mental decompression period. This can make a big difference in creating a satisfying retirement.

Early Retirement

So we've already muddied the waters on the question of retirement. Retirement no longer means "not working." What does *early* retirement mean?

Yep, let's look at another recent study. This one tells us that 76 percent of baby boomers and 81 percent of Gen Xers (you're a Gen Xer if you were born from 1964 through 1981) have a strong interest in retiring before age 60. Of the Gen Xers, more than half hope to retire before age 50!

This report also explains that early retirement doesn't necessarily mean "not working," either:

➤ 42 percent want to work part-time in a field they enjoy.

➤ 11 percent want to volunteer somewhere on a regular basis.

➤ 19 percent plan to start a business.

➤ 10 percent will work part-time for the money.

A Nugget of Gold

There's a historical precedent for early retirement. In many Eastern cultures, a man who had fulfilled his duties to his family—parents, wife, and children—and to his community left his village to embark on a new life of contemplation and study under the sages. He was free to become a seeker of wisdom in his later years.

Potholes

Thirty-six percent of current retirees retired earlier than planned to health problems or workplace changes, according to the *2000 Retirement Confidence Survey* (www.ebri.org/rcs). Despite a variety of federal and state anti-discrimination laws, older workers and those disabled in some way often find it difficult to become re-employed.

Let's see, that only leaves about 18 percent who plan to retire to a life of leisure at an early age. But 72 percent will have a creative retirement doing whatever they choose to do—because they want to do it, not because they have to.

What's "Early," Anyway?

Government reports (there we go again with the reports) show that the trend toward earlier retirement peaked in 1990 at an average age of 58. Since then, the age has begun to creep higher. If we take 58 as the average age, then 55 and earlier could be defined as early retirement. But you pick your own target. Pick 60, if you want, or 45. It's your target and your goal, and that's the key. You select your goal, and then you can make a plan to reach it.

Once you have a defined target, you can ask the right questions and seek the answers that apply to you. There's no one way to plan on retiring early. For you, there's only your way. We'll help show you what questions you need to ask and how to find your answers.

Make It Your Choice

Whether you stop working at 45 or 75, make it *your* decision. Sure, sometimes life has other options that we have to follow because of illness, disability, and so on. But barring those events, you want to take control as much as possible when it comes to this decision.

We all have hopes and dreams for the future. But look back 10 or 20 years. Did you see yourself where you are now back then? Probably not. Life happens. When you plan and prepare to give yourself choices down the road, you have some say about your future. There's no guarantee, but it's better to have choices than not to. That's what planning is really all about.

Perhaps you love what you're doing today and really can't imagine retiring early or at all. So plan anyway. At 55, you might feel differently about working.

Because you gave yourself the ability to choose, you don't have to wait another 10 years to retire. Just go ahead and do it.

But It Ain't Necessarily So

The reality that will slowly but surely descend on tens of millions of baby boomers and Gen Xers is that it's not going to work out quite the way they hope. Only a small fraction of the 120 million or so baby boomers and Gen Xers will get to 50 or 55 with a real choice. Even saving enough to fund an early retirement that includes part-time employment will be a rough road for many. And deep down, most people have a healthy fear that they won't have enough money saved up to allow them to have a comfortable retirement.

We'll be running the numbers with you later in this book, but early retirement is going to be a major challenge. *Any* retirement is going to be a challenge for many people. But it can be done, and it *will* be done by many. There's no reason you can't do it if you really want to. But it's not going to happen by itself. We'll show you how to get started. It's up to you.

What Would You Do?

Thirty-five to forty years in retirement is a *long* time. When you stop working in midlife, you need a full plate of engaging activities that you want to spend hours, days, and years enjoying. You'll probably have to go back to fill your plate with seconds after a number of years as your interests change.

A successful, happy retirement at any age must include activities that provide you with a sense of purpose. A totally hedonistic lifestyle of self-gratification will not be fun for long. Preoccupation with yourself is a rough ride.

You keep alive with zest and enthusiasm for life when you have a productive purpose. Do you have an absorbing hobby or two? Get at least one before you retire:

From the Hammock

When Jim and his wife were about 30, she was miserable in her job and Jim was happy with his. So they made a plan that would give them the choice to work or to retire after age 40. By then, Jim was ready to stop working, and he did at age 45. His wife still works three days a week, by choice.

Potholes

Here are some of the realities that you may face as you approach your planned early retirement date:

➤ Your plan may not be realistic.

➤ You may have to work a few years longer.

➤ You still may have to work part-time.

➤ Your expenses in retirement may be higher than you think.

➤ You may have 30 to 50 years ahead of you when you retire early.

➤ Take up a creative art—painting, sculpting, or playing a musical instrument.

➤ Write the Great American Novel.

➤ Sign up for classes at your local high school or college.

➤ Get a degree in Egyptian hieroglyphics just for the fun of it.

➤ Volunteer in your community—you'll find lots of opportunities.

Potholes

If you want to retire early because you're unhappy with your working life, take extra care with the nonfinancial aspects of your retirement planning. You don't want to have an unhappy retirement, too. It takes effort to do it well.

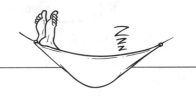

From the Hammock

When Jim turned 45, he thought he could finally figure out what he wanted to be when he grew up. Now he realizes that this is the wrong question. The real question is, "What do you really want to do, at any point in your life?" Then figure out what's necessary to give you the chance to do it. Live your life from the inside out as a "human doing."

You have to do something besides read the paper and watch the idiot box all day. Veg out too long, and you'll become a vegetable.

A third of retirees re-enter the job market within two years either for the money or because they're bored. Either reason is okay. We all need to face some challenges, to be with people, and to feel productive at every age. We need a sense of self-worth and usefulness to remain mentally and physically healthy.

Early retirement, by choice, and with a strong financial base to support you, gives you the freedom to re-create your life. You can do whatever you're capable of, and we rarely discover just how much that can be.

Your chances of a long, successful, and fulfilling retirement depend on how well prepared you are before you get there. Planning isn't just about the money. To bring your dream to fruition takes effort. It's okay to flunk total retirement if you have other options. Our idea of retirement is making sure you have options and choices.

What You Will Give Up

Obviously you give up the steady paycheck. That's the lifeblood of your cash flow during those many years in the salt mines. When you retire, you're leaving 10 to 20 years of increasing income on the table, your peak earning years. Let's say that you retired in 2000 at age 52 from a good corporate job. You earned $100,000 in your last year and could expect regular raises and a couple more promotions over the next 15 years if all went well. That's quite a change from the $10,000 you earned your first year out of college 30 years ago. Here are the numbers:

$1,450,000 earned over 30 years

2001–2010: $1,500,000 left on the table

2011–2015: $1,125,000 left on the table

That's $2.6 million or so that you won't earn by retiring at age 52 instead of 65. "Wait a minute," you say. "No one could retire if they made less than $1.5 million over 30 years after paying taxes, living expenses, mortgages, car loans, and more taxes!" Well, lots of people retired in 2000 and never earned close to that much in *45* years of working.

Use whatever numbers you have to work with in your career. No matter what you made, early retirement means forgoing serious money, even after taxes. And much of it would be *discretionary income*—money you could sock away for retirement at a later age.

What else do you give up? All those great bennies. The one you'll really miss is health insurance, even if you had to pay something toward the premium before retirement. You can buy into your old plan for 18 months when you leave at 102 percent of the total premium under *COBRA*. At the end of that time, you either convert to the insurer's non-group plan or find one of your own. It all comes out of your pocket when you retire—and it's not cheap. We'll take a closer look at this in Chapter 3, "Exploring the Issues."

You also give up whatever passes for a social life at your place of work. You may not fully appreciate this until after you've been home for a few weeks and those turkeys are still slaving away in your absence. Make sure that you have regularly scheduled social contacts in the community, several times a week, to maintain your sanity. Just doing the grocery shopping isn't enough.

One of the most important things you give up is your identity. You're going to feel awkward in some social contexts when a new acquaintance inquires, "And what do you do?" or when an old friend you haven't seen for a while asks, "So what kinds of exciting things are you up to at work?"

Say What?

Discretionary income *is the money that you choose how to spend. It's what you have left after you pay the income taxes due on it.*

Say What?

COBRA *is the Consolidated Omnibus Budget Reconciliation Act of 1985, a federal law that requires your employer to maintain your enrollment in the group health plan for 18 months after you leave the company. However, you must pay 100 percent of the premium plus 2 percent for the paperwork shuffling. Group premiums are usually cheaper than nongroup premiums for similar levels of coverage. COBRA is often used for people between jobs so that they can maintain health insurance coverage until they take a new job and qualify for benefits. But you can also use it when you retire before age 65.*

You're no longer a star widget salesman or a project manager, or whatever it was you did. Now they won't know what you are, and you'll notice that you don't, either.

Where Retirement Came From

In the nineteenth century and well into the twentieth, you worked if you were able, either for yourself or for someone else. In 1890, 75 percent of all men over age 65 were employed. The other 25 percent were disabled, physically or mentally.

Let's look at the number of people over 65 at various times to get a feel for these numbers.

Year	People Over Age 65
1900	3 million
1950	12 million
2000	35 million
2020 (projected)	53 million
2030 (projected)	70 million
2050 (projected)	82 million

Every year from 2010 through 2040, 3.5 million to 4.1 million people are expected to turn 65 in the United States. Some will retire earlier, some later, and a few never. Some, of course, will have never worked at all.

A Nugget of Gold

Prince Otto von Bismarck of Germany created paid retirement on a large scale in 1883. His purpose was to weaken the attraction of socialism by holding out the carrot of a secure retirement at age 70 for government employees and the armed forces. Because life expectancy at birth in Germany was only 45 at the time, it wasn't a very expensive program.

Retirement today is a phenomenon of the last 50 years or so. It's a product of three factors:

➤ An increasingly healthy population

➤ Social Security

➤ Pensions

Some observers believe that because the last two factors are destined to decline in importance to retirees, within 20 years we'll have more, and healthier, seniors, but they'll have less income from pensions and Social Security. Instead, they'll be more reliant on their own savings or work income to survive their golden years.

The New Deal

President Franklin Roosevelt's administration introduced Social Security in the mid-1930s during the Great Depression. Socialist ideas were becoming attractive as unemployment rose to 25 percent or more. Under this new law, covered employees would be allowed to retire at age 65 with the promise of a monthly check.

Because life expectancy was only 60 for men in the United States in 1935, the government was more concerned about the buildup of money in the trust fund than the expense of paying it out. Too much money in the fund was thought to be dangerous (you know how Congress is around a pile of extra money) and a restraint on economic growth. However, the immediate purpose was served: Unemployment dropped quickly as older men left the work force and collected Social Security.

A few large companies and a couple of states had already established pension plans by the 1930s. After World War II, the unions caught on, and by the early 1950s they were allowed to bargain for pensions. They discovered that it enabled them to recruit younger, more assertive members as the older ones were persuaded to retire with pensions.

More companies bought in to the pension idea when the government permitted mandatory retirement at age 68. They felt that they could clean out some dead wood and bring in new saplings to work harder and cheaper. Finally, the government penalized people who worked past age 70 by reducing their benefits if they were collecting and working at the same time.

Still later, the penalty age for working while collecting Social Security was lowered to 62; the penalty was removed for those over age 70. Then, in 2000, the government lowered the penalty-free age to 65, recognizing that older people wanted (and often needed) to work. A shortage of labor also figured into this decision.

Now the penalty is only on those who decide to collect Social Security from age 62 through 64. In 2000, it's a $1 reduction for every $2 earned over $10,080. This amount is increased each year by the change in the Consumer Price Index, a measurement of inflation over the previous year. In the year that you reach full retirement age (currently 65), the penalty is $1 for every $3 earned up to $17,000 until the month you turn 65.

A Good Deal

The structure and form of retirement continues to change. We've seen that there's no one way to do it. That leaves the decision whether to retire early, and what "early" is, up to you. Allow yourself the possibility of retiring early 10, 20, or 30 years down the road. Look at retirement as a continuum, not an end of one life and a beginning of another. What you choose today and in the future gives you new choices later.

From the Hammock

A friend recently asked for advice on how to retire at age 27. That he was now 50 presented a problem! Age 27 isn't too early to start planning retirement at 50, but we can't find a way to make the numbers work the other way around.

It's not all golf, gardening, tailgate parties, and windsurfing. But you knew that. It's up to you what your retirement will be. And if you really want an early retirement, you can earn it. We can help you do that.

Setting your goal doesn't restrict your choices in the future. On the contrary, it gives you greater choices to create your own retirement on your own terms. The alternative to not having a goal and not planning is likely to be no choice at all. You'll have a financially limited, late retirement—or, worse, an unexpected and unwanted early retirement due to circumstances beyond your control.

The Least You Need to Know

➤ A creative retirement may include part-time work to help make ends meet and allow you to ease into full retirement.

➤ A financially successful retirement at any age isn't enough: Plan to make it an emotionally satisfying one, too.

➤ Have a firm plan to keep mentally and physically active with hobbies, volunteering, travel, and regular exercise.

➤ No matter when you retire, the decisions that you make between now and then will determine how successful your retirement will be.

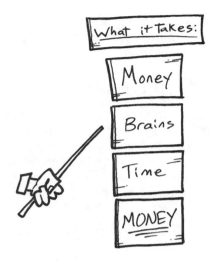

Chapter 2

What It Takes

In This Chapter

➤ You need a lot of money to retire early

➤ Wanting to retire early is necessary, but not enough

➤ Learn to make wise choices that balance your goals

➤ Procrastination delays reaching your goal

➤ Protect yourself so you don't have to take big risks

Did you ever want something so bad you could taste it? Well, if you want to retire early, or at least have the choice, you need to feel that ache. You need it to drive you forward to reach your goal.

Now's the time to find out what it takes to give you that choice. In this chapter, we'll lay out the five D's that you need:

➤ Dough

➤ Desire

➤ Decisions

➤ Discipline

➤ Defense

A Nugget of Gold

If you're one of the 28 percent of Americans who think playing the lottery is a better way to become wealthy than saving and investing (according to the Consumer Federation of America), think again. Ten dollars a week invested at 10 percent a year for 30 years will guarantee you more than $100,000. The same $15,600 for lottery tickets guarantees only that you spent that money with lousy odds at just winning it back.

Say What?

We'll skip the economic mumbo-jumbo. **Inflation,** for our purposes, is measured by the Department of Labor's Urban Consumer Price Index. It attempts to measure by how much the cost of a large, diverse "basket" of consumer goods and services increases over a period of time.

You've got to have all five; four out of five won't cut it. The good news is, most people can have all five if they make up their minds to do so.

Dough: A Pile of Money

"Money makes the world go 'round," the song says. And it's money that will help to define the quality of your retirement. Supporting yourself in retirement is very different from doing it on a steady paycheck. What you want is enough dough-re-mi to allow yourself to maintain your preretirement standard of living without going to work if you don't want to.

We all know about the two easy ways to get rich (legally): inherit a fortune or get fantastically lucky on a lottery ticket. By now, you have a pretty good idea of the chances of either of these happening to you. There's a third way that puts the odds in your favor—combining the other four D's (which are within your control) with a steady, growing income. You need only a little bit of luck to reach financial freedom.

If you run into some luck along the way, great. But don't plan on getting lucky to reach your goals, and don't waste your time or money on get-rich-quick schemes. *You're* not the one who gets rich.

If You're Planning on a Pension

People who qualify for an early pension get some help when they retire early. Some pensions may even start at age 55 or are improved as part of an "early retirement offer" from your employer. But, outside of government and big corporations, pensions are fast disappearing.

Don't let the lure of a pension at an early age tempt you into retiring early without thinking it through. Only 4 percent of pensions are indexed or set to increase to keep up with the cost of living. At 4 percent *inflation,* that nice pension that you get today loses half its buying power in 19 years and two thirds of its value in 28 years. That won't be enough. Many companies also reduce an early pension when you begin collecting Social Security.

Too Little, Too Late

The retirement age for receiving reduced Social Security benefits is scheduled to increase along with the age at which you can collect full benefits. Currently, you can begin collecting about 80 percent of your full benefit at age 62. Note that although the benefit increases yearly to keep pace with inflation, it remains at 80 percent of full benefits for the rest of your life.

If you were born between 1943 and 1954, you qualify for full benefits at age 66. This age continues to increase by two months for each later birth year until 1960, when the age is 67. You can still collect early retirement benefits at age 62, but, beginning in 2000, the benefit is slowly reduced each year from 80 percent of full benefits down to 70 percent by 2022. These ages may be raised again before you get there, under future legislation aimed at reducing the strain on the Social Security system.

Retirement Age for Full Benefits

Birth Year	Age
Before	
1938	65 and 2 months
1939	65 and 4 months
1940	65 and 6 months
1941	65 and 8 months
1942	65 and 10 months
1943–1954	66
1955	66 and 2 months
1956	66 and 4 months
1957	66 and 6 months
1958	66 and 8 months
1959	66 and 10 months
After	
1959	67

On the other hand, the benefit increases the longer you wait beyond 62 to file. From age 66 to age 70, the benefit increases 6 percent a year. There's no increase beyond age 70, except for annual cost-of-living increases that affect all benefits.

Even then, plan on Social Security covering only 20 to 30 percent of your expenses in retirement. Through Social Security and Medicare (see Chapter 4, "Life in the Slow Lane," for more on Medicare), the U.S. government won't be in a position to give you any extra help. The rapid increase in the number of people over age 65 will put a serious strain in the budgets of all developed Western countries. Governments, including the U.S. government, will run increasing budget deficits for Social Security and healthcare programs as the twenty-first century unfolds.

How Much Dough?

The following example doesn't relate to you or to anyone in particular, so don't say, "That's not how I live!" Just hang in there with us. It's for Donna and Charley, but we hope it will give you an idea of what it takes to retire early. The following information outlines their financial situation as they begin the first phase of their retirement. We'll come back to Donna and Charley in later chapters to see how they're doing down the road. Here's the setup:

➤ Donna and Charley retired in 2000 at age 50. Their preretirement expenses were $61,000 a year, after paying income taxes. They'll save on work-related expenses, but they plan to do more traveling. They just paid off the $700-a-month mortgage on their house, but now they'll pay that much for a good health insurance policy. So let's call it even. They'll spend $61,000 in their first year in retirement, too.

➤ They have 13 years to go until they're 63 and can collect Social Security at 75 percent of full benefits. We'll put their federal tax bracket at 15 percent. (We didn't forget state income taxes. A 15 percent federal tax bracket and a 5 percent state bracket will net out to around 15 percent after you take the standard deduction and personal exemptions.)

➤ To have $61,000 to spend after taxes, they'll need $72,000 in income. They don't want to break into their nest egg early because it has to last 40 years—maybe more. And they don't want to touch their tax-sheltered retirement plans until they are required to. They know that they need to let these keep growing. And, except under certain conditions, there's a 10 percent penalty on withdrawals before age $59\frac{1}{2}$ in addition to regular income tax.

➤ Donna and Charley are invested in money market funds and bond and stock mutual funds in order to get an 8 percent return on their money. Find your calculator. Divide $72,000 gross income by .08 (that's 8 percent expressed as a

A Nugget of Gold

Tax-sheltered retirement plans such as 401(k), 403(b), and various Individual Retirement Accounts (IRAs) are designed to help you save for retirement while you're working. When you retire, you want to live off your taxable savings and investments for as long as possible. This allows the tax-sheltered plans to continue growing through compound interest. If you can hold off until age 70, your next 25-plus years will be funded much better. (We'll look closely at 401[k] and 403[b] plans in Chapter 20, "Keep the Taxman Waiting While You Work," and at IRAs in Chapter 21, "The IRA: Your Personal Tax Shelter.")

decimal). You should get $900,000. That's how much they have in investments outside their tax-sheltered retirement plans.

➤ In their tax-sheltered retirement plans, Donna and Charley have $535,000 at age 50. This money is invested in stocks and stock mutual funds that they hope will return an average of 10 percent a year.

Wow! Donna and Charley have $900,000, not counting retirement-plan money. That's a lot. But it gets worse. We haven't counted inflation. Let's use a 4 percent average annual rate of inflation. (That's a bit high for the decade of the 1990s, but it's low for the 1980s.)

By age 60, Donna and Charley are living about the same as they did when they retired, but at 4 percent inflation, their expenses have grown to $90,294. To produce that much money at 8 percent a year would require almost $1.3 million. And by the time their Social Security checks start coming in three more years, those expenses will have grown to $101,569.

But Donna and Charley had only $900,000 in taxable accounts to start with. They'll have to dip into this money to cover annual expenses over $61,000. After 13 years, their nest egg will have fallen below $600,000. At 8 percent, that provides only about $49,600 a year in 2013.

Let's give them $26,000 in Social Security at age 63. Now they're short only $37,300 that year. That shortfall also comes out of their dwindling nest egg, which will be under $29,500 when they hit age 71. Fortunately, Donna and Charley still have their retirement-plan money that they'll begin drawing at age 70. They can keep the $130,000 or so left in their taxable account for an emergency and cash cushion. (At age 70, their expenses are $139,000 a year.)

Donna and Charley will make it to age 90 if their tax-sheltered retirement plan totals have grown to $3.6 million by age 70. That means that the $535,000 they had there when they retired at age 50 must average a 10 percent annual return for the next 20 years.

Potholes

Never forget the taxman because he'll never forget you. When you're living off interest, dividends, and some capital gains, the taxes count. Quick and simple calculations will work. Take your federal tax bracket—say, 15 percent, or .15—and subtract that from 1.00. You'll get .85. Divide your expenses by .85 to get the pretax number. In our example, 61,000 ÷ .85 = 71,765.

It Might Not Be Enough

Donna and Charley started with a total of $1,435,000, counting that $535,000 in their retirement plans. But suppose they run into major problems such as these:

➤ A long stretch of stock market underperformance

➤ A period of high inflation

➤ Large expenditures for an emergency of some kind

➤ Reduced Social Security payments

➤ Soaring out-of-pocket medical expenses

➤ Nursing home or assisted-living expenses for one or both

If no problems occur, they're on schedule to run out of money in 2041, at age 91. Any major financial disasters are likely to cause them to run out of money earlier. If they live longer than 90 with none of the previously listed problems, they'll be living on Social Security alone. They will have outlived their money.

This quick-and-dirty number-crunching says that Donna and Charley needed closer to $1,650,000 when they retired in 2000 to safely make it until age 95 or longer. About $1 million in their taxable accounts and $650,000 in their retirement accounts would provide the cushion they need. They could work three more years and save enough to reach those numbers.

Alternately, they could scale back their standard of living in retirement to make the cash last longer. But that's not what you look forward to—40 years of retirement wishing that you had just a little more so you could do the things you want. In their 80s, when they discover that the money is running out, neither one is likely to be able to get a part-time job.

We think that Donna and Charley should have had $1 million in their taxable accounts when they retired in 2000 to comfortably cover their expenses until they started drawing on their retirement account money. If you plan to retire at age 50 in the year 2020, you will need $2 million to cover the same level of taxes and expenses in retirement. This accounts for 4 percent inflation per year, and your first-year expenses in 2020 dollars will be $133,659 just to pay for the same things that $61,000 covered in 2000.

If you're willing to bet on 3 percent inflation over the next 20 years, you'll need only $1.62 million in taxable accounts, but that's not a bet you can afford to lose. The target numbers that you come up with in Part 2, "Planning the Path to Wealth," may be lower or higher than these. It depends on the expenses that we'll help you project in your retirement. You'll set your own goals for financial freedom and make your plan to fit them.

Desire: You Gotta Really Want It

Desire to reach a goal is what keeps you going through thick and thin. Desire translates a dream into a goal. Without it, it's easy to get sidetracked.

Pat Riley, the coach of the Miami Heat basketball team and former L.A. Laker coach who guided his team to the NBA Championships, has written: "It's about an image.

It's about visualizing where you want to be and seeing yourself there someday. Every day you visualize it, you dream about it, you think about it, you work on it, and you keep striving for it."

We're not suggesting that you become obsessive about retiring early. Obsessive behavior suggests an unhealthy, unbalanced life. Keep your desire on simmer. It's great to have goals to work toward, but remember that it's the journey that counts, not the destination. The satisfaction from achieving your goals is not measured just in dollars. It comes from knowing that you're doing a good job planning and executing your plan for the future.

If you can't find the necessary level of desire today to retire early, there's nothing wrong with that. You probably have more important goals that need to be accomplished first. Whether you retire early or late, a comfortable retirement is something that you want when you get there. Following our advice will help you either way. You choose your priorities in life. Desire enables you to have your choices.

It's Been Said

"To accomplish great things, we must not only act, but also dream; not only plan, but also believe."

—Anatole France

Decisions: Tough Choices

Once you decide that you want the choice to retire early and you have the necessary desire, decisions become part of your daily life. You learn to look at the choices you have each day in the light of your goal.

Many choices won't affect reaching your goal. Recognize the ones that will. They're not all decisions about money, although sometimes the secondary consequences of your decisions do have significant financial consequences. Think through the important choices so that you don't act impulsively and regret your decisions later.

Some decisions involve family: marriage, divorce, children, parents, where to live, where to vacation, and so on. Others are work-related: this job or that one, stay or accept a transfer, get more training and education or not. You'll recognize all these because they are usually major life decisions. Before you make them, consider how they'll affect your choice to retire early.

You constantly make lifestyle decisions, large and small. Many are made without any thought—it's who you are or want to be. Question them, even the little ones, and make them conscious decisions. These are often called habits. Some are good, and some are bad. They, too, are decisions that you can consciously make or change.

For instance, a weekly outing for the family at MacDonald's with two Happy Meals and two Big Mac Value Meals costs about $14.50. You can make the same meal at home for about 6 bucks including the cookies. You'll save $442 a year. If you invest that amount at 10 percent for 20 years, it grows to $25,300! That could cover a couple years of room and board at college.

The bigger lifestyle decisions often involve big bucks: which house, in which neighborhood; which cars; and which toys for big kids as well as little ones. We all want things, and we work hard so that we can get them. Go for it. Just be sure to look at the variety of options you have and the financial consequences of each, both now and down the road.

One hundred dollars compounded at 10 percent a year grows to $4,530 in 40 years.

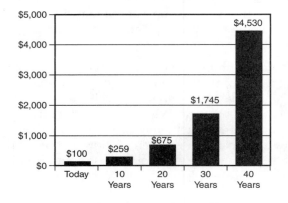

Say What?

Compounding has been called the eighth wonder of the world. You earn a return on your initial investment, and then you earn a return on your return. That's how compounding works. In the first few years, it doesn't look like a big deal, but it picks up a lot of steam later.

The price you pay for the freedom to retire early in the future is not getting everything you want today. These can be difficult decisions for many people. That's where desire and the knowledge of the cost of your choices come in. A dollar that you spend today represents a lot of dollars that you can't spend later.

The amazing phenomenon behind the growth of money is *compounding*. Compounding is what makes your retirement possible at all. Your relatively small savings grow at an increasingly faster rate. As long as the results keep ahead of inflation and taxes, then your numbers and also the buying power of your money increase.

We're not counseling you to become a miser. Balance your impulse to live for today with the goal you've set for yourself in the future. It gets easier the more you do it and the further you go. You'll start to see the money grow into serious sums, and you'll feel yourself getting closer to your goal.

Discipline: A Lotta "Round Tuits"

We're all pretty good at recognizing when we need to do something, but we're also good at telling ourselves "I'll do it as soon as I find the time to get around to it." Sound familiar? If retiring early is a choice that you really want down the road, it's important to make the time. Then get a good supply of "round tuits" so that you won't have a reason to procrastinate anymore.

Your decision isn't to totally deny yourself what you want today. You choose what you need and want as part of a continuum with what you want tomorrow. After all, today you also want to be able to retire early. Life is about trade-offs. The shrinks call it deferred satisfaction. You can't have it all—at least, not at the same time. You wouldn't know what to do with it all anyway!

So get that double hot-fudge sundae with the whipped cream on top once in a while. Take that great vacation to the Caribbean or wherever every five years. You don't need the sundaes every day—that's not good for your health. You don't need that first-class vacation every year, either. Get creative and take some day trips while you relax around the house instead. After all, you're already paying to live there, so enjoy a quiet vacation at home once in a while.

If you take the attitude that you're denying yourself the pleasures of life for some unknown and far-off, uncertain future, you aren't approaching this with the right attitude. It won't work. You want to develop a healthy balance between what you want today and what you want tomorrow. That will provide you with the discipline to make your decisions and still feel good about your life now.

Discipline also means not procrastinating. This is a critical factor in whether you will reach your goal of early retirement or the financial freedom to make that choice. When you put off necessary decisions and actions, you completely undermine your chance of success.

From the Hammock

Let's say you need to buy a car. There's a classy Volvo that caught your eye, the reliable Honda your friend Tom raves about, or the low-priced Kia you saw advertised on the tube. There's maybe $10,000 difference between each today. But at a 10 percent per year average return for 30 years, that's not a $10,000 difference—it's a $175,000 difference! We might pick the Honda and drive it for 10 years, but we'd probably check out a 3-year-old Volvo for around the same price first. In a year, they're all used cars, and who else remembers whether you bought it new or used?

It's Been Said

"The secret of getting ahead is getting started. The secret of getting started is breaking your task into small manageable tasks, and then starting on the first one."

—Mark Twain

As you read this book, you'll see where and how you need to set goals, make plans, and carry them out. It's critical to get into the habit of following through on a timely basis. Sooner is better than later. Now is best.

Defense: The Best Offense

If you're a sports fan, you've probably heard it said that the best offense is a good defense. Defense wins games. Sure, you need offense to score, but you don't have to score often if you can keep the other side from scoring at all.

The same principle holds true in the rest of life. You play defense here by protecting what you have and carefully evaluating the risks you do take. You want to reduce the chance that you'll take a big hit that sets you back financially. If it's big enough, you may not recover in time to reach your goal of retiring early.

When a team falls behind in a game, the players are motivated to play harder to try to catch up. That's good. But they also have to take bigger chances to score, and that's not so good. In hockey, the coach might remove the goalkeeper and add an extra skater to try to score a goal if the team is behind near the end of a game. That leaves no one guarding the goal, but it's a risk they have to take.

The difference between sports and your life is that the team has another game and another season. The players get to start over again. You don't. There's no practice time for life, no dress rehearsal, and no "wait 'til next year." Your defense is designed to prevent you from falling so far behind in your game that you have to take high risks. When that happens, the odds will be against you, and you'll likely fall further behind. A good defense keeps you in the game if something goes wrong. Then you steadily regain your position without exposing yourself to great risks.

When you understand where you can prevent taking a big financial loss, you can play good defense. You put the odds of succeeding in your favor. You'll find out what some of these risks are and how to defend against them in Part 2, "Planning the Path to Wealth," and Part 4, "A Safari on Wall Street," of this book. They'll include investing risks as well as risks that you can lay off on someone else. Let them take the hit—that's called insurance. We'll also look at other choices you can make that limit your exposure to losses as part of your defensive plan.

Let's get your game plan together and look at the options you have, the decisions you will need to make, and the risks and challenges you face. Then you can add an intelligent defensive strategy that fits your overall plan. You may never have to play catch-up against long odds because you'll be winning the big game with good defense and good offense.

The Least You Need to Know

➤ Before you retire, make sure you have enough money to last as long as you do.

➤ Financial freedom is a choice within your control if you want it enough to make the tough decisions.

➤ You have to be financially disciplined in your lifestyle choices. You need to be willing to trade off something today so you can have a long, comfortable early retirement later.

➤ Success is a result of preventing big losses that keep you from reaching your goal.

Chapter 3

Exploring the Issues

In This Chapter

➤ Early retirement brings on unexpected emotional changes

➤ You are what you do; plan to do something

➤ How outside professional financial advice can help you with your plan

➤ Couples don't always retire at the same time

Retirement at any age is a fundamental change in lifestyle that opens a whole bagful of financial and emotional consequences. You need to be well-prepared for both kinds. When you retire early because that's what you wanted to do and planned for, you may be spared some of the difficulties facing older retirees and people who must retire unexpectedly. On the other hand, early retirement brings other challenges.

A financially and emotionally successful early retirement doesn't happen by accident. Just as you need to plan well to afford early retirement, you should thoroughly investigate all the consequences. You certainly don't want to reach financial freedom and find yourself miserable in retirement. In this chapter, we'll throw out some of the hurdles and problems you may face so that you can start thinking about them years—or even decades—before you retire.

A Midlife Crisis

Racy, red convertibles and sweet young things were the hallmarks of the stereotypical midlife crisis for 35- to 45-year-olds in the past. Because middle age these days is more like 40 to 60, early retirement brings on a new definition of midlife crisis.

Potholes

You don't have to be a lofty executive to get accustomed to power and status. When you're working, you manage people and projects, and you make things happen. You're somebody, and your ego likes it. When you retire, though, you're just the guy who takes out the trash or the woman who walks the dog. It used to be said, "No man is a hero to his butler." We'll bet that your spouse doesn't treat you like you're the boss, either. Don't take your status at work too seriously; it disappears in a flash.

During the last few decades, retirement was one of the most troubling life events for almost half of retirees. The younger they were, the more difficulty they had. And the higher their power and status at work was, the greater the stress of adjusting to retirement was. As an early retiree, you probably had a good income and the power and status that went with it. This means that you must pay careful attention to these issues well in advance.

Who Am I?

You are what you do. The identity you have now comes in large part from your job, profession, and career. To your co-workers and acquaintances, you certainly are what you do. And you buy into that identity over the years much more than you think you do. You'll see when you retire just how much that really is.

You're not giving up just the title and job identity; you're giving up your major productive contribution to society (we'll leave it up to you to determine how much that is). That package gives your life a big part of its meaning. It defines some piece of your self-worth. You'll leave it all behind when you retire.

Because you are what you do to such a great extent, make sure that you have plenty to do with all that free time in retirement. Make an activity plan that is an extension of your current leisure pursuits. If you don't have many hobbies, don't retire until you do. These activities, especially volunteering in your community, will form the basis of your new identity.

You will want to have a fairly structured day and week planned, similar to what you had at work. Plan these activities before you retire for at least the first year or two. The rest of your life will develop from this period if the first two years go well. You'll find new interests, new friends, new activities, and new priorities as you move on.

A lack of a structured action plan may lead to boredom, anxiety, depression, heavy drinking, or worse. It happens to many retirees. Don't fantasize about what you're going to do; make a written plan for the things that you want to spend more time on—the more detailed, the better.

Retirement is particularly stressful for men. They often define their lives through work, whereas many women divide their energies (and identity) among pursuing a career, raising children, and maintaining the household. Just because these are stereotypes doesn't mean that they aren't true in many households.

Single early retirees don't even have the contact with another person at home. Are your friends still working? Find new playmates. That makes it imperative to plan some of your activities outside the home with other people.

What Have I Done?

Around birthdays that have zeros in them, you'll find yourself evaluating your life to date. You will face disappointment over opportunities lost, chances fumbled, and mistakes made. For some reason we tend to express remorse rather than gratitude at such times. Be sure to acknowledge your accomplishments, choices that worked out well, and the good things that have happened in your life to balance the negatives.

You may also experience a fuzzy fear or anxiety about the future around your 40th or 50th birthday. Are you making the right choice to retire early and do the other things you plan? Perhaps you'll discover that you're in a rut, too set in your ways to be comfortable with major changes. You certainly can change if you push yourself. You're not mentally ready to retire until you've worked through these feelings and are ready for—and even eager for—big and somewhat unknown changes in your life.

These are all normal emotions in midlife. Don't try to avoid them—they'll just keep hounding you. Instead, get comfortable with them and move toward your goals of early retirement and beyond with happiness and satisfaction. It's no shame to get professional help here if you don't have someone else to share these feelings with. You don't want to allow these emotions to ruin your plans.

It's Time to Grow Up

For many people, retirement causes emotional changes similar to those in adolescence. Your life changes abruptly after so many years of working hard. Your daily routine is disrupted, and you no longer have the identity that you had in the working world. These affect how you feel about yourself more than you think they will.

It takes some people years to learn to adjust to a whole new life in retirement. Some never do, and, unfortunately, many people die an early death because of it. The mental and physical aspects of our bodies work closely together and affect us in mysterious ways. Think of your work as an addiction or a dependence that you must break in order to successfully change your life. Even if you don't consider yourself a workaholic, cold-turkey retirement is rough for a lot of people.

From the Hammock

Jim planned a phased retirement over four years: four-day work weeks for the first two years and then three-day weeks for almost a year. He followed that with limited "consulting" over six months. After that, he gave himself a full year to learn to relax, to read, to play tennis, and to pay more attention to his investments. No major new commitments. After that year, he evaluated his experience and how he felt. Only then did he allow himself to make any serious commitments to new activities. Find out what works for you.

27

Try out the idea of retirement in your mind several times before you retire—and not just fun fantasies. Perhaps you'll be able to identify some of the emotions that you'll encounter ahead of time. That's not the same as the real thing, of course, but the dry run will help when the curtain goes up on your new life. Be ready for some degree of emotional trauma and a real feeling of loss—even if you didn't like your job.

In the years before you retire, talk to some retired folks you know, whether they retired early or not. Ask them these questions:

➤ What emotions did you experience?

➤ How did you handle them?

➤ What did you do and not do in the first year?

➤ What do you wish you had done or not done?

Set up your own informal support group of retirees based on these conversations. You don't have to hang out with them when you retire; just ask if you can call them or meet to discuss what's bugging you. They've been there, and many are willing to talk about their experience if it would help another person.

A Nugget of Gold

There's no free lunch. Any professional in any field is in business to make money. Whether you want medical, legal, or financial advice, be prepared to pay well for quality. But do your homework first. Ask friends and co-workers who they use and how satisfied they are. Then check relevant Web sites such as these:

➤ The Certified Financial Planner Board of Standards, at www.cfp-board.org

➤ The North American Securities Administration Association, at www.nasaa.org, to find your state's regulatory agency

➤ The Better Business Bureau, at www.bbb.org

➤ The National Fraud Exchange, at 1-800-822-0416 (no Web site yet)

Then make an introductory appointment and interview the person for the job. (There's more on hiring a planner in Chapter 11.)

Get a Financial Physical

When you hit age 50 or so, it's a good time to take a long, careful look at your goals and your financial position. If you're planning to retire at 50 or earlier, then perform your financial physical at age 40. Do a complete financial review. Be sure that the following is true:

➤ Your goals are still your goals.

➤ Your goals are realistic.

➤ You refine your goals if they're still fuzzy.

➤ You're financially on track to meet your goals.

Say What?

Your investment **portfolio** is your collection of stocks, bonds, mutual funds, and other investment securities you own in your taxable and tax-deferred accounts.

If you're in good shape, keep doing what got you here. However, you may want to enlist the assistance of a financial planner if you don't already have one you work with regularly. It's worth your time and money to get real peace of mind—or to discover that you overlooked or miscalculated something important in time to remedy it. (See Chapter 11, "Finding and Using a Financial Planner," for more on how a financial planner can help you.)

A fee-only financial planner charges for his time reviewing your goals and financial position and meeting with you. It's a hefty hourly fee, but you want to know that you're getting objective and experienced advice. Fee-only planners are scarce. Other planners are commission-only or fee-and-commission (sometimes called fee-based). Both earn commissions by selling a variety of financial products and investments.

Say What?

A **will** is a legal document that descibes how your property is to be distributed upon your death. It's part of your **estate plan,** which is a formal set of documents to manage your property both before and after your death for the benefit of you and your heirs. Chapter 23, "Your Estate Needs a Plan, Too," covers both subjects.

Getting Help

If you haven't been working with a financial planner, you don't want to have one who is interested in selling you something at this critical review. A fee-only planner can suggest changes in your investment *portfolio* and help direct you to make any changes that you agree would be desirable. But there's no commission for the planner involved, and you make the changes yourself.

If you've been working with a commission-based or a fee-and-commission planner already, that's good. You should use your planner for a serious checkup, too.

Presumably, this person already knows your goals and plan thoroughly and has helped structure your portfolio to achieve them. That's part of what you paid for all along. Either way, a financial professional is an experienced outsider who can help you in this review.

This is also a time to start thinking about long-term issues that you will need to decide on or change early in retirement. Maybe you should reduce your life insurance and use the money to buy long-term care insurance. Maybe not. It's also time to review your *will* and start doing serious *estate planning*. Yes, you already have an estate; it's everything you own and owe. Make these kinds of issues part of your financial physical, too. Your planner will have a good list to cover.

When the Paycheck Stops

Retiring from a high-paying job or from your own business means that you're giving up doing what you do well. That's what got you to financial freedom at an early age. Don't think that you're going to replace that much income by spending more time with your investment portfolio. Unless you have a proven track record of superior returns in managing your stocks and funds, more time doesn't mean better returns. In fact, quite the opposite can happen. More time can mean more buying and selling, and more trading has been shown to reduce returns.

Prove that you're a good enough investor with market-beating returns over 5 or 10 years before you retire, and maybe it will work. Take 20 percent of your portfolio and actively manage it for this long. If you can beat the relevant market indexes consistently, then maybe you can plan on producing better returns for a larger portion of your investments. If not, leave most of the decisions up to experienced financial managers, and spend your free time more productively.

There are good reasons why you don't make any major changes in your portfolio or in how you manage it when you retire. That's why you should already have a solid financial plan in place and stick to it. (We'll look at investing more closely in Part 4, "A Safari on Wall Street.")

One Works, the Other Doesn't

With 80 percent of couples both working today, it's natural that many of them have different ideas about early retirement. Increasingly, even without major age differences, the man retires early while the woman keeps working. Perhaps her career didn't get off the ground until after the kids were in school, and she's just hitting her stride. With more husbands filling the Mr. Mom role (about two million, at last estimate), the wife might be the family breadwinner. Or maybe the idea of early retirement just doesn't float her boat today.

For whatever reason, this situation requires the willingness of both parties to communicate ideas and feelings early and often. It also requires a willingness to accept and respect the other's decision. Compromises may have to be worked out in many areas. We're all in new territory here, but, as mature adults, you should be able to handle this.

Retirement brings role changes, and when one partner continues to work, the stresses on both people change and can even increase. Responsibilities around the home, such as housework, may come into play. The retired spouse has time to do more but may feel that these duties should continue to be shared. He didn't necessarily retire to become a full-time cook, housekeeper, and groundskeeper. A realignment of responsibilities may be in order, but this should be thoroughly discussed. A mutually agreeable program decided well in advance of the retirement prevents problems later.

The retired spouse may want to spend more time with grown children and grandchildren. The working spouse feels left out and resentful. Or perhaps aging parents need increasingly more attention and support. The retired spouse has the time but may come to feel that the burden isn't being shared. Conversely, the working spouse experiences guilt at not pulling his weight.

While these issues are by no means exclusive to working/nonworking couples, they always add stress to a relationship. The emotions aroused in situations like these need to be shared, not bottled up and allowed to fester. Often these situations develop *after* retirement; planning for them was minimal. But when you have kids and parents, the possibilities exist ahead of time—and so should some discussion of potential issues.

Still Bringing Home the Bagel

When one partner retires while the other works, one still has a paycheck. Subtle or not-so-subtle issues of money and power surface even though the financial situation allows both to retire. If the wife works, the husband's loss of status from his former job may be compounded at home because he's no longer a co-breadwinner. Meanwhile, his wife may feel that because he's no longer "contributing," she gets more say in financial matters as well as other decisions.

Again, the solution is to communicate ahead of time. However, these feelings are often subtle and not easy to identify without some effort. The working spouse needs to acknowledge that the retired spouse earned and contributed money to their investments. That money is providing income and is growing to meet future needs. Retiring early or not retiring are choices to be made when financial freedom is achieved.

Certainly, the continued income stream from the working partner will improve your financial outlook even more. But your plan should incorporate that income and should be flexible enough to change when the second partner retires.

A Nugget of Gold

When the wife keeps working while her hubby retires early, she's providing additional security for herself that she needs for retirement. If she earned less money, worked fewer years, or is much younger, continuing to work will directly benefit her. She'll build up higher future Social Security payments as well as retirement plan or pension values. Because women can expect to live four to six years longer than men, these benefits will help ensure her financial comfort in later years when she may be alone.

Finally Retired Together

Eventually, both of you will be retired and looking forward to fulfilling all the plans that you only talked about before. But now there are new adjustments to make. The house that was big enough for two or more when one or both worked is suddenly too small. You're not used to getting in each other's way 24×7.

Again, this is where both of your planned schedules of activity come in handy. Some of these activities may be with each other, but it's important to have time apart. Activities with friends or by yourself enable each person to continue the life and identity that he had before. You don't suddenly have a mind meld when you retire. You married for better or worse, but not necessarily for breakfast, lunch, and dinner every day.

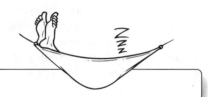

From the Hammock

Jim's wife telecommutes part-time. They share a large office space at home, but they also have other places around the house to retreat to when the desire to be alone strikes. Dee and her husband have separate home offices; his is downstairs and hers is upstairs. They e-mail or call each other to make lunch arrangements, and they always knock before entering the other's office. Respecting your spouse's space is important.

You may also find that you each need time and space to be alone at home. His and her dens, offices, or studios converted from a spare bedroom can solve this. When you're not accustomed to being together all the time, having the ability to retreat to a private space for a couple hours contributes to overall harmony. You don't want to feel like you have to leave home to get some space.

When the extra income stops, more financial issues may arise. The budget plan needs to be reviewed, and a renewed understanding of how spending decisions are made and how much gets spent should be shared. You may be wealthy, but chances are good that you can't spend it as fast as you can think of ways to do it. If you find a need for separate discretionary spending accounts, put it in the plan ahead of time.

Plan on reviewing finances and investment performances together once or twice a year. When one party keeps the books, the other shouldn't be kept in the dark. The person who's not in charge of the finances may be glad not to have to keep track of all the money and investment details, but the overall picture needs to be shared.

At some point, odds are good that one of you will be left to carry on alone. Uncovering and understanding the financial situation shouldn't be an additional burden when that time comes. Your financial plan should have included this possibility so that the surviving spouse knows where everything is and how the plan goes forward. Both partners need to feel an adequate level of control and understanding of the finances and investments at all times.

You may be starting to realize that a plan for early retirement is not just making sure that you have enough money to retire. Planning doesn't end at retirement, either. The plan looks ahead for many decades. This plan is a living document, evolving as circumstances and plans evolve. It's not too early to begin thinking and discussing some of these topics in addition to the finances. If you have a spouse or a partner, you may discover that it ends up improving your relationship now, too.

The Least You Need to Know

➤ Communicate with your partner early and often for a smoother journey toward and into early retirement.

➤ Formally schedule your activities ahead of time for your first year or two in retirement.

➤ Be sure that your plan includes some out-of-the home activities with other people.

➤ Include time and space to keep out of each other's way when you're both retired.

➤ Your financial plan needs careful attention before and after you retire.

Life in the Slow Lane

Early retirement opens the door to new and enriching possibilities in your life. To reach your goal of financial freedom in middle age with health, wealth, and happiness is as good as it gets. But early retirement isn't all peaches and cream. As we've already noted, it's still life.

You'll face decisions in early retirement that may be as difficult as those you had to make before. They may or may not be different choices, but they still have consequences that require close examination. With possibly 40 years or more of life yet to go, the choices are critical. With no paycheck to buffer you, the nature of your cash flow has changed.

The Life of Riley

We don't know why Riley belongs here. He didn't retire early, and he only lived in the imaginary world of TV. But someone who's living the life of Riley is thought to be doing well and enjoying himself or herself immensely. That's your goal.

From the Hammock

Before you put your home on the market, take a long trip to your desired area at a time when the season is not ideal. Pretend that you live there. Check out the neighborhood, the activities, and the overall ambiance. Talk to the natives. Do you feel comfortable? Some places are great to visit in high season, but you wouldn't want to live there year-round.

Potholes

Check out the tax status of your retirement plan distributions before you begin withdrawals. States with high or progressive tax rates will take as much as 9 percent on top of the federal tax. If you're expecting large distributions after age 70 (and we hope you will be), the state tax could add $10,000 to $20,000 to the bite. You might want to move (again) before then. Some states with an income tax don't tax retirement plan distributions.

Financial freedom means that you can live the lifestyle you've grown accustomed to—minus the job, if you so choose. The quality of that lifestyle will rise as you use all that free time to pursue your interests and activities. You can finally do what you want!

Well, within some limits, you can. Just because you have a million or two wisely invested doesn't mean you can freely spend money. You budgeted for living expenses, travel, and other activities that you didn't have enough time to do before. You have a thoroughly thought-out financial plan. Don't dump it in retirement.

Where to Live

The biggest question you have is where you want to call home. Although 90 percent of traditional retirees stay in the same area—and often the same home—early retirees may have other plans. Perhaps your travels have already suggested a new locale. The weather suits your activities, and the pace of life will match your new schedule. Sell the house, pack up, and go, right? Not so fast.

Look closely at the cost of buying a house or condo in your target area, including paying real estate taxes, income taxes, sales taxes, and, in some areas, what amounts to wealth taxes. For instance, Florida has no income tax, but it levies a $1/10$ of 1 percent tax on financial assets except those held in qualified retirement plans. New Hampshire taxes interest and dividends above a relatively low level, but it currently has no income tax. Every state is different.

States are going to get money from you one way or another. How the particular combination of taxes is structured will affect you differently depending on these factors:

➤ Interest and dividend income
➤ Property value
➤ Capital gains
➤ Holdings of securities
➤ Purchases
➤ Pensions and Social Security
➤ Retirement plan distributions

It will pay you, literally, to look into all of these before you pull up stakes and move. You could discover annual differences in your total taxes of $5,000 and up—sometimes way up. Contact the state department of revenue for income and sales tax information, the town or city hall for property taxes, the registry of motor vehicles for auto taxes and fees. Certain cities and counties also may impose income taxes that can add as much as several thousand dollars a year to your tax bill.

If you have a financial planner, ask for help with all of this information. Or, make an appointment for a review of these taxes with a planner while you're visiting the area you're interested in. You can visit the state revenue departments by going to www.nasire.org/StateSearch/ and clicking on Revenue. You'll see a link to each state's revenue office.

Housing Costs

There are also big differences around the country in the cost of a house or condo. The median house price between states can differ by more than a factor of 2. The real estate mantra, "Location, location, location," says it all. Differences in price between similar properties can vary 100 percent even in adjacent towns and neighborhoods within a town. It pays to do your homework.

With so many years ahead of you, it's likely that you'll move more than once in retirement. Whether you choose houses, condos, or apartments, do careful research and spend time in the area first. Mistakes in moving are correctable, but no one likes to go through the process too often.

Perhaps you'll decide to spend a year or two as a vagabond. Sell your home, put your stuff in storage, and go. Buy a land cruiser, or just move every few months from apartment to apartment until you decide where to light for a longer spell. Meanwhile, invest your house proceeds in a good money market fund, and use the income to augment your budget until it's time to put down roots again. Then you can use that money to buy a new place.

From the Hammock

Wherever Jim travels, he picks up the local real estate guides and studies them. After spending some time there, he gets a feel for prices and values. You don't have to travel to do this. Web sites such as www.realtor.com show homes for sale in all areas, with multiple screens to allow you to focus on what you want. You can also order local guides for many locations at www.harmonhomes.com, or see apartments at www.aptguides.com. However, nothing beats a visit in person before you actually get serious about buying.

A Nugget of Gold

If you owned and occupied your home for at least two of the last five years before you sell it, you don't owe tax on the first $250,000 of the gain if you're single and $500,000 for couples filing joint returns. And as long as the sales are two years apart, you can do this more than once. Any gain over these amounts is taxed as a capital gain.

Potholes

You may have noticed that the U.S. healthcare system is in turmoil. Where we live in New England, the landscape has been changing every few months or less. We expect this transition period to last for many years, and we have no idea what it's transitioning to. Well before you retire, start the task of researching the healthcare options that may be available to you at that time.

If You Have Your Health ...

One of the biggest shocks to early retirees today is how confusing it is to sort out their healthcare options—health maintenance organizations (HMOs), preferred provider organizations (PPOs), indemnity plans—and how much they all cost. As it now stands, you can't get Medicare coverage until age 65. You're on your own until then. Plan on spending a good chunk of time researching your options. Your state's department of insurance is a good place to begin. You don't want to have your early retirement torpedoed by huge uninsured medical bills.

Rates and coverage vary widely within locales and between locales. If you don't convert from your previous employer's group plan to a nongroup plan offered by the same insurance company (and that is often your best choice), you may face a long waiting period or delays in coverage for preexisting conditions. If so, increase your emergency fund to carry you through this period, and hope nothing serious happens.

It Will Cost You Now

Our health doesn't usually improve with age. Like it or not, it's a downhill slope, although we hope a gradual one.

The increase in life span we've seen over the last 75 years is due, in part, to improving healthcare. But it comes at a price. Modern health can correct and improve conditions and illnesses that formerly shortened life or reduced the quality of the life remaining. You can expect continued improvements in healthcare that will extend our life span—and higher costs to pay for them.

Depending on where you live today, a good nongroup healthcare policy runs $250 to $400 per month per person for people in their 50s. That's about $6,000 to $9,000 a year for a couple.

The sobering numbers in the following table underline the fact that your health care costs in retirement are likely to be one of your biggest expenses.

Projected Health Insurance Costs at 7 Percent Inflation

Current Cost	In 10 Years	In 20 Years	In 30 Years
$6,000 per couple	$11,800	$23,200	$45,700
$9,000 per couple	$17,700	$34,800	$68,500

Pick yourself up off the floor. It may be worse, or it may be better. No one knows. Until you do know, plan on it being expensive, although not as expensive as self-insuring.

It Will Cost You Later

When you qualify for Medicare, or whatever may exist in its place when you get to the qualifying age (currently 65), you're not in the clear. Medicare was created by Congress in 1965 to provide a basic level of health care to people over age 65. It is managed by the Health Care Financing Administration. Medicare is covered more thoroughly in Chapter 22, "Social Insecurity and Mediscare."

Medicare covers only a limited range of healthcare costs, primarily those associated with hospitalization. The premium for the *Part B* elective part of your Medicare insurance is deducted from your Social Security check each month.

You will also want to buy Medigap insurance to cover many of the healthcare costs not included in Medicare. The average Medicare recipient without Medigap coverage was recently paying $3,000 a year in out-of-pocket healthcare costs. As many as 10 levels of Medigap insurance policies currently are available in many states. These are private insurance company policies that must conform to federal guidelines on what they offer. You pick the level of coverage that you want at the price offered by a variety of companies.

Today you can also join a Medicare HMO in some areas (fewer every year, however). The HMO augments your Medicare coverage similar to a Medigap plan. These HMO plans started out free, but now they charge more every year. Medicare reimburses them for the Medicare-covered costs. The U.S. Congress adjusted the reimbursement rate schedule down so low that most HMOs are losing money and are rapidly raising rates or canceling coverage.

The bad news is that the cost of the best Medigap insurance premiums is also high. They're in the same range today as are the premiums that we just looked at for regular health insurance for people in

Say What?

Part A of what is called Original Medicare covers hospital costs for a period of time subject to a deductible. This is basic Medicare, and it is what you paid for all those years out of your paycheck. **Part B** coverage currently costs about $50 a month. It covers doctor bills while you're hospitalized, outpatient care, and some services.

From the Hammock

If you want to check out what's currently available in your state with regard to Medigap coverage, go to www.Quotesmith.com and click on the Medicare Supplement tab. Fill in the information requested for your location, and you'll get quotes by company and policy.

their early 50s. So don't expect a break when you turn 65. Put numbers in your budget forecast that reflect this reality.

We'll look at other Medicare issues as well as long-term care insurance in Chapter 22. No matter how you look at it, your healthcare is likely to be your biggest ongoing expense throughout your retirement. And the quality of your health will be your major concern, if not your major topic of conversation. (We hope not!)

Die Broke—or Not

Popular book titles in 2000 counseled people to plan to spend every penny they had while they were alive and to bounce the last check for the funeral—or to plan on stretching out their money and leave an estate. Entertaining arguments were presented on either side, but this decision is up to you—sort of. The basic problem, as you may have already figured out, is that you have no way of knowing in advance when you're checking out. That makes it impossible to plan perfectly either way.

Our advice is to plan on living to age 95, and cover all your expenses as best as you can project them through then. You don't want to outlive your money. That's the biggest risk you face. If your money outlives you, that's what your will and estate plan are for (see Chapter 23, "Your Estate Needs a Plan, Too").

You've seen how your health insurance expenses are likely to increase. Other expenses will go up, too, although probably not at the same rate. You may cut back on the travel and high living later in your retirement, but other expenses are likely to take their place. There are too many unknowns to create an accurate plan well in advance, but that's no excuse not to create one. Build in a fudge factor to keep your finances healthy. It's a lot easier to find ways to get rid of excess cash in your old age than it is to find ways to get more.

Potholes

If you're in great financial shape with more than you'll ever want or need, and you're notified that you'll get an inheritance of some size, check with your financial planner first. You may want to disclaim it—pass it up—if that means it will pass to your children instead. That keeps it out of your estate but enables you, in essence, to give it to your children.

You need to do this within nine months of the death of the person who left you the money—except for IRA or 401(k) accounts. New rules extend the deadline to December 31 of the year after the death of the IRA or 401(k) account holder.

What Will Your Parents Think?

We talked earlier about the issue of caring for aging parents. Just when you're off gallivanting around the world in your retirement, they may be looking for more physical, emotional, and financial assistance. The current median-income retiree today is living on $12,000, including Social Security, and will see her income decline from there in real dollars while expenses keep growing. That could be one or more of your parents.

A parent should be proud that you've done so well in life that you can afford to retire early and follow your muse. That parent may also derive a sense of security knowing that you'll be able to provide for her if and when the time comes. And you probably want to be able to help. Just make sure that your help doesn't sink your ship.

If you have parents who may need financial help down the road, you need to explore this possibility alone, with your partner, and with your parents when you're close to retiring. You may have to do financial planning with them, or for them, or help them seek outside financial planning.

Moving an elderly parent in with you, and providing care and support, is the time-honored custom in many cultures. It's probably happening in your family or neighborhood. If it comes to assisted-living or nursing care facilities for one or more parents, can you afford to help? It may come down to yours later or theirs now. What are you going to do? These kinds of decisions are very difficult emotionally and financially for everyone involved. Each person will face his and her own questions and issues around them. They should be part of your plan.

Often parents aren't comfortable sharing the details of their financial lives with adult children. They may be willing to talk with a professional who can help them look at the issues without the emotional involvement. You can't force them to do any of this, and some folks just won't do it. That doesn't help you very much, but that's the way it works.

On the other hand, maybe your parents are wealthy, or at least well enough off to finance their own retirement. Although they may still need financial planning assistance and other support at some point, you shouldn't have concerns about your own finances being disrupted.

Neither should you plan on an inheritance to augment your finances. Your parents may live long and spend much of their money one way or another. Or, perhaps your siblings will get the bulk of their estate because your parents recognize that they haven't done as well as you in the money game. Inheritances can be tricky, and you shouldn't expect much, if anything. If you get something, fine. Fold it into your plan and make any adjustments as needed to your investments. Just don't count on it.

What Will Your Kids Think?

If you will still have children under the age of 20 when you retire, who knows what they think about anything, anyway? If you've covered whatever

A Nugget of Gold

If you included in your plan an option to be able to lend your kids a hand financially, with either buying a house or setting up a college education fund for your grandchildren, let them know. This way, they'll know what they can expect. You don't want them to think they're on easy street, though. Check with your tax adviser before you do any of this kind of planning.

college expenses you have planned for, tell them whatever else you're comfortable sharing. Your actions and behavior will communicate more to them over time.

More likely, your children, if you have any, will be young adults when you retire early. You should discuss aspects of your retirement plan with them so that they understand that retiring early is a positive choice for you. At a minimum, you'll be setting a good example for starting to save and invest early so that they, too, can have a choice to retire early.

While you may discover in later years that you've accumulated more money than you'll need (that's when it's time to revisit your estate plan), you don't want to be overly generous in the early years of your retirement. That could jeopardize your situation after age 80, and you could run out of money. Any changes need to be thought out carefully.

The Least You Need to Know

➤ Financial freedom doesn't mean that you can forget about your budget and spend money with no thought of tomorrow.

➤ Where you choose to live in retirement can have a major effect on your taxes and housing costs.

➤ Your healthcare options will be confusing and expensive, requiring lots of research before you retire.

➤ Most early retirees will have both aging parents and young adult children who may need or expect you to help them. You need to carefully consider what you can do ahead of time and let them know.

Chapter 5

From Money to Wealth

> ### In This Chapter
>
> ➤ Wealth is measured by net worth, not income
>
> ➤ When you're financially free, you're wealthy
>
> ➤ Emotions can sabotage your plan
>
> ➤ Live in the present, but plan for the future
>
> ➤ Don't allow your money to be lazy

How do you define wealth? Many would say that a wealthy person is someone who makes more or has more than they do. For such people, it doesn't really make any difference what they have in terms of a dollar amount. According to a Phoenix Home Life Mutual Company survey, half of the people with a *net worth* of $1 million to $4 million think that they need more than $5 million to be "wealthy"!

Wealth is *not* about how much you make. If you spend every penny you have, you may be broke. You're living paycheck to paycheck, one step away from disaster. Wealth comes from what you have left after taxes and expenses. That's how you build wealth, and that's how wealth is measured.

Many people who live in big, expensive houses with two or more flashy cars have a big income. They also usually have big debts. They may be broke—or worse. If they owe more than they own, their net worth is negative. Their neighbors, their friends, and even their families might think that these people are rich. Don't bet on it.

The Difference Between Wealthy and Rich

Malcolm Forbes, the late publisher of *Forbes Magazine,* said, "True wealth gives you freedom." That fits with our theme. Your goal is to reach the point of financial freedom where you have the choice to retire or not, as you wish. How much money that requires depends on how much you want to spend to live. Because that amount varies widely from one person to the next, it's up to you to decide.

In 1999, the range of estimates of how many people have how much looked like this:

Net Worth Estimates in the United States

Number of Households	Net Worth
14–17 million	Over $500,000
3–7 million	$1,000,000
600,000–900,000	$5,000,000
55,000	$30,000,000

At the time of this writing, these numbers may be smaller because the plummeting stock market and the demise of dot.coms and stock options cleaned out a lot of paper wealth.

You're Wealthy!

A handy definition of wealth goes like this: You're wealthy if you can live comfortably on the after-tax income from your investments. In Chapter 2, "What It Takes," Donna and Charley had $900,000 invested in taxable accounts and no debt. That produced $72,000 of income at 8 percent, or $61,000 after taxes. This matched their expenses during their first year in retirement. By this definition, they were wealthy.

Say What?

Net worth *is simply how much a person owns minus how much she owes. Add up all your investments, property, and possessions, and then subtract all your debts. That's your net worth.*

As Donna and Charley moved forward, we decided that they really needed to have $1 million to get them safely to age 70. Then their retirement plans rode to the rescue and carried them to their 90s. Otherwise, inflation and unexpected problems were going to raise havoc with their plan and their lives.

When you create your financial plan and project your expenses into the future, you can find your threshold of financial freedom. You might invest a greater percentage of your money in taxable accounts, or more in your retirement plan accounts. If the combined amount gets you comfortably to your 90s, call yourself wealthy. But don't cut corners; higher estimates give you some cushion for unexpected events. The difference between wealthy today and broke tomorrow isn't very much when something goes wrong.

A Nugget of Gold

Wealth is the result of saving and investing well, not how much you make. In the book *The Millionaire Next Door* (Longstreet Press, 1996), authors Thomas J. Stanley and William D. Danko offer a rule of thumb to gauge whether you're as wealthy as you could be at your age. Multiply your age times your pretax annual household income from all sources. Divide that by 10. Not counting any inheritance, this is about where you could be if you've been a good saver and invested wisely. If you're not there yet, keep reading.

At age 38, Linda and George earn $90,000, plus they make $4,000 from interest and dividends a year. Their age (38 years) times $94,000 equals $3,572,000. Divide that by 10. According to this formula, they should have $357,200.

You're Rich!

Rich people live off the income from their investments forever without dipping into their *capital*. They'll die and leave an estate bigger than they have today. For Donna and Charley in 2001, that would mean about $2,550,000 to start. By age 90, it would grow to more than $6 million. That means starting with $1,115,000 more than they had. The total invested has to keep growing to keep up with inflation and taxes. Donna and Charley's expenses at age 90 will be almost $300,000, not including taxes:

Once they start to dip into their investments to pay expenses each year, their pile shrinks. As it shrinks, so does the income that it can produce. You don't need to be rich to retire early—just wealthy enough that you don't run out of money.

From the Hammock

The more stuff we get, the more stuff we want. That isn't the way to become wealthy. Getting and keeping more money is. Rethink wealth not as getting what you want, but as becoming comfortable with what you have. Then *more* isn't a problem, and we actually do end up with more because we can save and invest instead of spend.

Say What?

Capital is your wealth in the form of money or property that you use to produce more wealth or to pay your expenses.

Say What?

Fixed-income investments such as CDs and bonds pay you a fixed amount of interest periodically. CDs and bonds also return your principal at the end of the stated period. Bonds and bond funds experience changing values reflecting fluctuations in the market rate of interest, but only bonds pay back your investment at maturity—bond funds don't. Bond funds usually have no maturity.

6 percent on $6,000,000	= $360,000
Minus 20 percent taxes	– 72,000
Net income	$288,000
Minus Expenses	– 292,000
Difference	–$4,000

You want to have more income than you need in the early years of your retirement. The extra income gets reinvested to increase future income. As inflation pushes up your expenses, it's likely that eventually you'll have to begin taking money out of your pile. The reinvestment also provides a cushion to cover unexpected expenses and years when your return isn't up to snuff. It isn't "extra" money.

In later years, you may want to lower your exposure to stock market volatility and put most of your money in *fixed-income investments* such as certificates of deposit and bonds. You no longer need growth (and the risk that comes with it) at age 85 or 90; you need secure income. We reduced Donna and Charley's return on their money to 6 percent before age 90 to reflect this. You'll do what works for you in your plan. (We'll show you how to do that in Part 2, "Planning the Path to Wealth.")

How You Feel About Money

What a loaded topic. You might not know how you really feel about having money. Sure, you want more—who doesn't? Yet you might find that when you get more money, you become a bit squirrelly about it, especially if you come from a family background where money wasn't very plentiful. This section is about not letting unidentified emotions become a barrier to reaching your goals.

Lucky

We define luck as the ability to recognize opportunity when it knocks and the willingness to answer the door and let it in. In this way, we can often make our own luck. Understanding this can alert you to become aware of and prepared for opportunity. We may not be in control of what kinds of opportunities approach, but we can control how we respond to them.

The actions of becoming aware and being prepared actually do influence the opportunities we get. The remote-control couch-potato cowboy limits opportunity to 1-800 numbers or infomercials. Not much happening there. Right now, you're learning about a major opportunity to achieve financial freedom because you picked up and are reading this book. If you follow our suggestions and eventually reach your goal, is that luck?

Guilty

Some people find that they feel guilty when they have money. This is especially true when it's "sudden money" from a big inheritance or a one-in-a-million lottery ticket. But even those who work hard and save can discover a vague feeling of guilt. You might wonder, "Why me? I don't deserve to be wealthy," or, "Why should I have so much while others go hungry?"

These are legitimate questions, and you need to face these feelings and work them out. Perhaps you can resolve these issues by thinking, "I do deserve to become wealthy if I've worked for it," and, "I can make a commitment to help others who have much less than I do with my time and money."

If you don't deal with these kinds of emotions, they may undermine your motivation and your plan. You'll find some excuse to stop saving and start spending so that you can feel better. It may make you feel better, but you sabotage yourself and your goal.

Secure

The other side of the coin is for those who see money as security. And who'll argue with that? But, beyond a certain point, it becomes unhealthy. Clutching tightly to their big wad like Scrooge McDuck, these people become miserly and suspicious. They won't spend their money on anything, including themselves. You may have heard about the millionaire bag ladies living out of shopping carts. They're true stories.

Potholes

The effect of inflation is devastating. Six million dollars after 40 years of 4 percent inflation has only the same buying power as $1,550,000 did in the beginning. It looks like a lot more money, but it isn't. Don't underestimate inflation's effect when you create your plan.

A Nugget of Gold

Higher incomes have only a weak positive impact on happiness, according to a National Bureau of Economic Research study covering 1972 through 1998. The study said that married folks are the happiest, men are becoming happier, and women are less happy in general than they used to be. Happiness peaks at age 18, they found, declines until age 40, and then starts to move up again. But money doesn't have very much to do with happiness.

There's a lot of space between the extremes we've outlined. In all cases, you should be sensitive to your feelings about money as you become wealthier. If you detect a sense of unease about having or spending money, look closely at why. Remember, money is only a medium of exchange—no more, no less. It literally has no value by itself, no matter how high you pile it in your bedroom. Its value is only in what you can do with it for yourself and others. It's your money; don't let it control you.

Potholes

"Send $2,000 for a special opportunity that can't miss!" When opportunity knocks, it usually doesn't ask for your money first. Invest in your education and experiences to create opportunities for yourself. Putting your money in these other "opportunities" will provide you with only an expensive education and less money.

It's Been Said

We're told that you won't find the line "Money is the root of all evil" in the Bible. But you will find that "Love of money is the root of all evil." There's a big difference.

The Big Picture Stuff: The Long Term

It's no longer true that young people aren't concerned about their retirement 30 or 40 years in the future. The Gen Xers are saving much faster than baby boomers were at the same age. In fact, some are saving more than many baby boomers are today. When you view your life as a long continuum connecting today with a far-off tomorrow, the wisdom of saving early becomes clear.

Find a balance between what you want today and what you want tomorrow. That's the way to understand the big picture. What you do today may determine your choices down the road. Some people don't seem to be able to do this. They get to age 60 and find out that they don't have much of anything saved up. Looming retirement sorta snuck up on them. All they can say is, "I wish I had started saving years ago." Hindsight is always clearer.

That doesn't have to be you. Foresight always works better. The dream of retiring early, or the financial freedom to have that choice, is obviously in your mind because you're reading this book. Keep stretching toward the future. You don't know what will happen, where you'll be, or what you'll be doing in a few decades. But the plan you begin today provides a framework that gives you options later.

Taking the long-term view of your life is also valuable for building and managing your portfolio. Cultivate the long-term view by looking at the big picture of your life. Then figure out each day what you can do to make the whole picture look a little bit brighter.

Same as Regular Retirement, Only Faster

Retiring early is the same as retiring later, only it comes at you quicker—and because it does, you need to plan earlier and fulfill your plan faster. Rules like, "Save until it hurts, and then save some more," are necessary to enable you to retire early.

We pointed out in Chapter 1, "It's About Having Options," that you're likely to be leaving a lot of money on the table by retiring early. The 10 years from age 55 to 65 are likely to be your peak earning years, and you're skipping the money to retire early. You also have 10 more years to add on to your retirement. To compensate for both of these, retiring early does become a pedal-to-the-metal sort of race. But the only way you can lose it is not to get there at all.

Because no one can predict the future, there are no guarantees in life. Your hard work and saving 'til it hurts have the best chance of allowing you the freedom to retire early. Even if your plan doesn't work as well as it looked like it would on paper despite your efforts, you will eventually get to the point where you're assured of a comfortable retirement. It may not be on your original schedule, but it will put you ahead of most people.

Make Your Money Work for You

Successful retirement, early or not, means that you learn to put your money to work for you. When you get enough of it, you achieve financial freedom. When your hard-working money makes more than you do working hard, you've made it. To get there, you need to follow these tips:

➤ Save until it hurts, and then save some more.

➤ Learn to manage your money.

➤ Invest wisely.

➤ Supervise the productivity of your money.

A survey for United States Trust Co. found that 150 baby boomers averaged 6.5 percent a year returns

From the Hammock

Frugality has its place. You spend carefully so that you can save more for your retirement. Later, you want to make sure that your money lasts as long as you do. Make a spending plan as part of your budget that allows you to be good to yourself without putting your future in danger. That gives you permission to spend. The last time we inquired, you still can't take it with you.

It's Been Said

"It requires a great deal of boldness and a great deal of caution to make a great fortune, and when you have got it, it requires ten times as much wit to keep it."

—Baron Nathan Meyer Rothschild

on their stock portfolios from 1973 through early 1999. Over that same period, the *S&P 500* returned more than 21 percent per year, and technology stocks returned almost double that. There's obviously a lot of lazy money out there. Opportunity knocked in the form of a great bull market, and many didn't know how to respond.

Money won't work by itself. Put a $10 bill in your sock drawer, and two years later, you still have a $10 bill. But it's worth only $9.22 after two years of 4 percent inflation. You allowed it to be lazy money.

Money sitting in a checking account or bank money market account earning little or no interest is lazy money, too. If you're not making the 4 percent a year, the money is wasting away. Sure, you need enough money in a checking account to pay your bills next month, but you can get good interest even on that money if you look around. (We'll show you where to put your money to work in Part 3, "Investing for Your Retirement," and Part 4, "A Safari on Wall Street.")

You may not have any clue today how to invest your money and manage it so that it works hard for you. We're sure you can learn, though. It takes some time and effort, but it's worth it. Watching money work hard for you beats working hard for your money, hands down. It's an attitude, a mind-set that you can adopt, that you want to invest in if you want to reach financial freedom.

Say What?

The **S&P 500** refers to an index of the stock prices of 500 major, mostly U.S., companies selected by a group at Standard & Poors, an investment research company.

The Least You Need to Know

➤ Never confuse income with wealth. Wealth grows from the money you invest after taxes and expenses.

➤ If you find that you're uncomfortable when you start to accumulate money, examine your emotions and work through them to reach your goals. Don't let emotions destroy your plan.

➤ We can often create our own luck by learning how to respond when opportunity knocks.

➤ A long-term perspective means finding the way to balance what you want today with what you want in the future.

➤ Make your money work as hard as you do. Lazy money wastes away.

Part 2

Planning the Path to Wealth

Financial planning shouldn't be a scary term. Financial planning is how you establish personal and financial goals, and then construct a plan to achieve them. It shows you how you can retire early, have choices, and reach financial freedom.

Financial planning isn't really about money and investing. Your plan transforms your hopes and dreams into the quality of life that you want in early retirement. You save, you invest, and you grow your money so that you can live your chosen lifestyle in the future.

You learn patience with financial planning as you see how your plan comes together and works for you over many decades and through your retirement. Life is a finite journey, so don't be in any rush to go through it. Money is life's way of preventing you from having it all at once. Be patient. Give your money enough time to do its work for you.

Chapter 6

Wealth: How to Get It and Keep It

> ## In This Chapter
>
> ➤ Creating a financial snapshot of your life
>
> ➤ Measuring your cash flow
>
> ➤ Good debt and bad debt
>
> ➤ How to protect your growing wealth

In a Princeton Survey Research Poll in 1996, more than 60 percent of Americans reported these among their biggest concerns:

➤ Paying for healthcare

➤ Not having enough money for retirement

➤ Paying for college for their kids

➤ Losing a home, or never being able to afford one

➤ Losing a job or taking a pay cut

While we all have other concerns, too, people often worry about not having enough money to meet life's biggest challenges. *Making* enough money isn't the major problem here; it's *having* enough. You're probably making enough to get by, but it might not take much of a bump in the road to upset your financial situation. This chapter shows you how to get your financial life in shape.

Are you ready to pass "Go"? Here's where you find out whether you're in position to build your plan for financial freedom. If not, you'll see what you have to do to get there. You don't erect a building without first constructing a sound foundation.

Get It Together

The first step is getting organized. See if you have good financial records of your income, expenses, assets, and bills and account statements for the following:

➤ Checking accounts

➤ Savings accounts and CDs

➤ Retirement plans

➤ Stocks, bonds, and mutual finds

➤ Insurance policies

➤ Credit cards

➤ Tax returns

➤ Bills

➤ Personal data and records

A Nugget of Gold

You can put many of your records on your computer with a program such as Intuit's *Quicken* or Microsoft's *Money.* This will keep some your financial information organized even better than paper files, if you update it regularly. But you still need to file the paperwork. If you do use your computer for record-keeping, back it up on disks each time you enter stuff.

If you throw these documents into a box or a drawer when they come in the mail and just let them pile up, you're not organized. Do you spend hours going through the pile when you need to find something? That won't work anymore.

Make a careful plan to organize all your documents in three-ring binders, manila envelopes and folders, file drawers, or covered plastic boxes. Add a small, fire-resistant safety box for really important documents. Spend $75 and a couple hours the next rainy Saturday, and you're organized. Then get into the habit of filing new stuff at least once a month. It takes 10 minutes. You're planning to become wealthy, and that will multiply the paperwork. Get a handle on it early.

Determining Net Worth

Now that you're organized, you can easily get your hands on all the documents that you'll need to assess your financial position. There are forms for you to use in Appendix A, "Financial Worksheets," for all the numbers that we'll cover here. Net worth is first.

Whatcha Got? Assets

First, list your cash assets. These aren't all cash per se (count cash if you have a lot on hand), but they are cash equivalents because they can be converted to cash in a couple of days:

➤ Checking accounts

➤ Saving accounts

➤ Certificates of deposit

➤ Money market accounts

➤ Savings bonds

➤ Traveler's checks

The next step is to create a list of your lifestyle assets. Lifestyle assets are things that you use and enjoy today as part of how you live. You probably bought them, and, if necessary, you could sell them. That sale price is the figure that you use to determine an item's worth. Your most reasonable estimate is fine if you can't find any other value. Include these items:

➤ Property

➤ Cars and trucks

➤ Furniture

➤ Jewelry

➤ Collectibles

➤ Other valuables

➤ Grown-up toys

Add anything not on the Net Worth form if you know that you could (legally) sell it.

Finally, assemble your other account statements to find what your invested assets are:

➤ Stocks

➤ Bonds

➤ Mutual funds

➤ Real estate other than your house

➤ Limited partnerships

➤ Ownership interest in a business

Include what is in your retirement plans such as 401(k)s and IRAs. Use your latest statements for all values—not how much you paid or put in.

Totaled together, these three categories comprise your assets.

What Do You Owe? Liabilities

On the other side of the ledger are your liabilities, or what you owe. Back to your files. Among other things on the Net Worth form, find out what you owe on the following:

➤ Mortgage

➤ Credit cards

➤ Auto loans

➤ Education loans

➤ Home equity loans

➤ Personal loans

➤ Taxes

➤ Bills, bills, and bills

When you've totaled these up, you may need to take a break. But come back—there's more to do.

When you subtract your liabilities from your assets, you get your net worth. Are you wealthy yet? Probably not. Like it or not, this is where you're starting from—and if you don't know where you are, you can't get to where you want to go.

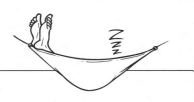

From the Hammock

It's not enough to know that you want to retire early and reach your other financial goals. You'll discover that once you know what your assets and liabilities really are, you'll find yourself motivated to reduce your debt and increase your net worth. Combine this with a concrete set of goals and it will be easier to take the steps you need to manage your cash flow to achieve your goals.

If your net worth is a positive number, you're in a much healthier position. A negative number means that you owe more than you're worth, and that ain't good. But knowing that you're behind the eight ball should be a good enough kick in the butt to get you to "Go."

Play Defense First

You increase your net worth, or turn a negative net worth into a positive net worth, by learning to manage your cash flow. Money comes into your hands, and money flows out. That's cash flowing. You need to play defense to keep the money from flowing out as fast as it comes in. To manage it, you first create another set of numbers called a cash flow statement. (What did you think we'd name it?)

Money Flows In

Refer to the Cash Flow statement in Appendix A as a guideline for totaling your income. Income is what you earn from your jobs. Also add investment income and any other regular payments that you can count on, such as these:

➤ Self-employment income

➤ Rental income

➤ Interest and dividends

➤ Alimony

➤ Child support

Don't count any capital gain on investments here because you can't be sure of this every year. Add all the others for the last year, using gross income for salaries, not take-home pay. The figure that you arrive at is what you have to work with and what you use to build wealth. This means that you must treat it carefully and protect it, not let it keep flowing out of your hands.

And Out It Goes

Where does it all go? To pay your expenses. Go to that organized pile of bills that you paid and checks that you wrote, for starters. You know the usual suspects. Add up what you spent in the last 12 months on items such as these:

➤ Groceries

➤ Clothes

➤ Rent

➤ Utilities

➤ Repairs

➤ Insurance

➤ Loan payments

Include everything else that you can put a firm number on—or use a good estimate, if you don't find the paperwork. The "Expenses" part of the Cash Flow form will jog your memory.

In addition to your basic expenses, you have what we'll call elective expenses. These are activities and things you could do without if necessary, but they often are what makes life more enjoyable. Nevertheless, they're the things you could cut back on or eliminate in a pinch or to improve your cash flow.

Add it all up for the year, and subtract it from your total income. Wow! Look at what you saved. *Didn't* you save that much in the last year? You wish. And if the number is negative already, there's trouble in River City.

We never accurately count all the cash that we spend every day in every way. Where do you get your cash? When you deposit your paycheck? From an ATM machine? Do you write checks for cash or take a cash advance on a credit card? You had paperwork for all these, and they're on your statements. Add them up, and you'll get a lot closer to discovering what you really spend.

Get Real

Now you know why you don't save so much. To build wealth and to increase your net worth, you have to ride herd on all your expenses. Keep track of every household and personal expense for everyone who handles household cash for three months. Explain to your family what's going on, and ask for weekly reports, in writing. If everyone on the team knows what the game plan is and why you're setting up a defense, the griping and complaining won't be too bad.

When these real numbers are in, redo the Cash Flow statement. Now you can make a long-term defensive plan to protect your cash flow. Look carefully at where you can cut back on elective expenses of all kinds, from the coffee and donut every morning and meals out, to household purchases and expenses.

You can implement some of these measures at once. Others, such as vacation expenses, holiday gifts, and car payments, may take some planning and discussion. Find ways to protect your cash flow and turn it into net worth. That's called saving. Set a goal for how much you need to save when you do the numbers in the next few chapters. No longer will you plan to save what's left over at the end of the month. You know now where that got you.

Say What?

When the value of an item or property increases over time, it is said to **appreciate** in value. Using debt for property that is likely to appreciate is usually good. Items that lose value are said to **depreciate**. Using debt to buy them is a bad idea, especially when they lose value faster than you pay off the debt.

Get Out of the Debt Hole

A negative cash flow creates a negative net worth. We can spend more than we earn because so many companies are happy to lend us money. Why? Either they get the money when you spend it and again when you pay it back, or they charge you rent for using it until you pay it back. What do you really get out of this? Debt.

Some debt is good debt. A mortgage on a house or other property is good debt if you can afford the payments. Over time (sometimes a long time), a house *appreciates* as fast as inflation, so you can at least get your money back. Borrowing money for education is good because more education gets you (or your children) a better income later.

A car loan is borderline good debt/bad debt. If you need the car to get to work to earn money, and that's the only way you can afford a car, it may be good debt—for now. We'll look at this question more closely in Chapter 7, "How to Be a Middle-Class Millionaire." There's really not anything else to consider in the good debt category.

The Rule of Debt

The rule of debt, as you can see from the previous examples, is *Make sure that you borrow only for that which improves in value or improves your cash flow in the near future.* Everything else is a losing proposition. It costs you twice—and, sooner or later, you end up with nothing to show for it. People who live on debt have a rented lifestyle that they can't afford. Net worth goes negative and life gets worse, not better.

To build wealth, you can't give your money away for nothing. Whether you pay 6 percent or 18 percent (or even more) interest on your loan, you're hurting yourself and helping someone else. You're going backward in the journey of life, and you're preventing yourself from reaching any of the goals that truly matter to you.

Get Help

If you have more debt than you can handle, there are ways to get help. The National Foundation for Consumer Credit is a network of 1,450 nonprofit community organizations that provide budget and debt counseling services, education on using credit, and help setting up a debt repayment program. Local members are called Consumer Counseling Services. For a local office, either call or use the Internet:

➤ Call 1-800-388-2227.

➤ Go to www.nfcc.org.

The Debt Counselors of America is a nonprofit Internet-based organization that uses certified financial planners to provide information and assistance with debt, credit, and other financial problems. Call 1-800-680-DEBT, or go to www.dcs.org for more information.

A Nugget of Gold

The gold doesn't go to you if you carry credit card debt from month to month. Companies borrow at 6 to 8 percent and loan you the money at 12 to 18 percent. They have expenses and lose a few loans, but they usually manage to come out well ahead. For instance, a close reading of Sears's Annual Reports indicates that it earns 50 to 80 percent of its total operating profit in most years just from credit card interest. They almost give away the merchandise at cost so that they can earn money on the loan. Pay cash for the goods, and keep the gold for yourself.

It's Been Said

"Debt is the worst poverty."
—Thomas Fuller

Not only does bad debt cost you money and prevent you from making progress toward financial freedom, but it also puts you at risk for personal *bankruptcy*. More than one million people file for personal bankruptcy each year in the United States. Most are middle- and upper-class folks who had too much debt. Something went wrong—a job layoff, a medical problem, or a divorce—and they lost their ability to make payments.

Say What?

When you can't pay your bills, are beyond your credit limit, and can't sell enough to meet these obligations, personal **bankruptcy** is a legal option, but it costs money just to file. Chapter 7 bankruptcy eliminates all unsecured debt (you give back the stuff that you got with secured debt, such as your car or your sofa, unless you reaffirm your debt with the creditors). Chapter 13 bankruptcy allows you to create a plan to pay all your debts and attorney's fees. You'll have an extended period of time to do this through the court.

Play defense with your cash flow by limiting unnecessary expenses and carrying only a healthy amount of good debt. This is the second step toward improving your wealth. Even if it takes you a couple of years to pay off your bad debt and to implement your defensive plan, get started right away. Then you're closer to "Go."

Your 911 Fund

This is your second line of defense after you get a handle on your cash flow. With a 911 fund, you're covered when the car breaks down, the fridge goes on the fritz, or you lose a job. Call your 911 fund and pay it back afterward, as quickly as possible, out of your cash flow.

How Much?

How much should you put in your 911 fund? Aim for a minimum of three months' expenses (take your annual expenses from your Cash Flow statement and divide by 4). If you have two good earners in the family, that should be enough. With only one breadwinner and a child or two, go for six months or more. If you lose your job, get laid off, or become ill or injured, you could lose your paycheck for that long. Your 911 fund keeps you out of more serious financial trouble.

Where to Keep It

Keep three months' worth of emergency money in an account separate from your regular bank accounts. Even better, open a *money market fund* at a discount brokerage. Money market funds pay more than twice as much interest as most bank savings and money market accounts. Get checks with the account, and put the checkbook in your home fire-resistant safety box—leave it there unless it's truly for an emergency.

If you need more than three months' expenses in your 911 fund (and it can't hurt to have more), put the remaining amount in a *short-term bond fund* or a *balanced mutual fund* at the same brokerage as your money market fund. This money will earn a little more over time, and it's almost as secure as a money market fund. You can get the money transferred to the money market fund with a phone call and can write a check tomorrow.

Your 911 fund isn't "mad money," nor is it a vacation fund. You use it only to self-insure against the problems of daily economic life. It keeps you out of debt and out of trouble, and it provides security. It's also the buffer between your life and your investments. Build your 911 fund first, before you invest.

The Protection Game

You've done what you can to protect yourself against life's little—and not so little—financial hiccups. What can you do to protect yourself from major problems? You transfer part of the risk to the big-money guys—the insurance agencies. You handle the amount that you're prepared for, and they pay for the rest. That's what insurance is for, and you need a bunch of it. Just be glad that someone is willing to take the financial impact of these risks for you.

These coverages are necessary so that you don't get permanently derailed when something goes really wrong. This is a short summary of what you need to get to "Go."

Protect Your Income

Say What?

Money market funds are mutual funds that invest in very short-term loans (less than one year to pay back) to companies, governments, and government agencies. They pay close to market rates of interest monthly. A **short-term bond fund** buys bonds that come due in less than three years. The value of your investment moves up and down a small amount as market interest rates change. A **balanced mutual fund** invests in both bonds and stocks of large, stable companies that usually pay dividends. The value of your investment may change a bit more, but the bonds usually balance the stocks pretty well.

Disability is your biggest risk because you're twice as likely to be disabled for more than 90 days between the ages of 25 and 55 than you are to die. It may not be a complete and permanent disability, but once your 911 fund is exhausted, your growing investments are at risk.

Whether you're single or married, and whether you have a two-income household or one, every adult wage earner who isn't independently wealthy needs disability insurance. You may have some at work, but it might not be enough. Take a copy of the policy to an independent insurance agent who sells several lines of disability insurance for an analysis of what it covers and what you need.

Life Insurance

You insure your life to protect the income stream that you represent. You are what supports, or helps to support, your family. If you don't have dependents, you probably don't need life insurance. If you're married, you both have good jobs, and you don't plan on having kids, you don't need life insurance. Single people don't need life insurance, either.

Otherwise, you need insurance to support those who are, or will be, dependent on your income. A husband and wife who are parents, even if they're both working, should each have a policy to replace their income and cover the expenses of raising a family.

Potholes

When you discover you do need more life insurance, you can quickly become overwhelmed with the choices. Don't settle for the first insurance plan you get from a smooth-talking agent. Make sure you understand exactly what you're buying and how it works. Look at and compare several plans before making a decision.

We recommend that you first investigate term insurance policies. They provide straight life insurance for specific periods at a very low cost compared to other types of policies. Then, if you want to look at those other types, you have a basic plan with which to compare them.

Again, you may have some life insurance at work, but not enough. There's a worksheet in Appendix A to guide you. If you find that you need more, remember what you're insuring: your income stream if you die. At some point, you won't have dependents, you'll have a lot of money, and you'll be financially free. You won't need life insurance then. Buy what you need only for the period of time that you need it.

Property and Casualty Insurance

If you own a home, make sure that you have an HO3 homeowner policy and get a *rider* for replacement cost to cover both your home and its contents. The small extra cost is well worth it. If you have any valuable possessions, such as expensive jewelry, works of art, or rare coin collections, you also need riders to cover them specifically.

Renters need an HO4 policy to cover personal property and liability. Your landlord covers the building but not your stuff. Condo owners need HO5 for the same reason. The condo association covers the building, with part of the condo fees going to buy insurance (ask to see the policy) but not your possessions.

Umbrella Liability

When it rains, it pours. Once you have more net worth than your homeowner insurance and auto policies cover, your assets are at risk if you're sued or cause an accident with serious medical bills for someone else.

A million-dollar umbrella policy picks up coverage where the others leave off. To get an umbrella policy, you need high levels of liability coverage on both policies and high property damage coverage on your auto policy. That's okay—you should have high levels anyway to protect your growing wealth.

Say What?

A **rider** is additional insurance for a specific item or class of items, or a specified type of coverage, that "rides" on your base policy. Expensive furs, jewelry, artwork, antiques, collectibles, and other such items are excluded from basic coverage.

Health Insurance

You can't afford not to have health insurance, even if you're single. You never know when you'll become ill or have an accident, and medical costs are astronomical. The combination of large medical bills and loss of income is guaranteed to blow a huge hole in your financial outlook. Without insurance, you'll be charged the full rate for everything, not the discount negotiated by health plans.

If you have health insurance through work, you're in good shape. Get the family plan, if you have a spouse or children. Otherwise, research your options for nongroup plans with preferred provider organizations (PPO), health maintenance organizations (HMO), and traditional indemnity plans. You can usually get a large deductible with the latter to reduce your premium.

Without all these insurance coverages (except life insurance, if you have no dependents), you're leaving yourself vulnerable to financial catastrophe. Your goals will get trashed, and you may not be able to get back on track. Whatever your plan in life, protect yourself with insurance. Sure, it costs a lot—until you need it.

You can begin your research on many types of insurance on the web. The following sites provide information and quotes from a variety of insurance companies.

➤ www.insweb.com, a complete insurance marketplace

➤ www.quickeninsurance.com for quotes on many types of insurance

➤ www.quotesmith.com for more quotes

A Nugget of Gold

There are three main varieties of health insurance coverage available. The traditional indemnity plan allows you the most choices, but requires you to pay for the first $250, $500, or more each quarter or year. The premiums are usually higher than the other types of plans, too.

An HMO is an organization of healthcare facilities and personnel that provides medical services on a prepaid plan. You're limited to doctors and facilities inside the plan, but your premiums and out-of-pocket expenses are the lowest of the plans.

A PPO consists of a network of healthcare providers and hospitals who agree to provide services to members at rates negotiated by an insurance company. Like an HMO, you pay a small coinsurance payment per service or visit but your choices are wider. You may even choose a doctor or hospital outside of the network, but your benefit coverage will be reduced.

The Least You Need to Know

➤ You can't get started until you know where you are now. Get organized, and then create a Net Worth statement and a Cash Flow statement.

➤ A complete defensive game plan starts with getting control of your cash flow—your expenses.

➤ There's good debt and bad debt. Identify the bad debt in your financial life, and pay it off quickly.

➤ Protect your financial plan for your life with an emergency fund and insurance before you start investing.

Chapter 7

How to Be a Middle-Class Millionaire

In This Chapter

➤ Millionaires aren't what you think they are

➤ How to think and act like a millionaire

➤ Why it's more important to be a good saver than a good investor

➤ How to manage your cash flow

A million dollars certainly isn't what it used to be, that's for sure. Inflation constantly erodes the buying power of the dollar. Your first million (you're going to be a millionaire before you retire—can you get comfortable with that idea?) is still a major milestone on your path to financial freedom, but it won't be enough to allow you to retire early. You'll have to become a multimillionaire if you want that choice.

The first million is the hardest because you start with virtually nothing. You have no money working hard for you, so you have to do all the work. As you save and invest over the years, you get a partner, your money, working for you. You're also likely to earn more money than you are now through raises, promotions, and new jobs, as well as more experience, training, and education. Don't get discouraged today if a million dollars looks like a too-distant goal. You'll get there.

If a million dollars isn't what it used to be, neither are millionaires. Even multimillionaires likely aren't who or what you think they are. Most don't live in big, fancy houses and drive expensive, flashy cars:

➤ They are 45 to 60 years old.

➤ They have a median income around $150,000.

➤ They are usually married, with children.

➤ They were raised in middle-class or poor families.

➤ They are self-made, first-generation wealthy.

➤ They live comfortably, but not flamboyantly.

➤ They save 20 percent or more of their income.

You get the picture—they're just folks who work hard, spend carefully, save money, and invest for the long term. After 20 or 30 years of doing this, they became millionaires. And they keep on doing the same stuff that got them there. Becoming wealthy didn't change who they are or how they live. Financial freedom is more important to them than keeping up with the Gateses and spending money to display their status.

Think Like a Millionaire—Don't Act Like One

When the whole world knows you're rich, or thinks you are, they'll beat a path to your door—and to your wallet. Money makes the world go 'round, and it's your money everyone is after. It's their job to separate you (in honest, legal ways) from your money.

A Nugget of Gold

In 1999, the U.S. Census Bureau estimated that there were 7.2 million millionaires in the United States. The Bureau defined a millionaire as one who had a million dollars or more of net worth—not including a primary residence, just investable assets. The Bureau also reported that this was four times more millionaires than in 1990. There were millionaires popping up everywhere during the 1990s, and the Bureau expects that to continue.

You don't have to let this happen to you, even if you don't have a million dollars yet. If you let your money be lured from your wallet or purse very often, you never will become wealthy. Start thinking like a millionaire who wants to stay a millionaire. Take a few lessons from the majority of people who became millionaires: They don't look, dress, or behave as you think they would.

Focus your thoughts and actions on steadily increasing your invested assets:

➤ Make careful spending decisions.

➤ Save at least 20 percent of your income.

➤ Learn how to manage and invest your money.

Your family—parents, brothers and sisters, children, and in-laws—don't need to know how well you're doing. They'll know if you're comfortable and doing all right just by being around you enough. Adult children should know what a parent has. For example, a friend of ours figured that she had to take care of her parents and altered her lifestyle dramatically. She found out only when one became incapacitated that her parents were millionaires!

Obviously, when you retire early, your family and friends will see that you are well off. A few may be somewhat envious, but they will also be happy for you because they know that you worked for it. If some show concern for your welfare and whether you're making the right decision, assure them that you have saved and invested well with a plan that allows you to retire early and live comfortably. That's all they need to know.

You Can't Spend Yourself Rich

The "dis-ease" of always wanting more than you have doesn't go away just because you get more. Our culture and our consumer-based economy are built around having more stuff and buying more services. This "dis-ease" is most dangerous when we can't afford what we want but we buy it anyway. This puts us further in debt.

There's nothing wrong with wanting a better life and a better lifestyle. In fact, that's exactly what we're talking about: a comfortable lifestyle now and for 30 or 40 years in retirement. But a dollar spent today is many dollars that won't be available to spend in your future. Get into the habit of taking the long-term view of your life, not just focusing on what you want today.

The millionaire mind-set understands this. Careful spending decisions help ensure that you spend your money cautiously with much thought, not on the spur of the moment just because you want something now. Even when you can afford to buy something and pay cash, think the purchase through. Do you really need it, and is it worth spending this money today rather than having it grow for your needs in the future?

Learn to train your mind to think about all your money decisions. Learning to make small decisions carefully will make the bigger decisions that you make later easier. And they're more likely to be better decisions. You don't get smarter just because you have money, but you will have more money if you learn to make smart decisions.

Potholes

Money isn't the answer to all our prayers; it's only a tool to achieve our financial goals. We can't fill our emotional or spiritual needs by having or spending money. We have to find other ways to meet those needs.

Lifestyle Choices: Live Well for Less

Life can be an economic struggle when you're just starting out on your own; there's so much you don't have. Life is more than a roof over your head and three square meals a day, but sometimes that's all you can afford. Most people start out this way, even millionaires.

The big difference between those who become wealthy and those who don't isn't how much they make; it's what they do with their income once they've met their basic needs. This is when you make lifestyle decisions that affect how you manage your cash flow. A high-living lifestyle costs money:

1. First, it's expensive to acquire stuff.

2. Second, you have to maintain it.

3. Third, you want to replace it or trade up to an even higher level.

This is an expensive road to travel, and it's difficult to get off this road and go in another direction once you're on it. You quickly get used to a higher standard of living and want even more.

Pay Cash

We saw in Chapter 6, "Wealth: How to Get It and Keep It," that, except for education and a mortgage, going into debt is not a winning proposition. This leads to the first rule of living well for less: Pay for your purchases in cash. We don't mean that you should show up at the car dealership with a suitcase full of dead presidents; a checkbook is fine. If you want, use your credit cards instead of carrying around a wad of cash. Just be sure that you pay the charges when the bill comes due next month.

Paying for purchases in cash often means that some time elapses between your wanting to buy something and actually buying it. You have to make the decision to buy something and save your money. For true emergencies—car repair or appliance breakdowns and the like—you have your emergency fund if you don't have cash available. Anything else that you need is worth saving for, or it's probably not really worth having.

This philosophy is obviously considered old-fashioned today. It started to go out of style in the 1950s, but it never disappeared because it actually works. Part of financial planning is anticipating the big and small things we want, and making a plan to save the money to pay for them ahead of time. Manage your cash flow so that you save for the things that you want now as well as what you want in the future.

Spend It or Save It

The decisions you make about spending your income directly affect how much you save. If you want to retire early, it's more important that you become a good

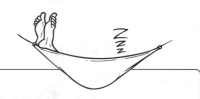

From the Hammock

When Jim and his wife married, her mother counseled them that as long as they were both working, they should try to live on only one income and save the other one. That way, if they started a family, lost a job, or became ill and couldn't work, their lifestyle wouldn't be forced to change for financial reasons. Meanwhile, they would be building a healthy savings and investment account. It didn't quite happen this way when they were just starting out, but it was a goal that they did achieve after several years.

saver than a good investor. Obviously, you have to have something to invest. But you can't control how your investments perform; you can control how much you save.

Some people grow up in an environment where saving and investing for the future were just not part of the picture. If you were brought up this way, you've already taken a big step on starting to change how you think about your life and your money by reading this book. Keep your mind open to the reality that you will likely have a future and that you can plan for it today. You can take some measure of control over what your future can be.

Pay Yourself First

Some people like to use fairly detailed budgets to manage their cash flow. We certainly understand if you're not one of them. There is an alternative that doesn't require as much budget detail, but it does require just as much discipline.

A Nugget of Gold

A 1995 U.S. Bureau of Labor Statistic study reveals that households with an average after-tax income of more than $70,000 save more than 27 percent of their income each year. Sure, it's easier to save when you have a high income, but we suspect that most of these people started saving a large percent early.

In your financial-planning process you determine how much you need to save from each paycheck to reach your short-term and long-term goals. Then you arrange to save it under any circumstance. This strategy is called "pay yourself first." Paying yourself first can be accomplished in several ways:

➤ By having deductions taken from your paycheck for your retirement plan

➤ By automatically writing a check on payday to your investment account

➤ By having an automatic deduction from your checking account deposited to your investment account

You can usually set up one or more of these choices through your employer, and you can always write a check to pay yourself first. Financial planners often use 10 percent of your pay as a target number to save for retirement. However, if you want to retire early, you need to bump that up to at least 20 percent. You have many fewer years in which to save and many more years to live in retirement.

How much you need to pay yourself first to meet your goals is part of what you will discover when you use the forms in Appendix A, "Financial Worksheets." It depends on your age, your income and expenses, and how many years are left until you want to retire. It's also critical to consider how many years you'll have in retirement. You may have half your life ahead of you when you retire early. Obviously, the later you begin saving, the bigger the amount you'll need to put away, so it pays to start early.

What's left over after you pay yourself first (and pay your income taxes) is what you live on, as well as what you use to save for your nonretirement goals. These goals could easily run another 15 to 20 percent of your pay to build a down payment for a house and to pay something toward college for your children. Let's see where that would leave you.

Hypothetical breakdown of a paycheck.

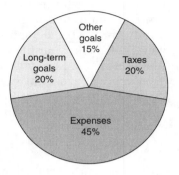

In this example, you cover all your expenses today with 45 percent of your income. You adjust your lifestyle to match this amount. The other 35 percent of your income that doesn't go to the government (including Social Security and Medicare taxes) is money that you save for future needs and wants. This apportioning may look severe, but keep in mind that you're not depriving yourself—you're paying yourself so that you can have what you want later. That's the only way you'll get it.

If you find you're running short of money and can't pay all your bills each month, review your expenses closely and find out how to cut back on them in the future. You probably will need to set up and monitor a budget until you adapt your lifestyle and spending habits to the amount you have to live on. After a couple of years, you may find that a quarterly review of expenses is all that you need to stay on track.

A Comfortable Lifestyle

You can have a better lifestyle than you think, despite living today on half your income or less. There are ways to stretch the dollars you have to live on as well as the ones you save for nonretirement goals. They're part of the careful spending process. Your plan should be to live a reasonably comfortable lifestyle that you can maintain or slowly improve up to and throughout your retirement years.

From the Hammock

Using those supermarket cards and coupons regularly can save you 15 percent or more on your grocery expenses every year, with little effort. Enlist your kids in clipping coupons, and split the savings with them. Put their share in a savings account each month. At the end of the year, transfer the money into mutual funds, where it will grow until they graduate from high school. They'll learn and earn while you save.

There are hundreds of ways to save money on your normal, daily living expenses. These ways may take a little work or research to uncover, but there are many good books to help you. There's no reason to spend more than you have to, and the dollars add up. Check out *The Complete Idiot's Guide to Being a Cheapskate* and *The Pocket Idiot's Guide to Living on a Budget*.

The best way to save money, of course, is not to spend it in the first place. Make careful spending decisions in the process of balancing what you want today with what you want in the future. This will often lead you to scale back your purchases or forgo some altogether without noticeably reducing your lifestyle.

Save on House Costs

Two thirds of American households own their home. That's part of the American Dream for many people. It's often a good financial decision for three reasons:

➤ You get a tax deduction for mortgage interest.

➤ You pay no capital gain tax on the first $500,000 of any gain on the sale ($250,000 for singles).

➤ The house may appreciate in value at or above the rate of inflation over a long period.

Say What?

When you put less than 20 percent down on the purchase of a house, you're usually required by the lender to buy **private mortgage insurance** (PMI). You pay the premiums in addition to your monthly mortgage payment. This insures the lender for the money you owe on the house if you should stop making payments for whatever reason.

Once your equity in the house exceeds 20 percent, ask the lender if PMI can be dropped. New federal laws allow this, and some states require the lender to notify you. You'll probably have to pay for an appraisal of your property if there's any question about the value.

A house should not be considered an investment; historically, you could make more money in the stock market. With this in mind, there are points to consider when you're thinking about buying a house or trading up. You can save a ton of money over 20 or 30 years by making careful decisions when buying a house. Consider the following:

➤ Don't buy as much house as you can afford. Mortgage lenders may let you borrow up to three times your annual household income. Don't stretch your budget this far—aim for around two times your income.

➤ Put down 20 percent, even if you have to wait a couple of years to save enough. This way, you'll save on interest payments and you won't be required to buy *private mortgage insurance* (PMI). You're only insuring the lender with PMI in case you default on the loan.

➤ Get a 20-year instead of a 30-year mortgage. On a $100,000 mortgage at 8.5 percent, you'll save $68,531 in interest. A 15-year mortgage will save another $30,977. The monthly payments are $99 a month higher for the 20-year and $216 a month higher with the 15-year mortgage. If you didn't stretch the budget to buy it, you can probably swing the extra money.

➤ Refinance when mortgage rates fall by 1 percent or more. Look for a good deal on refinancing costs, and pay whatever fees you can't avoid up front. When you refinance, perhaps you can reduce the term to 20 years or even 15 years.

➤ When you buy or trade up, remember that every extra $10,000 worth of house you buy could cost you $30,000 to $40,000 more over 30 years for more interest cost, higher real estate taxes, a higher insurance premium, and higher maintenance costs. Here's another reason not to stretch too much: Every $10,000 that you invest in an S&P index fund at 11 percent return over 30 years grows to $228,923 before taxes. Taking all these points together, an extra $10,000 in the house leaves you poorer by almost $230,000 after 30 years. And that's after the house appreciates by 4 percent a year on the extra $10,000. This could be money that you use to retire early.

Save on Autos

Automobiles are a necessary evil for most people and a constant drain on your cash flow. Because they depreciate—lose value—quickly during the first two years, you shouldn't use borrowed money to buy cars. Dealers may make more on the loan than they do on the car, and you end up paying 10 to 15 percent more for it.

If you must borrow money to buy your next auto soon, or if you're already making payments on a vehicle that you bought in the last couple of years, consider the following strategy:

➤ Limit yourself to a three-year loan.

➤ Keep the car for six to eight years.

➤ When the loan is paid off, keep making payments to "My Auto Fund" for the next three to five years. A money market fund will work fine for this. Don't use the money for anything else.

➤ When you finally buy a new auto, pay cash from your auto fund.

➤ Buy a two- or three-year-old better-quality car that's in good shape with low mileage. Keep it for three to six years, and keep making payments to your fund. After a year, they're all used cars anyway.

➤ Never lease a car unless it's for business and you can deduct the payments on your tax return.

Once you pay cash for a car and begin making payments to "My Auto Fund" toward your next car, you're way ahead of the game. You may find that after 20 or 30 years of doing this, you can pay cash for his-and-her Mercedes—or put some of the money toward early retirement.

Pay for College

Few parents today can afford to pay in full for their children's college education. These expenses are paid through a combination of savings, grants-in-aid, scholarships, and loans. By the time the kids are old enough for college, your household income should be higher, too, and the student can work to help pay expenses.

The College Board reports average tuition and room and board for the 2000–2001 year at $21,400 for private four-year colleges and $8,100 for public four-year colleges. With tuition and expenses rising at an average of 7 percent a year in recent years, a baby born in 2001 will face costs of $67,600 and $25,600 a year, respectively.

"College aid" is a term that covers many types and sources of money for college. And there's a lot of it out there. Spend the year before your child begins applying to colleges exploring these sources. Other online information sources are listed here:

➤ www.petersons.com

➤ www.finaid.org, www.ed.gov, and www.fafsa.ed.gov, the Department of Education's sites

➤ www.wiredscholar.com

➤ www.salliemae.com (Sallie Mae is the leading supplier of education loans)

The U.S. Congress has created other programs through the Treasury Department (including your friends at the IRS) to help you pay for college. We

A Nugget of Gold

You can visit the College Board Web site at www.collegeboard. org for more information on college costs. There are financial calculators to help project future costs for college at www.financenter.com, www.quicken.com, and www. moneycentral.com.

can't cover all the usual booklets of rules and regulations that apply to each of the following, but you can order IRS Publication 970, "Tax Benefits for Higher Education," at www.irs.gov. They're all worth looking at, so you can cut the out-of-pocket costs down to more manageable amounts.

Here are some options you should consider:

➤ Think about buying education bonds. U.S. Treasury I Savings Bonds and EE Savings Bonds purchased after 1990 can be used for college education expenses. The program allows the holder of the bond to exclude interest from federal tax when the bond is used to pay tuition and related fees. The bonds must be in a parent's name. The rules phase out the tax break for joint returns between $81,100 and $111,100, and for singles between $54,100 and 69,100 for 2000. The limits are indexed to increase each year by the rate of inflation.

➤ The Hope Tax Credit covers tuition and related expenses for eligible students in their first or second year of a degree-granting program. You claim a *tax credit* on Form 8863 filed with your 1040 return for the first $1,000 paid, plus 50 percent of the next $1,000.

➤ The Lifetime Learning Credit, also claimed on Form 8863, doesn't have the restrictions of the Hope Credit. It covers any post-secondary education at eligible institutions, including graduate-level courses. This credit is 20 percent of the first $5,000 paid for tuition and related expenses, for a total of up to $1,000 per student per year.

➤ An Education IRA has nothing to do with an IRA for your retirement. You can set up a savings plan for children under 18 and contribute a maximum of $500 per year per child. The contribution isn't tax-deductible, but the income compounds tax-free if it is used for college tuition and related expenses. The account must be set up as an Education IRA and must be in the child's name. The money can be transferred to another child later for the same purpose. If it's not used by age 30, the money becomes taxable.

Say What?

A **tax credit** is better than a deduction. You subtract the tax credit dollar for dollar from the amount of taxes you owe at the end of your Form 1040. You have to file the information form to support the tax credit. In the case of education credits, Form 8863 is the one you need.

Potholes

You can't take both the Hope and the Lifetime credits for the same student in the same year. And both credits are phased out for modified adjusted gross incomes of $80,000 to $100,000 on a joint return, and $40,000 to $50,000 on a single return.

➤ Prepaid state tuition plans, called 529 plans, are better than they used to be under new rules that Congress passed in 1997. Each state has its own plan, usually run by a large financial institution. Money invested grows tax-deferred until a child begins college. The earnings are taxed at the child's tax rate, which should be lower than the parents' rate. Most state plans are open to nonresidents, and the money can be used at most colleges and universities around the country. Check out all state plans, and look carefully at the expenses and investments used before you jump in. You can't fund both an Education IRA and a 529 plan in the same year.

The discipline that you bring to these decisions, fueled by your desire to have the choice to retire early, is what will make your plan work. If you're having difficulty making these decisions, spend more time thinking about your goals and how important they are to you. Then, with practice, the decisions to sacrifice a little now will get easier to make, especially when you see the money piling up for the goals you want tomorrow.

A Nugget of Gold

To check out prepaid state tuition plans, start at www.collegesavings.org, the College Savings Plans Network, and www.savingforcollege.com.

The Least You Need to Know

➤ Most millionaires didn't start out rich or make it big in the stock market.

➤ You become a millionaire through careful spending and saving regularly over a long period of time.

➤ Financial freedom is a result of living below your means so that you can save for your goal.

➤ Aim early for a lifestyle that is comfortable but not too comfortable. It must be one that you can afford for 30 or 40 years in retirement.

Chapter 8

Estimating Your Retirement Costs

In This Chapter

➤ Estimate your expenses in retirement

➤ How inflation affects your expenses

➤ Health insurance—maybe your biggest expense in the future

Retirement means that you'll have a lot of free time on your hands. That was the goal, right? Retirement also means that you don't have a steady paycheck coming in. This will be a radical change in your cash flow. All your expenses will be paid from the money that you already have and what that money earns working for you. This is why, in creating your financial plan, we start with the costs that you will face in retirement. You find out how much you'll need based on how much you'll spend.

In Chapter 7, "How to Be a Middle-Class Millionaire," we stressed saving and careful spending as you work toward retiring early. The careful spending part doesn't stop after retirement. No, you don't have to scrimp and budget for the early-bird specials at the local diner; that's not why you retired early. Your financial goals allow you the freedom to choose early retirement when you have enough money to live in the style you choose.

It isn't easy to project expenses in retirement when that day may be 20 or 30 years away. But you need a reasonable, working estimate to build your plan around. As you get closer to retirement—say, within five years—you'll want to refine your estimate. The expenses that you project then will be a lot more accurate. You'll use them to carefully test your plan to make sure you're on track.

A Nugget of Gold

Many financial plannners make a rough estimate of expenses in retirement of 70 percent of your pre-retirement income. You shouldn't rely on this one-size-fits-all shortcut, especially if you plan to retire early. Your pre-retirement expenses may have been a lesser percent of your income because you were saving more than the average person. On the other hand, your expenses in early retirement may be higher as you pursue new interests and travel more. Make your own estimates and you'll feel more comfortable with your entire plan.

At that time, if your plan reveals problems, you still have time to correct the situation:

➤ Save more.

➤ Work a year or two longer.

➤ Plan to secure a part-time job for a few years after you retire.

For now, we just want a ballpark number to get started on a plan and to give you an idea of what the challenge is. By the end of this chapter, you'll have three estimates for the three stages of retirement, which you'll enter into the Expense Summary form at the end of the chapter. In Chapter 10, "Achieving Your Retirement Goals," you'll match these against your projected income from Chapter 9, "How to Pay Your Expenses in Retirement." In these three chapters you'll have a variety of mostly short forms to fill in. Dust off your calculator and your seventh-grade arithmetic. They're all easy.

Inflation Is Your Worst Enemy

We defined inflation as the rate of price increase in a diverse basket of consumer goods, as measured by the Department of Labor's Urban Consumer Price Index. Almost every year, prices of many goods and services go up. Another way of looking at inflation is that the value, or buying power, of a dollar decreases. This means that you need more dollars to buy the same stuff that you bought last year.

Over the last 25 years, the buying power of a dollar has fallen to 27¢. What you pay a dollar for today cost 27¢, on average, in 1975. This is a result of an average annual rate of inflation around 5 percent since then. The rate of inflation has been lower than this since 1990. For the last 100 years, the rate of inflation has averaged about 3 percent.

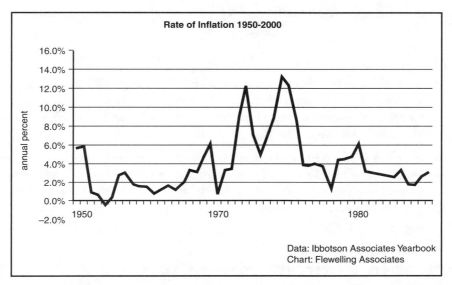

Rate of Inflation 1950-2000

Data: Ibbotson Associates Yearbook
Chart: Flewelling Associates

The rate of inflation from 1950 through 2000. Note how big the changes in the rate of inflation can be from year to year, and how it can change direction quickly.

No one has ever shown much success at predicting the rate or even the direction of inflation from year to year. That doesn't stop economists from trying, but it's just a guess. For this reason, we picked a 4 percent rate of inflation as a tool for projecting numbers in a financial plan. We hope that the rate is lower than this, but it's better to be safe than sorry.

What if 4 percent turns out to be high? You'll have a comfortable margin of safety built into your plan in case something else doesn't work out as well as expected. The exception that we'll make to the 4 percent inflation rate is for projecting health insurance costs. We'll use 7 percent here. Healthcare expense increases have gyrated wildly, from 3 percent a year to as much as 15 percent in some years. They're even harder to predict than inflation.

Inflation is what we call a silent risk because it slowly, quietly, and relentlessly works against you. This is true in your expenses as well as in your investments. If you're 35 now, you have to factor inflation into your calculations for the next 60 years! But remember that, although the numbers you'll be projecting look huge, they're based on today's dollar values plus 4 percent annual inflation. They aren't as monstrous as they appear, but you should take them seriously.

A Nugget of Gold

Many people who were retired during the years 1973 through 1981 were happy to rollover their bank certificates of deposit at interest rates as high as 15 percent. When the rate of inflation headed back to 3 or 4 percent, they were quite upset. A 6 percent interest rate made them feel poorer.

However, the important fact to remember is that the real rate of interest is the difference between inflation and the interest rate you're paid. A CD at 13 percent with inflation at 14 percent is a negative real rate of 1 percent! Interest at 6 percent when inflation is relatively steady at 3 percent is a positive real rate of 3 percent.

Expenses in Retirement—by Stages

If you or your partner works part-time in retirement, the only major effect on expenses may be health coverage. However, few part-timers today get health insurance benefits. We'll assume that you'll have to foot the bill yourself.

Potholes

Note that under current law, you aren't covered by Medicare until age 65. You still have to pay for your healthcare and insurance until then. This is a very expensive but very necessary expense.

When you retire, you'll redo your cash flow numbers periodically to account for changing circumstances. We don't expect you to know today exactly what your life will be like way into the future. You'll look at your expenses and make projections for them in three stages:

➤ Retirement to age 62

➤ Age 62 through age 70

➤ After age 70

Your income will likely change at age 62 when you (currently) are allowed to collect Social Security. If you qualify for a pension, that will also change your income in the year you begin collecting it. Another major change in your income begins when you're required to start taking distributions from your retirement plans, such as IRAs and 401(k)s, after you turn

70. You usually want to wait until then to allow your money to compound without taxes cutting into the gains each year. The only exception to this is a *Roth IRA*. (We'll look more closely at the Roth IRA and all types of retirement plans in Part 5, "Tools You Should Use.")

During your retirement, you can generally expect your expenses to rise steadily due to inflation. If you change your activities, that may also increase expenses. When you sell your home and rent someplace else, your expenses will again increase. Without any changes, your expenses will look like this on a graph.

Say What?

A **Roth IRA** resembles a regular IRA, except that you use after-tax money. You can't deduct it from your income taxes when you contribute.

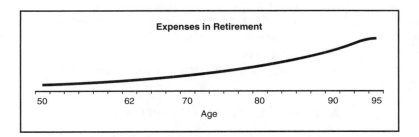

Expenses in Retirement

Age

50   62   70   80   90   95

Your expenses will rise steadily and relentlessly in retirement solely due to inflation unless you change how you live to reduce them.

Retirement to Age 62

What major changes other than health insurance premiums do you anticipate when you retire? Obviously, if your children are grown and have finished college, childcare and education expenses disappear (for them—you might go back to school, however). Gifts to your grown children or grandchildren are a subject that you can decide later, when you're retired. Here's a list to consider now:

➤ **Mortgage**—If you own your home and plan to stay there, we strongly suggest that you pay off the mortgage before you retire. That will remove a big drain on your cash flow.

➤ **Work-related expenses**—Clothing and auto expenses will drop if you bought good clothes every year or so for work, and if you commuted long distances.

➤ **Life insurance premiums**—Unless you decide that you want life insurance for estate planning, you no longer need it. You have no one depending on your continued earned income because you have none.

➤ **Disability insurance**—Drop this as of the day you retire, if you haven't already. No job, no income, no payoff. You should drop disability insurance as soon as you can afford not to work, even if you choose to continue working. You don't need to insure against the loss of income after you reach financial freedom.

➤ **Income taxes, including Social Security and Medicare deductions**—No earned income, no payroll tax deductions, and no tax. You'll still owe federal and state income taxes on your investment income in taxable accounts.

Potholes

When you stop getting a pay-check, you can no longer cover your income taxes with payroll deductions. You will need to file estimated tax returns (including returns to your state, if you live in a state with income taxes) and send a check four times a year. Then you'll file your regular return by April 15 when you know exactly what you owe. The IRS (and state revenue departments) assesses interest and penalties for underpayment of taxes during the year. (You can order IRS Schedule 1040-ES and IRS Publication 505 at www.irs.gov, or call 1-800-772-1213.)

➤ **Travel**—You may plan to travel a lot more in retirement. This becomes a big expense for many active retirees. Talk it over with your partner, and pick a dollar figure (in today's dollars) that you'd like to spend each year for travel. Review it carefully a few years before you retire.

➤ **Hobbies**—Whether it's golf, gardening, painting, or stamp collecting, with more time, you'll spend more money on activities that you enjoy. You might not have any active interests that cost much money today. You need to put something here so that you can pursue whatever turns you on in your newfound free time.

Estimate Your Expenses

Using the previous guidelines and your Cash Flow Worksheet numbers from Appendix A, "Financial Worksheets," estimate your expenses for your first year in retirement in today's dollars. Enter them under "Current Cost" in the form Expenses for Year One in Retirement, which follows the Cash Flow form in Appendix A.

Using the following guidelines, use your "Current Cost" expenses to create your "Cost at Retirement" expenses.

As we crunch the numbers here and in the next chapters, we'll be following a hypothetical couple, Linda and George, as they do the same. Their figures will be used in our example in each form. Don't worry if your figures aren't like theirs—you're planning *your* retirement.

Linda and George, a 38-year-old couple with two teenagers, a mortgage, and a combined $90,000 earned income, spent $68,600 in 2000. They hope to retire in 12 years, at age 50, when their kids have finished college. They project their expenses for the first year in retirement, 2013, at $72,800. They've paid off the mortgage and have no other debts. Health insurance, at $17,800, will be a big, new expense for them.

Inflate Them

How many years do you have until your targeted retirement date? Pick a year that seems reasonable now. The results of your financial plan calculations will tell you what you need to do to make it work, or tell you to reconsider your date and do the numbers again.

Decide on the number of years to go, and match that with the inflation factor in the following table. If it's an odd number, use the next-higher even number. Multiply your Subtotal of Expenses in the "Current Cost" column of the Expenses for Year One in Retirement form by this factor to determine how much those expenses will cost in your first year of retirement. Enter the result under "Cost at Retirement" on the Expenses for Year One in Retirement form.

Inflation Factor

Years to Retirement	Inflation Factor	Years to Retirement	Inflation Factor
10	1.48	22	2.37
12	1.60	24	2.56
14	1.73	26	2.77
16	1.87	28	3.00
18	2.03	30	3.24
20	2.10		

At the bottom of the Expenses for Year One in Retirement form is a line for health insurance costs. Enter a number from the following "Health Insurance Inflation Factor" table under "Cost at Retirement." These numbers project average per-person health insurance costs from 2000. Count how many years until you plan to retire from the year 2000 to get the proper inflated health insurance cost. These costs are *per person,* so be sure to double them for a couple.

Health Insurance Inflation Factor

Years to Retirement	Health Insurance	Years to Retirement	Health Insurance
10	$7,800	22	$17,600
12	$8,900	24	$20,100
14	$10,200	26	$23,000
16	$11,700	28	$26,400
18	$13,400	30	$30,200
20	$15,300		

Add the subtotal expenses and health insurance numbers under the "Cost at Retirement" column. Enter the result as total expenses. Now you have your estimate of expenses for your first year in retirement. These expenses will increase at more or less the rate of inflation from the time you retire. Therefore, we'll calculate the next two stages based on these numbers, increased at 4 percent and 7 percent per year. The following graph shows how expenses keep rising in retirement.

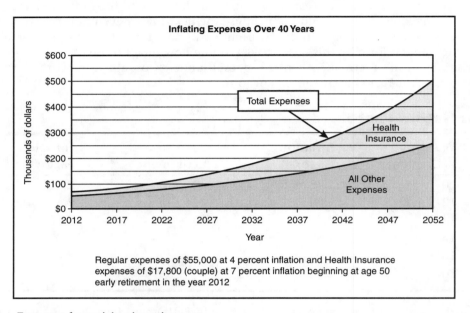

Inflating Expenses Over 40 Years

Regular expenses of $55,000 at 4 percent inflation and Health Insurance expenses of $17,800 (couple) at 7 percent inflation beginning at age 50 early retirement in the year 2012

Expenses keep rising in retirement.

At the end of this chapter is an Expense Summary form. (You'll use the three key numbers that you come up with in this chapter in Chapter 10.) Enter the "Total Expenses" figure in the first line of the Expense Summary form.

Age 62 to 70

Unless you change your housing situation during this period, the only major change in expenses occurs at age 65. You qualify for Medicare at age 65 under current laws and can drop your regular health insurance. However, it's not clear whether you'll save money, as you'll see here. Medicare is long overdue for an overhaul to put its cash flow on better footing for the future. No one knows what changes may occur, but we wouldn't be surprised if a *means-testing* plan is put in place at some point. The qualifying age may also be raised to keep up with the increase to age 67 for full Social Security benefits.

At this time, Medicare Part A, hospital insurance, is what you pay for in payroll taxes all the years that you're working. The amount that you're paying is currently

1.45 percent of gross pay from you and 1.45 percent from your employer. You're automatically enrolled when you begin collecting Social Security.

Medicare Part B, covering doctors' fees and some tests, costs additional money. If you sign up for Part B, the premium (about $50 a month in 2001) is deducted from your Social Security check. You're also automatically enrolled in Part B when you file for Social Security benefits unless you notify Social Security that you don't want this coverage. Both Part A and Part B have deductibles and coinsurance payments.

However, even with Part A and Part B, you're still exposed to a variety of medical and healthcare costs, including prescription drugs. To cover most of these expenses, you can choose to enroll in a Medigap insurance plan. These plans are offered by private insurance companies, not the government. Plans differ widely from state to state in terms of coverage, cost, and type of plan.

We'll assume that you want one of the better plans, which currently costs $3,000 to $4,000 a year per person. This cost, plus Medicare Part B premiums, may be close to the same per-person cost for regular health insurance that you paid before age 65. That depends on the coverage that you elect and your general health. However, you may still incur more out-of-pocket costs than you do today, so we'll continue the current cost and inflation pattern.

Your expense calculations build upon the amounts that you generated in the preceding Expenses for Year One in Retirement form. You'll see how much inflation increases your expenses even though you don't change your lifestyle. To complete the following form, Expenses at Age 62, follow these steps:

1. Enter the subtotal of the expenses that you calculated in the "Cost at Retirement" column of the preceding form, "Expenses for Year One in Retirement," on the "Expense Subtotal" line in the first column of the following Expenses at Age 62 form.

From the Hammock

Dee and her spouse and Jim and his spouse pay their own health insurance costs for a PPO. The premiums are currently over $8,000 a year per couple. Not only will they increase due to rising inflation in health care costs, but the premiums are based on age, too. Therefore, they will increase periodically as they all grow older. Age 65 is still a long way off and they have to plan for healthy increases in the premiums each year until then.

Say What?

Government programs and IRS provisions already are designed to phase out benefits at or within certain income levels. You qualify for the benefit only if your income is below the specified level. This is referred to as **means-testing** because it's based on your means, or level, of income. The government assumes that you have the means to get by without that benefit if your income is above that level.

2. Pick the expense factor from the "Inflation Factors from Retirement to Age 62" table following this form, and enter it in the second column. The inflation factor is based on how many years you have from your target retirement year until age 62.

Potholes

Complication arises when there's an age difference between spouses. You must be 65 or older to be covered under Medicare. The younger spouse must still buy regular health insurance until age 65. And if the younger one still works and has health insurance coverage from the employer, the 65 year-old spouse can no longer be in that plan.

3. Multiply the amount in the first column by the factor in the second column. Enter the result on the "Expense Subtotal" line in the third column.

4. Enter the health insurance figure from the last column in the preceding Expenses for Year One in Retirement form in the first column of the Expenses at Age 62 form.

5. Select the healthcare inflation factor from the "Inflation Factors from Age 62" table, and put it in the second column.

6. Multiply the number in the first column by the factor in the second column, and enter the result in the third column.

7. Add column 3 to get your total expenses at age 62.

Expenses at Age 62

		Example		Yours		
Expense subtotal	$55,000	1.54	$84,700	$_____	____	$_____
Health insurance	$17,800	2.10	$37,380	$_____	____	$_____
Total Expenses	**$72,800**		**$122,080**	$_____	____	$_____

Enter the total expenses from this form in the second line of the Expense Summary form at the end of the chapter.

Inflation Factors from Retirement to Age 62

Years from Retirement Until Age 62	Expense Factor	Healthcare Factor
2	1.08	1.15
3	1.12	1.22
4	1.17	1.31
5	1.22	1.40

Years from Retirement Until Age 62	Expense Factor	Healthcare Factor
6	1.27	1.50
7	1.32	1.61
8	1.37	1.72
9	1.42	1.84
10	1.48	1.97
11	1.54	2.10
12	1.60	2.25
13	1.67	2.41
14	1.73	2.58
15	1.80	2.76
16	1.87	2.95
17	1.95	3.16

Age 70 and Beyond

You still have a joint life expectancy of about 20 years at age 70, and we suggest that you plan on 25 years in your calculations so that you don't outlive your money.

Again, you don't know how active you'll be after 70, whether you'll settle down and travel less, or what the state of your health will be. We'll use the same expense pattern updated from age 62 by 4 percent a year, to keep it simple. Healthcare expenses and insurance are increased by 7 percent per year.

To complete the following form, Expenses at Age 70, follow these steps:

1. Take the expense totals from the first two lines of the third column on the preceding form, Expenses at Age 62, and enter them in the first column of the following form.

2. The inflation factors are already entered in column 2 because everyone who makes it to age 70 from age 62 lived eight years.

3. Multiply the amounts in the first column by the inflation factors, and enter the results in the third column.

4. Add the third column to get total expenses at age 70.

Expenses at Age 70

	Example			Yours		
Expense subtotal	*$84,700*	*1.37*	*$116,039*	$_____	1.37	$_____
Health insurance	*$37,380*	*1.72*	*$64,294*	$_____	1.72	$_____
Total Expenses	*$122,080*		*$180,333*	$_____		$_____

Enter the total expenses from this form in the last line of the Expense Summary form at the end of the chapter.

Now you have beginning expenses for the three stages to match against projected income in Chapter 9. The numbers probably look pretty high to you, and they are compared to current expenses. That's the effect of inflation.

It's Been Said

"Inflation is when your nest egg no longer has anything to crow about."

—Jimmy W. Marsh

Remember that your income and investments will grow, too. For you to retire successfully, early or not, your income and investments must grow faster than inflation. You'll need to save a lot over the years to cover these expenses, but the growth of your investments will do much of the work for you. You can do it! Don't let the big numbers discourage you.

You might wonder why we don't inflate expenses within each stage. After all, they'll continue increasing each year after you retire, as well as after ages 62 and 70. Simplicity is the main answer; these are ballpark numbers to give you an idea of what you need at each of these stages of retirement. Within each stage, you'll cover the increases in the following ways:

➤ **To age 62**—You'll use your taxable investment accounts. We'll show you how this can work in Chapter 11, "Finding and Using a Financial Planner." You'll be reducing your total investments as Donna and Charley did in Chapter 2, "What It Takes," but that's what you have this money for.

➤ **From age 62 to 70**—You'll use your Social Security or pension income. Social Security payments (but not most pensions) are indexed to inflation each year. This won't cover all of the increase, but you'll still have taxable investments to draw from.

➤ **Beyond age 70**—Your Social Security benefit keeps increasing, but now you have large annual distributions from your retirement accounts. Even after taxes and expenses, you should be able to reinvest some of this money most years to cover your expenses later.

You will use your expense projections from this chapter in Chapter 10. You'll match them against expected income at the beginning of each stage of retirement. To make these numbers easier to find, enter them in the following Expense Summary form.

Expense Summary

Source	Example	Yours
In first year of retirement	*$72,800*	$_____
At age 62	*$122,080*	$_____
At age 70	*$180,333*	$_____

The Least You Need to Know

➤ Estimating your expenses in retirement is the key to your financial plan if you want to retire early.

➤ Inflation relentlessly increases the dollars that you will spend every year, especially for healthcare. Without earned income when you retire, you need to cover these expenses from your investments for many decades.

➤ You can't rely on Medicare to cover your healthcare expenses, even when you qualify for coverage at age 65.

Chapter 9

How to Pay Your Expenses in Retirement

In This Chapter

➤ Where your income will come from

➤ How your income will change in retirement

➤ What you may get from Social Security

➤ Tax hazards to watch for if you plan to work part-time

Still overwhelmed by those big expense numbers in Chapter 8, "Estimating Your Retirement Costs"? Try to forget about them until Chapter 10, "Achieving Your Retirement Goals," where we'll show you how you'll pay for them. In this chapter, you'll project what your income will be for each stage of retirement. By the end of the chapter, you'll have three estimates for the three stages of retirement, which you'll enter into the Income Summary form at the end of the chapter. We'll ask you to make some decisions in each of these periods, but we won't hold you to them when you retire.

Tiered Income Changes

This chapter looks only at outside sources of income, such as these:

➤ Part-time work

➤ Pensions

➤ Social Security

➤ Rental and other income

The difference between outside income and your expenses is what you will need to pay. That money will come from your investments in taxable accounts and in tax-sheltered retirement accounts over the course of your retirement. When you find out how much you'll need to save and invest in Chapter 10, you'll have your financial goals in dollars and cents.

Your income stream in retirement will change significantly at various times. For many, these changes will come at age 62 and age 70, for reasons covered in the last chapter. You may also qualify for a pension or other employer retirement plan benefits at some point after you retire. You'll include that, too, in the calculations.

Your income stream during retirement may look a lot like this figure, with jumps at several points. If you work part-time in retirement, there will also be a dip when you stop.

Income in early retirement tends to increase in jumps when you begin collecting social security and when you begin withdrawals from retirement plans.

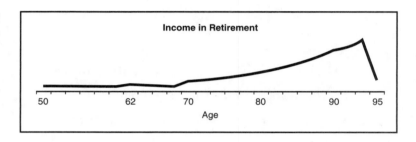

Collecting Social Security

A Nugget of Gold

If you begin collecting your Social Security benefit at age 62, your benefit will always be that reduced percentage of your potential full benefit. The dollars will increase with the rate of inflation each year, but you won't qualify for a higher benefit later once you begin collecting.

Under current law, you're allowed to collect reduced Social Security benefits at age 62. By 2022, the benefit at age 62 is scheduled to be 70 percent of what your full benefit would be at age 67. The minimum benefit is being slowly reduced from 80 percent in 1999 to 70 percent by 2022. At the same time, the age for receiving full benefits rises a little each year to age 67 in 2027. However, a widow or widower may begin to collect on the deceased spouse's benefit at age 60.

Do you plan to work part-time after you turn 62? If you think that you'll be making less than $10,000 in today's dollars, it is usually best to start collecting reduced benefits at age 62. The five years of reduced benefits may make your early retirement plan possible. Of course, if you really don't need the income to cover expenses, you can wait. However, if you wait until age 67, you won't break even until age 78. Let's find out how that's possible.

If you were born in 1960 or later, you could retire at one of these points:

➤ Age 67, with full benefits of, say, $29,000 a year

➤ Age 62, with 70 percent of full benefits, or $20,300 a year

➤ Any age between 62 and 67, with a benefit in between

The difference between benefits at 62 and 67 in this example is $8,700 per year. Five years of the reduced benefits totals $101,500. If you wait until age 67 to collect full benefits, you would collect $8,700 more each year. But to make up the $101,500 head start that you would have had at age 62 at the rate of $8,700 a year will take you 11.7 years, when you're 78 years and 8 months old. If you were born before 1960, the break-even point is even longer.

If you're collecting Social Security checks and working part-time between the ages of 62 and 64 today, the IRS is all over you like fleas on a dog:

➤ Your part-time earned income over $10,680 (or $980 a month) in 2001 reduces your benefit by $1 for every $2 that you earn over that limit.

➤ The year you reach your full retirement age, you lose $1 for every $3 on earnings over $2,084 each month until your birthday month. After that, there's no penalty.

➤ If your total income is $25,000 to $34,000 single, or $32,000 to $44,000 married filing jointly (including Social Security, pensions, and interest from tax-free municipal bonds or funds), you're taxed 15 percent on half of your Social Security benefit.

➤ If your total income is over the higher amounts in these ranges, you're taxed on 85 percent of your Social Security benefit at regular income tax rates.

Your plan to work part-time after age 62 and collect Social Security benefits may be expensive. The combined effect of these rules could cost you as much as 73.8 percent of your benefit. If you're in the 28 percent tax bracket, you pay that rate on 85 percent of your benefit. Then you're penalized $1 of your benefit for every $2 that you earn (50 percent) over $980 a month. And you still pay taxes and payroll deductions for Social Security on what you earn. It might not be worth it.

Potholes

If you qualify for Social Security benefits and you also have a pension from a job that wasn't covered by Social Security, your Social Security benefit will be reduced by a complex formula. This is called the set-off provision, and it can come as quite a shock to people who planned on both amounts in full to pay for their retirement.

Pensions

If you think that you are due a pension sometime after you retire, check with your employer's benefits office to find out some important information:

➤ How early you can begin to get checks

➤ About how much the check will be

➤ Whether your check will be adjusted for annual cost-of-living increases

➤ How much and when you could get a lump-sum payout.

The last question is important. In Chapter 20, "Keep the Taxman Waiting While You Work," we'll look at pensions and lump sum payouts. You could roll a lump sum payout over to an IRA and manage it yourself. That could give you more money over time than the pension checks. You also would be in control of the withdrawals—subject, of course, to your uncle in Washington.

Many public-sector employees in state and local government pension plans can begin to collect a pension at a much younger age than private-sector employees. Check with your benefit office for full information on your options.

Retirement to Age 62

These will be the years when you're on your own. You can get money from your retirement plans, but then what will you live on for the last 15 to 30 years of your life? Let that money grow, compounding on a tax-deferred basis. Pay all your expenses from taxable accounts as long as you can, preferably until age 70. That's part of becoming financially free. This may mean reducing the size of your investments during this period, not just spending the income—but that's what they're for.

If you withdraw money from a retirement account such as a 401(k) or IRA before you turn $59\frac{1}{2}$, you owe a 10 percent penalty in addition to regular income tax. You can avoid this penalty in a few limited hardship-type circumstances; we'll cover those in Chapter 21, "The IRA: Your Personal Tax Shelter."

You can also arrange to take substantially equal payments for at least five years or until you turn $59\frac{1}{2}$ under one of three schedules approved by the IRS. You avoid the 10 percent penalty, but you still owe the regular income tax, of course. You should consult a tax professional before you elect to do this. We don't recommend it as a way to fund early retirement. Who's going to pay for your later years if your money's all gone?

A Nugget of Gold

Money left alone to compound at an average annual rate of 10 percent a year will double every 7.2 years. If you don't touch your retirement account from age 50 until you turn 70, $500,000 (for example) will grow to almost $3.4 million! That's how you pay those inflated expenses later in life.

How Much You'll Make

Do you think that you or your partner will be working part-time in retirement? Enter a reasonable projection of what you think you might earn in the following form, Income in Year One of Retirement. Remember, part-time work usually doesn't pay as much as full-time work for comparable hours worked. If you plan to consult in your area of expertise, that doesn't guarantee income at all unless you have a client.

If you're unsure right now about earned income after you retire, don't include it. Keep it in mind as an option that you have. When you're done crunching the numbers, you may decide that it's an option that you don't need. On the other hand, you may discover that it becomes a desirable option.

If you do expect to have some part-time income when you retire, or if your partner still expects to work, will this income stop before you turn 62? If so, you'll need to make up this income from your investments. You may want to perform a second income calculation to reflect the adjustment in projected income for the years after you think it may stop. Use the additional columns to the right of "Year 1" on the Income in Year One of Retirement form. Label them to reflect which year in retirement you think the changes will occur.

Other Income

If you can collect a pension before age 62 and as soon as you retire, enter this amount on the following form, Income in Year One of Retirement. If you find that you'll have to wait several years to collect a pension because you retired early, do another income projection calculation for that year. You may also find that your pension is higher if you can afford to hold off a few years.

Do you have rental property? Do you plan to keep it after you retire? Make a reasonable projection of the rental income that you can expect when you retire. If you've been raising rents to keep up with inflation, increase today's net income at 4 percent a year through the year you plan to retire.

Other income that you expect from outside sources, not your investments, may be entered here only if you are absolutely sure of getting them. Possibilities include alimony, trust fund income, or income from a *retirement annuity* plan from a previous employer.

The tax rate of 10 percent (or 90 percent of income after tax) approximates a tax rate of 15 percent on taxable income after the standard deduction and

Say What?

If you have a 403(b) plan, your main option is to get a **retirement annuity** payment after a certain age. With a 403(b) plan, you have a choice, but see Chapter 20 to find out how to exercise that choice. If you have a 457 plan, the retirement annuity is your only choice. You receive a set sum of money each month for as long as you live.

personal exemptions are applied. If you have significantly more taxable income, your tax rate will be higher.

Income in Year One of Retirement

Income Source	Year 1	Year __	Year __
Part-time work	$_____	$_____	$_____
Partner's income	$_____	$_____	$_____
Pension (annual)	$_____	$_____	$_____
Rental income (annual)	$_____	$_____	$_____
Other (guaranteed)	$_____	$_____	$_____
Total Income	$_____	$_____	$_____
Minus taxes	× .90	× .90	× .90
NET TOTAL INCOME	$_____	$_____	$_____

You may come up with zero income here. You're okay, so far. You know what you can count on from outside sources now, even if it's zero. That's what Linda and George, our couple from the preceding chapter, discovered. They know that it may not work that way, but that's their expectation. Don't put down anything that you're not reasonably sure of at this time.

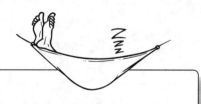

From the Hammock

Apply for Social Security online at www.ssa.gov or call 1–800–772–1213 for an appointment at the nearest office several months before your birthday.

Enter the net total income for the Income in Year One of Retirement form in the Income Summary form at the end of the chapter. If you have more than one total in the form, enter them all and note the year of the change at the top of each column.

Age 62 to 70

Now you can begin collecting Social Security. Hallelujah! Social Security may cover part of the growing shortfall between your income and expenses for a few years. Even though Social Security increases each year to keep up with inflation, you'll probably still be spending down your investments until age 70. You should still have money left in your taxable accounts at age 70, unless the market has a losing stretch of several years during this time.

Part-Time Work and Other Income

Are you or your partner expecting to still be working after age 62? Keep in mind that employment income during these years will reduce your Social Security benefit if the income exceeds the rather low threshold of $10,680 (in 2001 dollars). This calculation is applied to each individual; you could collect Social Security while your spouse continues to earn income.

The income range that affects how much of the Social Security benefit is subject to taxes is figured based on your tax filing status. If you're filing a joint return, all the incomes are taken together. The benefit of one spouse may be taxed at a higher rate because of the income of the other spouse. You can't get around this even if you're married and filing separately.

If you have rental income, project how much it could grow from the number that you entered in the preceding form, Income in Year One of Retirement. Follow the same guidelines suggested there, or use 4 percent a year for estimated inflation as a rate of increase.

If you have a pension, you can certainly collect it at age 62. If you already planned to collect your pension before age 62, use the number that you entered previously. If you plan to start collecting it at age 62, use the projection that you received from your employer's benefits office for age 62.

Any other income that you entered on the form for your first year in retirement should be entered here if you're sure that you'll be getting this amount at age 62. Don't include any investment income here; we'll figure that in Chapter 10.

Estimate Your Social Security Benefit

We'll try to make an estimate of your Social Security benefit at age 62 (of course, you might plan to hold off collecting this until later). If both you and a partner will qualify at about the same time, fill in the form Calculating Your Social Security Benefit, which follows the tables later in this section, for both of you. Otherwise, recalculate for a later year when both are collecting.

A spouse with limited income may collect a larger benefit by filing to collect on the other spouse's benefits. A Social Security formula increases the total benefit to 50 percent of the higher spouse's benefit amount. However, both spouses must be collecting for this to occur, except in cases of death or divorce. More rules apply then (go to www.ssa.gov for more detailed information).

Because Social Security benefits are calculated based on your highest 35 years of income, you penalize yourself when you retire early. Those last 5 to 15 years of high income that you give up when you retire early would boost your benefit considerably.

To calculate your Social Security benefit, follow these steps:

1. In the first table, find the age closest to your age in 2000. Pick the number on that line from the column that is closest to your annual income that year. Enter it on line 1 of the Calculating Your Social Security Benefit form that follows the tables.

2. Select your target retirement age from the second table. Enter the reduction factor next to it on line 2 of the form.

3. Multiply the amount in line 1 by the factor in line 2. Enter the result on line 3.

Social Security Benefits Estimate: Retire at Age 62

Age in 2000	Earned Income in Year 2000				
	$30,000	$40,000	$50,000	$60,000	$76,000+
25	26,200	32,300	36,300	38,300	42,400
35	21,500	26,500	29,800	31,500	34,800
40	20,000	24,500	27,400	28,900	32,000
45	17,700	21,800	24,500	25,900	28,600
50	14,600	17,900	20,200	21,300	23,500

Reduction in Benefits Due to Early Retirement

Target Age to Retire	Reduction Factor
45	.70
50	.75
55	.80

Calculating Your Social Security Benefit

	Example	Yours	Spouse
1. Number from first table	*$31,500*	$_____	$_____
2. Factor from second table	× *.75*	×_____	×_____
3. Line 1 × Line 2	*$23,625*	$_____	$_____

George made $60,000 in 2000 and is 38 years old. He uses the estimated number for a 40-year-old. Because he won't be working after age 50, he uses a reduction factor of .75 (75 percent of the benefit). The Social Security benefit projections assume that you will continue working until age 62 or beyond. George's benefit will be smaller because he retires early. Linda made $30,000 in 2000, so her estimated benefit at age 62, $20,000, is also reduced to $15,000 by the same factor.

Your Income at Age 62

Now calculate your outside income from various other sources and enter the numbers in the next form, Income Projected at Age 62.

1. Enter any income that you expect after age 62 for part-time work from you or your partner income if you expect that either one of you will still work.

2. Enter pension information, if any, from the earlier Income in Year One of Retirement form. Use this number unless your employer benefits department showed you that it is guaranteed to increase.

3. Enter rental income and any other income that you are absolutely sure you will have.

4. Enter your estimated Social Security benefits from the preceding Calculating Your Social Security Benefit form for you and your partner, if applicable.

5. If you or a partner will receive benefits from a retirement plan other than Social Security, such as the federal government Thrift Plan or other government/non-profit contributory retirement plan, enter the employer's estimate of the annual income that you can expect from it under "Other."

6. Total all income.

7. Multiply by 92$\frac{1}{2}$ percent (.925) to cover taxes if you don't expect any outside income, or 90 percent (.90) if you do. These rates take into account your deductions and personal exemptions.

Income Projected at Age 62

Source	Example	Yours #1	Yours #2
Part-time work	$ 0	$_____	$_____
Partner's income	$ 0	$_____	$_____
Pension (annual)	$ 0	$_____	$_____
Rental income (annual)	$ 0	$_____	$_____
Other (guaranteed)	$ 0	$_____	$_____
Social Security	$23,625	$_____	$_____
Spouse Social Security	$15,000	$_____	$_____
Income	$38,625	$_____	$_____
Minus taxes at 7.5% or 10%	×.925	×.925	×.90
NET TOTAL OUTSIDE INCOME	$35,728	$_____	$_____

Enter the net total outside income in the Income Summary form at the end of the chapter. If you have more than one total in the form, enter both and note the year of the change at the top.

Beyond Age 70

You might make some changes in your lifestyle after age 70. You might not be slowing down; you might just be conserving your time and energy for important stuff. Here are some things you might consider doing:

➤ You might sell your home and invest the proceeds to cover rent somewhere else.

➤ You might drop old activities and take up some new ones.

➤ Perhaps you'll travel the world less and visit with your grandchildren more.

You don't need to make any of these decisions now. You'll make those adjustments to your life and your plan in retirement. We'll assume the same inflating level of expenses here, to keep it simple.

We'll also assume that neither you nor your partner is working at all. If you have rental property and still want to hang on to it after age 70, refigure the rental income that you can expect then. Or, plan on selling it, paying some taxes, and investing the rest.

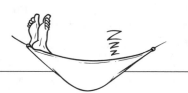

From the Hammock

Don't assume that you'll be settled in the rocking chair after age 70. A friend of Jim's golfs, skis, bowls, plays tennis, and takes long bike rides on a regular basis, depending on the season. He also volunteers, has two engrossing hobbies, and is beginning a new one. At age 80, he shows no signs of slowing down. He hasn't escaped the challenges of aging; he just doesn't let them get in the way of his fun for very long. He's an ideal role model for an active retirement.

To update your Social Security benefits to age 70, follow these steps:

1. Enter your rental income, if any, on the following form, Income Projected at Age 70.

2. Enter any pension and any other guaranteed income from your Income Projected at Age 62 form on the appropriate lines here.

3. Bring your estimated Social Security benefits up to age 70. If you planned on starting at age 62, take the figure(s) for Social Security that you used in the preceding Calculating Your Social Security Benefit form, and multiply by 1.369. This adds 4 percent a year to your payment at age 62. Enter this figure on the following Income Projected at Age 70 form. For Linda and George, this would be $35,728 \times 1.369 = \$48,912$. See the note following step 6 if you or your partner didn't begin collecting benefits at age 62.

4. Repeat steps 1 through 3 for your partner's Social Security estimate.

5. Total all sources of income.

6. Multiply by 92¹/₂ percent (.925) to cover taxes.

Did you or your partner begin collecting less than eight years before you turned age 70? And did you do a second income calculation on the preceding form to cover that possibility? You should do so if you think this will be the case. Then take the figure(s) that you came up with for that year and multiply by the factor(s) from the following table that corresponds to the number of years before age 70 that the benefits began. Enter the result.

Updating Social Security Benefits to Age 70

Years Collected Before Age 70	Factor
1	1.040
2	1.082
3	1.125
4	1.170
5	1.217
6	1.265
7	1.316

Income Projected at Age 70

Source	Example	Yours
Pension (annual)	*$ 0*	$_____
Rental income (annual)	*$ 0*	$_____
Other (guaranteed)	*$ 0*	$_____
Social Security	*$32,343*	$_____
Spouse Social Security	*$20,535*	$_____
Income	*$52,878*	$_____
Minus taxes	× .925	× .925
NET TOTAL OUTSIDE INCOME	*$48,912*	*$*_____

Enter the net total outside income in the Income Summary form at the end of this chapter.

In Chapter 8, you projected expenses in retirement for three stages. Now you have projected income from outside sources, covering the same three stages. In Chapter 10, you'll match the expenses and incomes by stages and then find out what to do to cover the gaps.

Potholes

Your taxes will be increasing overall as your retirement plan withdrawals increase each year. You may be taxed on 85 percent of your Social Security benefit during this period instead of on only 50 percent of it unless Congress raises the current fixed ranges and indexes them. For simplicity, we've continued to calculate the tax on only half of your benefit.

We hope that this issue will be resolved in the future. You already paid income taxes on the money that you "contributed" through payroll deductions. Once should be enough, but means-testing seems to be the wave of the future, so we suspect that 50 percent of the benefit will continue to be exposed for "high"–income taxpayers.

We suspect that these gaps are pretty big, even if they are inflated dollars. Financial planning is the way you get a handle on these shortfalls you will face when your earned income severely drops or disappears altogether. Only then can you make a realistic plan to pay for your retirement.

The numbers that you've come up with in this chapter and the last one are only rough projections, but they're better than picking numbers out of the air. We said we won't hold you to them because they're just your educated guesses as of today. So are our projections of inflation, taxes, and Social Security benefits—but they're the best that our cloudy crystal ball can provide.

The responsibility to cover your expenses in retirement, early or not, is largely yours. Social Security and Medicare aren't designed to do the job. That isn't their purpose. They provide a foundation upon which you design and build your own financial plan for retirement.

Income Summary

Source	Example	Yours 1	Yours 2	Yours 3
In first year of retirement	*$ 0*	$_____	$_____	$_____
At age 62	*$35,728*	$_____	$_____	$_____
At age 70	*$48,912*	$_____	$_____	$_____

The Least You Need to Know

➤ Part-time work may enable you to retire early, but tax problems can arise when you also collect Social Security.

➤ Collecting Social Security at age 62 permanently reduces the level of your benefits—but it may be the option that allows you to retire early.

➤ You need enough money in taxable accounts when you retire early to cover the expense gaps until age 70.

➤ It's usually wise to delay withdrawals from your tax-deferred retirement accounts until age 70, to allow them to grow enough to support you for another 25 years.

Chapter 10

Achieving Your Retirement Goals

> **In This Chapter**
>
> ➤ Determining your financial goals
>
> ➤ What to do to achieve your goals
>
> ➤ How to pay for early retirement
>
> ➤ When and how to tap into retirement plan money

What's it going to take, in real money, for you to achieve financial freedom and retire early? If you completed the expense and income forms in Chapter 8, "Estimating Your Retirement Costs," and Chapter 9, "How to Pay Your Expenses in Retirement," you're ready to move on and generate some answers.

The forms in this chapter aren't complicated, but there are quite a few of them. They take you step by step through the process of creating your financial goals for early retirement. Have your calculator handy, and take them slowly, one at a time. If your eyes start to cross, take a break and come back to them another time.

Make a Plan or Plan to Fail

A financial plan is a lifelong process of setting realistic goals, attaching a dollar figure to them, and determining how to get from here to there. The "how" includes four points:

➤ How much to save

➤ How much your savings needs to grow

➤ How to invest what you save

➤ How to use your savings so that you don't run out of money

The title of this section says it all: Without a good plan, you don't know where you are now, where you're going, or when you'll get there. You probably won't get there—and, even if you did, would you know? Despite the roughness of the plan and the uncertainty of life, any plan is better than no plan.

This is your action plan. You follow it, you monitor it, and you change it when necessary. You also refine it as you go along. Your best estimates today are only rough projections for an uncertain future. Anything can change. Therefore, you review your plan annually and adjust it for any significant changes or new information.

Flying Solo

Single persons who want to retire early have both advantages and disadvantages. Your basic expenses may not be half of a couple's, but, unless you're a single parent, you don't have expenses for kids and their college education. You need to save as aggressively for retirement as a couple.

With only one paycheck now, one Social Security check later, and one retirement account to draw upon, it's all up to you. But it can be done using the same program—spend carefully, save early and often, invest wisely, and plan well. You may not retire as early as you want, but that's true for couples also.

The program and formulas are set up to carry couples through age 95. Odds are good that one of you will live to age 92, according to the National Association of Insurance Commissioners. For singles, odds are that you will live to age 86 (men to 83, women to 87). The program and formulas are designed to carry singles through age 90.

A single parent, whether receiving child support and alimony or paying them, is at a disadvantage in the quest for early retirement. There's no way around this fact. The expenses versus the income don't leave much room to save aggressively.

Single parents need a financial plan just as much as anyone else. Save whatever can be squeezed out of your cash flow. You may not be able to retire early unless your income is much higher than average, but you can—and will—retire. You need to plan and save for that day, whenever it comes.

Create Your Plan

Your financial plan started with your Net Worth statement and your Cash Flow statement covered in Chapter 6, "Wealth: How to Get It and Keep It." That's where you are today. Chapters 8 and 9 begin to define, in dollars, where you want to go. The expenses that you projected in Chapter 8, derived from your current cash flow, and your income projection in Chapter 9 are matched at the stages of your retirement.

We presented two sample graphs near the beginning of Chapters 8 and 9. When you put them together, you want them to look something like the following graph.

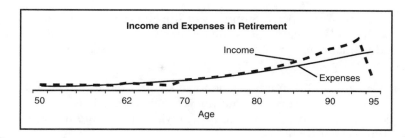

Income and Expenses in Retirement

Income

Expenses

50   62   70   80   90   95

Age

A goal of retirement planning is to match hypothetical expenses and incomes in retirement to achieve a relationship that looks like this.

Until you know how much money you need at retirement to support yourself during the three stages, your income line is way below your expense line. Your plan will determine how much you need to raise your total income in retirement to reach the expense line at the beginning of each stage. You create your financial plan to accomplish this as you work through the forms in this chapter. You may also discover some additional information:

➤ You need to work part-time for a few years.

➤ You won't retire as early as you hoped.

➤ You should scale back your expenses.

These are all options available to you when you make a thorough financial plan. If you wait until you think you're going to retire before you make a plan, these may not be optional; they'll be necessary. Half the battle is knowing what you need to do between now and then. Execution of your plan is the other half.

From the Hammock

While the stock market was falling in 2000 and early 2001, Jim occasionally wondered whether he had made the right decision to retire early. But a review of his financial plan and an update to the current values in his net worth statement reassured him. It all begins with a good plan. Then, a regular review of your plan (at least once a year), both before and after retirement, provides you with the confidence that you're on the right track. There's nothing that can restore your confidence better than a solid plan when events make you question your decision.

You'll need the numbers from your Expense Summary at the end of Chapter 8, and the Income Summary at the end of Chapter 9 in the following sections. As we did in Chapter 9, we'll make adjustments for projected taxes: They will be based on current tax brackets and rates as of early 2001, inflated by 4 percent a year.

Tax brackets, as well as personal and standard deductions, are indexed to the rate of inflation during the previous year. Because all your numbers are inflated at the same rate of 4 percent per year, the relationships between them will still be valid if inflation proves to be something other than 4 percent.

Retirement to Age 62

Enter your numbers from the first lines of your Expense Summary and Income Summary in the first year of retirement on the following form. Then subtract expenses from income and enter the result on the third line. If you used more than one set of figures because of changes in income, enter those, also.

Matching Income and Expenses at Retirement

Example	Yours Year 1	Yours Year___	Yours Year___
Income	*$0*	_____	_____
Expenses	*$72,800*	_____	_____
Difference	*–$72,800*	_____	_____

The difference, a negative number we're sure, is the shortfall in your income for your first year in retirement. You'll need to cover this amount from your taxable accounts each year until age 62.

Your income is not likely to change much during this period unless you take action:

➤ You work more.

➤ You stop working.

➤ You begin collecting a pension.

You had recalculations in Chapter 9 to cover these kinds of possibilities if you thought that one or more of them would be likely. Use them to cover changes during this period using the other two columns in the form. Your expenses, of course, increase each year at 4 percent unless you change the pattern of your spending during this period.

Linda and George, our 38-year-old couple from the two preceding chapters, don't plan to work at all in retirement. They hope to save enough in their taxable and retirement accounts to achieve financial freedom and not work in 12 more years. We'll see what it takes for them to reach their goal as we go.

How Much You'll Need

The next calculation determines how much money you'll need in your taxable accounts when you retire. It assumes that you're invested to average a 10 percent annual return in our Wealth-Builder investment portfolio for preretirement savings. This model portfolio, along with two others, all of which we'll detail in Chapter 12, "How to Pay for Your Goals," forms a basic investment strategy which you can use throughout your life. You'll pay taxes on the income and any *capital gain* each year.

Our model portfolio is designed to minimize taxes until you begin using this money to cover expenses. By then, you'll be in a lower tax bracket. Our basic investment strategy combines market returns, growth with safety over long periods, low costs, low taxes, and low maintenance. We'll also look at other strategies and investments that you can use in Part 4, "A Safari on Wall Street."

On the following Target Savings at Retirement, Taxable Accounts, form, do the following:

1. Enter the amount of the difference from the previous form, Matching Income and Expenses at Retirement, on the first line as a positive number.

2. Divide this amount by the factor on the following Expense Coverage Factor at Retirement table that corresponds to the number of years from your age on your birthday in your first year in retirement until you turn age 62. Linda and George will be 51 in their first year of retirement. Eleven years later they will turn 62.

3. Enter the result on the third line.

Say What?

When you sell a stock, bond, or mutual fund for more than your cost (including reinvested dividends), the difference is a **capital gain.** Under current IRS law, if you owned that investment for more than a year and a day, the gain is considered long term. Long-term gains are currently taxed at 8 percent if you're in the 15 percent tax bracket, and 20 percent if you're in a higher bracket. Beginning in 2006, a gain on an investment that you held for more than five years is taxed at 18 percent if you're in a bracket higher than 15 percent.

Target Savings at Retirement, Taxable Accounts

Example	Yours, Year 1	Yours, Year ___	Yours, Year ___
Difference	*$72,800*	_____	_____
Divided by	*÷ .07*	÷ _____	÷ _____
Target amount	*$1,040,000*	_____	_____

Expense Coverage Factor at Retirement

Years Until Age 62	Factor	Years Until Age 62	Factor
2	.123	9	.077
3	.112	10	.073
4	.103	11	.070
5	.095	12	.068
6	.089	13	.066
7	.084	14	.063
8	.080	15	.062

If you used several calculation years due to projected changes in your income, you should aim for the highest target amount to be safe.

This target amount is the dollar amount that you'll need in your taxable accounts the day when you retire or your earned income ceases. You have your first financial goal. This amount is invested to earn an average of 10 percent annually, or 9.3 percent after taxes. The net investment earnings will cover the shortfall in your income during the first year of your retirement. After the first year or so, you may need to use part of your investments in addition to the earnings. We'll explain how in Chapter 12.

How Much to Save

How do you get there from where you are today? Well, how much do you have in taxable accounts today? From your Net Worth statement, add up the value of your nonretirement plan investments today. If you are also saving money to help pay for college for your children, exclude that amount. It won't be available when you retire. In the next table, "Growth of Current Taxable Savings," you'll grow that amount at 9.3 percent, after tax, until you plan to retire.

The following steps apply this 9.3 percent average annual growth to your current taxable savings until you retire.

1. Enter your total of taxable investments from your Net Worth statement on the first line of the following Growth of Current Taxable Savings form.

2. From the table that follows, select the growth factor on the line that corresponds to the number of years until you retire. Enter it on the second line of the form.

3. Multiply the amount on the first line by the factor on the second line. Enter the result on the third line.

Growth of Current Taxable Savings

	Example	Yours
Taxable savings	*$268,100*	_____
Growth factor	*× 2.906*	× _____
Result of growth	*$779,130*	_____

Growth Factor, After Taxes

Years to Go	Growth Factor	Years to Go	Growth Factor
1	1.093	16	4.147
2	1.195	17	4.533
3	1.306	18	4.955
4	1.427	19	5.416
5	1.560	20	5.920
6	1.705	21	6.471
7	1.864	22	7.073
8	2.037	23	7.731
9	2.226	24	8.450
10	2.433	25	9.236
11	2.659	26	10.095
12	2.906	27	11.034
13	3.176	28	12.060
14	3.471	29	13.182
15	3.794	30	14.408

Linda and George started saving early and often. At age 38, their taxable investments, not counting money saved for college, is $268,100. That would grow to almost $780,000 when they retire in 12 more years. How much more do you need to generate in order to reach your target amount?

To find out, do the following:

1. Enter your target amount from the form Target Savings at Retirement, Taxable Accounts, on the first line.

2. Enter the "Result of Growth" amount from the preceding form on the second line.

3. Subtract the amount on line 2 from your target amount. Enter the result on the third line.

Amount Needed to Reach Retirement Target Amount

	Example	Yours
Target amount	$1,040,000	_____
Result of growth	–$779,130	– _____
Still need	$260,870	_____

You need to generate this amount from savings and return on those savings between now and your retirement.

The following Annual Savings Needed in Taxable Accounts form enables you to calculate how much you need to save each year. Then you need to invest the savings at the after-tax average annual return of 9.3 percent to reach your goal.

To calculate how much you need to save each year, follow these steps:

1. Enter the amount that you still need to save from the preceding form on line 1 of the following "Annual Savings Needed in Taxable Accounts" table.

2. From column 2 in the following "Annual Savings Factors" table find the taxable savings factor that corresponds to the number of years until you plan to retire. Enter the factor on line 2.

3. Multiply the amount on line 1 by the factor on line 2. Enter the result on line 3.

4. Divide the amount on line 3 by 12 for your monthly savings amount.

5. Enter your current gross annual household earned income from the Cash Flow statement that you completed in Chapter 6 (and Appendix A, "Financial Worksheets").

6. Divide the amount on line 3 by the income on line 5. Enter the result on line 6 as a percent (multiply it by 100).

Annual Savings Needed in Taxable Accounts

	Example	Yours
1. Need to save	$212,000	_____
2. Annual savings factor	× .046	× ._____
3. Annual savings required	$9,572	_____
4. Divide by 12 = monthly savings	$813	_____
5. Current household earned income	$90,000	_____
6. Percent of income to save	10.84%	_____%

Annual Savings Factors

Years Before Retire	Taxable Savings Factor	Retirement Savings Factor	Years Before Retire	Taxable Savings Factor	Retirement Savings Factor
5	.157	.154	18	.025	.022
6	.1245	.122	19	.023	.020
7	.1015	.099	20	.021	.0176
8	.0845	.082	21	.019	.0158
9	.071	.069	22	.017	.014
10	.061	.0585	23	.015	.013
11	.053	.050	24	.014	.0116
12	.046	.0435	25	.013	.0195
13	.040	.038	26	.012	.0095
14	.035	.033	27	.011	.0086
15	.031	.029	28	.010	.0078
16	.0275	.026	29	.009	.0071
17	.0245	.023	30	.008	.0064

If That's Too High

Now you know the monthly savings that you need to invest in your taxable accounts. Can you save this much now? What percent is this of your household income? If it's less than 15 percent, you can do it. You'll find ways to cut your expenses over the next year so that you can save this much.

As you get raises and bonuses, you can put the same dollar figure in your investments if you start with this amount now. Then you can spend the extra money, or invest more and retire earlier, or become wealthier. You're in good shape if you execute the plan.

Linda and George still need to save $1,000 a month, not counting college savings or retirement plan contributions. This $12,000 a year represents 13.33 percent of their gross income, but it's less than 15 percent. They're in the habit of saving, so their goal doesn't restrict their lifestyle.

If the annual savings required is more than 15 to 20 percent of your annual household income and you're under age 35, don't sweat it. This is a number you'll grow into. You should aim to hit this number in less than 10 years. When you can save this much, take the percent of your income that it represents that year and stick to that percent from then on. You'll be adding more dollars every year this way.

You have some catching up to do because you didn't start with the annual savings that you needed each year. This strategy will catch you up over time. If you're over 35 and you want to retire in about 15 to 20 years, you need to hit that number within five years and then hold your savings at that percent of your income each year.

113

From the Hammock

It's never easy to scale back your level of spending so you can increase your saving, but it's a necessary component of your plan to retire early. You'll soon get used to it and you'll see your investments growing toward your goal. If you expect to get regular increases in your pay every year plus a bonus or a promotion once in a while, plan to put all of the new income into your savings. Hold your spending steady until you find that you're ahead of your plan. Then you can cut yourself some slack for a job well done.

Age 62 to 70

Now we'll move to the next stage in your planned early retirement. If you, like Linda and George, elect to begin collecting Social Security benefits at age 62, your income will jump. They'll need it to cover their rising expenses.

Remember that both of these numbers you'll enter in the following steps are only your best estimates today of your future Social Security benefit and your expenses.

1. Go back and get your numbers from the second line of your Income Summary and Expense Summary from Chapters 8 and 9.

2. Enter these numbers in the following form.

3. Subtract expenses from income, and enter the difference on the third line.

Matching Income and Expenses at Age 62

	Example	Yours Year 1	Yours Year ___	Yours Year ___
Income	$35,728	_____	_____	_____
Expenses	–$122,080	_____	_____	_____
Difference	–$86,352	_____	_____	_____

This difference, expenses after your net Social Security benefit, will be paid out of your taxable accounts each year. Your investment pile will continue to shrink as you use it to support yourself in retirement. Social Security or your pension money can help, but it's not nearly enough to live on, as you can see.

A Nugget of Gold

States differ widely in their treatment of your income in retirement. Some even tax the following:

➤ Social Security benefits

➤ IRA and 401(k) distributions

➤ Certain kinds of pensions

➤ State and federal government retirement benefits

You'll have to do research in the state where you live when you begin collecting these kinds of income. You can start by visiting www.nasire.org/ StateSearch/ and clicking on Revenue to find a link to the revenue departments for each state. If you do your research ahead of time, you may decide to move to a state that is far kinder in its tax treatment of retirement incomes.

Your taxable investments should last until age 70, with room to spare. When you turn 70, the remaining money becomes your cash cushion and your 911 fund. In Chapter 12, we'll show you how to manage your investments using our basic model portfolio.

Beyond Age 70

One more time, go back to your Income Summary and Expense Summary, and enter the numbers from the third line in the following "Matching Income and Expenses at Age 70" table on the appropriate lines. Subtract expenses from income, and enter the difference on the third line. It's still a negative number, bigger than before.

Matching Income and Expenses at Age 70

	Example	Yours Year 1	Yours Year ___	Yours Year ___
Income	$ 48,912	_____	_____	_____
Expenses	−$180,333	− _____	− _____	_____
Difference	−$131,421	_____	_____	_____

From now on, you'll cover this shortfall each year with your required minimum withdrawals from your retirement plans. To find out how much you'll need there at age 70, fill out the following Target Savings in Retirement Plans at Age 70 form.

Target Savings in Retirement Plans at Age 70

	Example	Yours
Difference	*$131,421*	_____
Divided by	÷ .05	÷ *.05*
Target amount	*$2,628,420*	_____

This is the target amount for the growth of your tax-deferred retirement accounts. Because you stopped contributing when you stopped working, the money that you contributed had to do all the heavy lifting itself. Good old compound interest again!

Say What?

You are advised to name someone— a spouse, children, a relative, or a charity—as the **beneficiary** of any money left in your retirement plans in case you die before you withdraw all the money. This is your beneficiary, and you inform the company that holds your retirement plan, called the custodian, who it is. You may change the beneficiary at any time by notifying the custodian, or name more than one beneficiary if your plan allows you to. It's important to have a beneficiary; otherwise, your plan may name your estate the beneficiary. This will force your heirs to take the money soon after your death rather than allowing them to stretch out the distributions over their lifespans.

Tap Your Retirement Accounts

By April 1 of the year after you turn 70$\frac{1}{2}$, you are required to begin making annual minimum withdrawals from your tax-deferred retirement plans, such as regular IRAs and 401(k)s. We'll use age 70 as the year you begin making withdrawals.

The Treasury Department issued proposed new rules for calculating minimum distributions in January 2001. They were to take effect in 2002 and could be used for 2001 instead of the old rules if your IRA sponsor amended their rules to allow it in 2001. For 401(k) plans, your employer needs to update their plan before any new rules take effect. It is worth noting that the system has been running on a set of rules proposed in 1987 but never finalized!

These proposed new rules do a few things:

➤ They eliminate the need to make difficult choices about how you want to withdraw the money.

➤ They enable you to stretch out the period over which you take minimum required distributions so that you don't run out of money.

➤ They make changes to how and when *beneficiaries* are named.

They simplify the rules on how beneficiaries may withdraw the money.

While the proposed rules are designed to simplify the whole process, you should consult an experienced tax adviser before taking any withdrawals.

The IRS Tells You How

To begin tapping into their retirement accounts after age 70, Linda and George must follow strict IRS procedures to ensure they take at least the minimum required distribution each year. The IRS will impose a 50 percent penalty tax on a shortfall in any year. When Linda and George turn 70, they will calculate the value of all their retirement plans on December 31 of the year before. They'll divide this amount by an IRS-issued table. The old table used a joint life expectancy of 20.6 years. The proposed new table uses 26.2 years for a 70-year-old account owner. This would be used to calculate their minimum required withdrawal during the calendar year after they turn 70^1/$_2$, but they are taking it when they are 70 to avoid the double payment in the first year.

Linda and George each divide their retirement plans' total value, $2,628,420, by 26.2. Their first-year distribution is $100,321 under the new rules. They can take it out in a lump sum or in any amounts at any time they want during the year. You can often arrange to get a monthly check if you set it up ahead of time.

Under the proposed new rules, plan sponsors will also calculate the minimum required distribution for you in each account each year. They'll notify you and the IRS. However, you may take the withdrawals from any of your accounts if you have more than one. The total withdrawal for the year must equal or exceed the total minimum for all the retirement accounts you have.

It's Been Said

"I feel very honored to pay taxes in America. The thing is, I could probably feel just as honored for about half the price."

—Arthur Godfrey

A Nugget of Gold

If you wait until the calendar year after you turn 70^1/$_2$ to begin withdrawing, you must take two distributions that year—the first before April 1, and the second by December 31. This double withdrawal in one year is likely to raise you a tax bracket or two higher than one distribution would. We recommend that you start withdrawing the year you turn 70^1/$_2$ for this reason. You could save tens of thousands of dollars in taxes.

Each following year, Linda and George will take the number from the table corresponding to their age that year. For their second year, when they are 71, the calculation will divide the value of their retirement accounts on December 31 of the year they are 70 by 26.2 again, because they started at age 70 rather than the year after they turned 70^1/$_2$. The third year, the new number for age 71 will be 25.3.

It's Been Said

"If I have caused just one person to wipe away a tear of laughter, that's my reward. The rest goes to the government."

—Victor Borge

Potholes

Until the proposed rules are actually issued later in 2001, they can be changed. There is a formal hearing in June of 2001 on the new rules, but most experts expect the rules to go forward substanitally as issued in January 2001. It is also very possible that they will be changed again in the next 20 years. Consult a financial planner or tax attorney who specializes in retirement plan distributions before you make any decisions.

The proposed new minimum withdrawal table actually runs through age 115 and above. At that age, each year requires that the total be divided by 1.8 to calculate the minimum required distribution. So, if you take the minimum amount each year, you can't outlive your retirement plan money.

You can always take more each year. If Linda and George decide to use a 25-year withdrawal schedule starting at age 70, they'll always take out more than the minimum, and they'll plan on taking their final withdrawal at age 94.

Linda and George pay taxes on the withdrawal, plus half their Social Security benefit, at a projected 15 percent federal tax rate (yours may be higher, depending on your total income). After taking the standard deduction and their personal exemptions, they pay about 10 percent of the gross amount in federal taxes. They'll need the income from their remaining taxable investments and maybe a little of those investments to cover all their expenses that year.

During the following years, their minimum withdrawals will likely increase faster than their expenses because the average annual growth within the plan exceeds the minimum distribution amount. Even after taxes, they'll be able to increase their taxable investments by larger and larger amounts through reinvesting the surplus from their withdrawals until age 85. They shouldn't spend it all unless their circumstances require it. They may need this money after age 95, when their retirement plan runs out of money.

If you established a Roth IRA or converted a regular IRA to a Roth at some point (and paid the necessary taxes when you converted), when you take the money is up to you. There's no requirement to take any distribution while you're alive, and you don't owe any tax on it when you do. Take it when you need it. We'll look closer at traditional IRAs versus Roth IRAs in Chapter 21, "The IRA: Your Personal Tax Shelter."

How Much You Need

How much will you need to have in your retirement accounts when you retire? Remember, when you retire, you can no longer contribute to any retirement account because contributions are all based on earned income.

The following calculation will discount the target amount you calculated in the preceding form at 10 percent a year back to the year you plan to retire. This discount factor represents the 10 percent average annual growth of your retirement plan money from retirement to age 70.

1. Enter your target amount from the preceding form, Target Savings in Retirement Plans at Age 70, on the first line in the following Target Retirement Accounts Savings at Age 70 form.

2. From the following table, Growth of Retirement Accounts at 10 Percent per Year, find the number of years from when you plan to retire until you turn 70. Enter the retirement growth factor that corresponds to that number on the second line.

3. Divide the number on the first line by this growth factor. Enter the result on the third line.

Target Retirement Accounts Savings at Age 70

	Example	Yours
Target amount	*$2,628,420*	_____
Divide by growth factor	*÷ 6.12*	÷ _____
Target at retirement	*$429,480*	_____

Growth of Retirement Accounts at Ten Percent per Year

Years	Retirement Growth Factor	Years	Retirement Growth Factor
5	1.61	18	5.56
10	2.59	19	6.12
11	2.85	20	6.73
12	3.14	21	7.40
13	3.45	22	8.14
14	3.80	23	8.95
15	4.18	24	9.85
16	4.59	25	10.83
17	5.05		

Linda and George will retire at age 50, in 2012. In 2032, they'll begin withdrawing money from their retirement plans. On December 31, 2031, they will need $2,628,420 invested in retirement plans to cover their expenses for the following 25 years. They'll use the growth factor for 19 years because they'll start withdrawing at age 70 rather than after they turn 71.

119

How Much to Save

When you retire, you should have your target amount in your retirement accounts, including a Roth IRA if you have one. How do you get there from where you are now? How much do you have today? The following form grows your current retirement plan funds at 10 percent a year until the year you retire.

1. Enter the current value of all your retirement accounts from your Net Worth statement on the first line of the following "Growth of Retirement Savings" table.

2. Enter the retirement growth factor from the preceding "Growth of Retirement Accounts at Ten Percent per Year" table that corresponds to the number of years until you plan to retire on the second line.

3. Multiply the amount on the first line by the factor on the second line. Enter the result on the third line.

Growth of Retirement Savings

	Example	Yours
Current retirement plan value	$77,475	_____
Growth factor	× 3.14	× _____
Result of growth	$243,272	_____

Now, how much more do you need to reach your target amount at retirement?

1. Find your "Target Amount at Retirement" from the third line of the Target Savings in Retirement Plans at Age 70 form that you filled out earlier in the chapter. Enter it on the first line of the following Amount Needed to Reach Retirement Target Amount form.

2. Enter the "Result of Growth" of your current retirement savings from the third line of the preceding Growth of Retirement Savings form on the second line of the following Amount Needed to Reach Retirement Target Amount form.

3. Subtract the amount on the second line from your target amount on the first line. Enter the result on the third line.

Amount Needed to Reach Retirement Target Amount

	Example	Yours
Target amount at retirement	$429,480	_____
Result of growth	−$243,272	− _____
Still need	$186,208	_____

This additional need is a combination of the following:

➤ What you contribute

➤ What your employer contributes, if any

➤ The growth of contributions until you retire

You break this down to annual and monthly contributions on the following Retirement Contributions Needed Annually form. You will need to refer to the "Annual Savings Factors" table earlier in this chapter; for this form, you will use the retirement savings factor in column 3.

1. Enter the amount that you need to save from the preceding "Amount Needed to Reach Retirement Target Amount" table on line 1 of the following table.

2. Enter the retirement savings factor from the "Annual Savings Factor" table that corresponds to the number of years until you retire on line 2.

3. Multiply this factor by the amount in line 1, and enter the result on line 3. This is the annual amount of your contributions needed until your target retirement.

4. If your employer contributes to your 401(k) also, enter the amount that would match your contribution.

5. Subtract your employer's contribution amount on line 4 from the amount in line 3, and enter the result on line 5. This is the amount that you need to contribute.

6. Divide the amount on line 5 by 12 to get your monthly contributions.

7. Enter your current household gross annual earned income from your Cash Flow statement on line 7.

8. Divide the amount on line 6 by the amount on line 7. Enter the result on line 8. This is the percentage of your gross annual income represented by that contribution.

Retirement Contributions Needed Annually

	Example	Yours
1. Need to save	$186,208	_____
2. Retirement savings factor	× .0435	× _____
3. Annual contribution required	$8,100	_____
4. Minus employer contributions, if any	−$2,700	− _____
5. Your contribution	$5,400	_____
6. Divide by 12 = monthly savings	$÷ 450	÷ _____
7. Current household earned income	$90,000	_____
8. Percent of income to save	6.0%	_____ %

Line 3 shows the amount that you (and your employer, if you have a 401[k] plan at work) need to put in your retirement plans each year until you retire. If your employer doesn't contribute to your retirement plan, you'll have to do it all yourself. This can be accomplished by any combination of the following from you and your spouse:

➤ 401(k)

➤ IRA

➤ Roth IRA

➤ 403(b) or 457

➤ Keogh, SEP, SIMPLE, or other contributory retirement plan offered by your employer

We'll cover all these plans in Chapter 20, "Keep the Taxman Waiting While You Work." Combined monthly contributions to any of these plans equaling the total from the preceding form, invested at an average annual return of 10 percent, will get you to your total. Chapter 12 will show you a basic investing strategy designed to earn this return.

Potholes

If you don't have a 401(k) or other retirement plan at work, your only retirement plan is an IRA, unless you have some self-employment income. (We'll look at self-employment plans in Chapter 20. You can contribute a maximum of $2,000 a year, per person, to an IRA.) Congress may get around to raising this amount, but, until then, you have to save the balance of the money in taxable accounts in order to retire early.

If That's Too High

If the amount in the preceding form exceeds 10 percent of your gross annual household earned income and you're under age 35, you should grow into it within 10 years. Then keep adding that percent of your income that you earn the year you hit this dollar amount every year thereafter until you retire. You'll catch up.

If you have less than 15 years to go to your target retirement year and this annual contribution amount seems out of reach, aim to hit it within five years and hold it at that percent of your income until you retire. If you can't do this, you'll have to move your target retirement date back until the numbers work. It takes a lot of saving to retire early. The earlier you start saving, the easier it is.

Percent of Total Income

For each of the two calculations that you performed in this chapter—how much you needed to save in your taxable accounts and in your retirement accounts—the forms asked you to figure what percent of your current annual income these amounts represented. Put these two numbers in the following form, and add them.

Required Annual Savings Percent

	Example	Yours
From line 6 of Annual Savings Needed in Taxable Accounts form	**10.84%**	_____%
From line 8 of Retirement Contributions Needed Annually	**6.00%**	_____%
Total Percent of annual earned income	**16.84%**	_____%

In Chapter 7, "How to Be a Middle-Class Millionaire," we suggested that you needed to save about 20 percent of your annual earned income if you wanted to reach your goal of retiring early. If your total in the form is less than 20 percent, you're doing well. Keep it up, and you'll make it.

A Nugget of Gold

It's always a good idea to have your plan and your financial status reviewed by a financial planner before the critical dates in your plan:

➤ Before you retire

➤ Before you begin collecting Social Security

➤ Before you begin withdrawals from retirement accounts

➤ At age 80

An outside review will confirm that you're on track and provide you with peace of mind, or point out problems that you need to address. This is also the time to review the laws and rules for each of these critical points in your retirement so that you can make the best choices for your situation. No two financial plans are the same; your plan is the one that works for you.

If your total is well over 20 percent, follow our earlier suggestions depending on whether you're under or over age 35 now. If the numbers are still out of reach in the 5 or 10 years that we mentioned, your target retirement date is too optimistic. You'll need to modify your game plan:

➤ Keep working several more years to make your savings targets.

➤ Work (more) after you retire.

➤ Reduce your spending both now and in retirement by enough to make the numbers work.

The Least You Need to Know

➤ Your financial plan is your action plan to a successful early retirement.

➤ Retiring early means that you have to save early and in large amounts.

➤ You are responsible for covering your expenses in retirement.

➤ Forty to fifty years in retirement takes a lot of money and careful management of cash flow.

➤ Income taxes take a bite of everything, sooner or later.

Chapter 11

Finding and Using a Financial Planner

> **In This Chapter**
>
> ➤ When and how to get help with your plan
>
> ➤ Interviewing planners
>
> ➤ Checking their credentials and background

How does your plan look so far? If, in the course of the last three chapters, it seems to have crashed and burned, don't give up. You might not like what you've learned, but it's better to have learned it now. Perhaps your plan needs more work, more money, or more time. You can rethink your plan and rework it so that it becomes realistic and achievable. This is how dreams become reality over time.

Professionals Can Help

If any of the calculations in the last three chapters have stopped you cold, you can get help. *Financial planners* are in the business of helping clients to identify and define personal and financial goals. A planner will work with you on the details and point out aspects that you might not have covered.

If you've got a handle on your goals, a planner can work with you to understand your Net Worth and Cash Flow statements. You still have to do the digging, but a planner can help with problems such as a negative cash flow. By going over the numbers with you, a planner learns who you are and where you are.

From the Hammock

A **financial planner** is a person who can advise and guide you through the process of creating and executing your financial plan. Dee is a Certified Financial Planner while Jim is a do-it-yourself type. A certified financial planner is a licensed professional who has passed a comprehensive exam administered by the CFP Board of Standards covering the major areas of financial planning. They also had to work for three to five years, depending on educational background, in the financial planning field before receiving a CFP designation and agree to abide by a code of ethics. After that, they must earn 30 hours of continuing education credits every two years.

There are other professional designations for financial planners based on their training and education. However, in most states, anyone can hang out a financial planner shingle. Look for the professional designations after the name. We'll explain what the major ones are later in this chapter.

Knowing this, and understanding your goals, a planner can help you with the next step. Here, the planner can do a lot of the number-crunching that we covered in Chapter 8, "Estimating Your Retirement Costs"; Chapter 9, "How to Pay Your Expenses in Retirement"; and Chapter 10, "Achieving Your Retirement Goals." Planners employ different and more sophisticated ways using computer programs. But the results should be about the same. You get the dollar amounts that you'll need over specified time horizons and the amounts that you need to save to reach your financial goals. Planners can also find ways around problems that might prevent you from achieving a goal.

If you did all the work so far but you aren't sure about the results, a planner can review it with you. Planners like clients who have already done the work and understand what's involved. They're happy to probe, test, check, and evaluate the numbers with you and help you refine your plan even more.

Several times in the course of the preceding chapters, we suggested that you may want to review your plan and your progress with a financial planner at different times in your life. Bringing one on board early is a good idea. As time goes by, you have someone who knows you and understands where you want to go. It's great to have a knowledgeable professional whom you're comfortable talking to about these things occasionally.

Types of Planners

In addition to a Certified Financial Planner, any of the following may also offer financial planning services to the public. Some may have more than one professional designation following their name. This can tell you what their primary area of expertise and interest may be. For general financial planning assistance, the Certified Financial Planner (CFP) designation described in the preceding "From the Hammock" sidebar is the best place to begin. To help you with the rest of this alphabet soup, we'll look at the major designations you're likely to see.

➤ **Registered Investment Advisor (RIA):** Individuals registered with the Securities and Exchange Commission who hold themselves out to be an investment advisor. This registration is required of anyone who gives advice, makes recommendations, issues reports, or furnishes analysis on securities either directly or through publications for compensation and as part of a business. If a planner is an employee of an advisory firm such as a brokerage house, the brokerage house will have a blanket registration for all employees with the SEC.

➤ **Certified Public Accountant (CPA):** This is an experienced accountant who has met educational, statutory, and licensing requirements of the state in which the practice is located. CPAs do auditing and tax returns and leave the financial planning advising to the Personal Financial Specialists in their field.

➤ **American Institute of Certified Public Accountants—Personal Financial Planning Specialist (AICPA-PFP):** Personal Financial Specialists are CPAs who have passed a financial planning exam, have practical experience in financial planning, and are members of the AICPA.

➤ **Chartered Financial Analysts (CFA):** This designation is awarded by the Institute of Chartered Financial Analysts to experienced financial analysts who have passed exams in economics, financial accounting, portfolio management, security analysis, and standards of conduct. They focus on investing and managing portfolios.

➤ **Chartered Financial Consultant (CFC):** Designation awarded by the American College of Bryn Mawr and is the insurance industry's financial planning designation. Consultants must meet experience requirements and pass exams covering finance and investing.

➤ **Chartered Life Underwriter (CLU):** Designation awarded by the American College of Bryn Mawr. The recipients must have business experience in insurance planning and related areas and pass national examinations in insurance and related subjects.

➤ **Enrolled Agent (EA):** This designation is controlled by the IRS. The person must have either passed an exam covering all areas of taxation, or have five years of experience in a technical capacity at the IRS. This designation gives the holder the right to represent taxpayers in tax court.

What You Want in a Planner

You're looking for a wide range of characteristics in a financial planner, and it may take a while to find one with all of these. The critical one is that you are comfortable talking about your life and finances with this person. You also want a planner who has these characteristics:

➤ **Acts as an educator.** You want to learn about the process of financial planning and how you can use it.

➤ **Acts as a communicator.** You want someone who can explain all this stuff to you so that you can understand it.

➤ **Acts a listener.** A good communicator also listens to you, hears your questions, and understands your hopes and fears.

➤ **Is trustworthy.** You're sharing your inner dreams and your private financial life with this person.

➤ **Is competent.** Look for a person with knowledge and experience in all areas of financial planning. That doesn't mean that this person knows everything; the planner will know when to refer you to a specialist, too.

➤ **Is committed.** You want someone who's on your side and is there when you have questions or problems.

➤ **Is objective.** You depend on unbiased advice and recommendations that are in your best interest.

A Nugget of Gold

It's well worth the time and effort you should spend to find a planner or adviser with whom you're comfortable. With luck, you'll work together for many years. You'll be trusting this person to advise you about your money, goals for you and your family, and how to reach them. Outside of your employer, this may be the most important inancial relationship you have in life.

How to Find a Planner

Begin by asking friends, relatives, and co-workers if they work with a financial planner. If you have an attorney or tax preparer you work with, ask who that person would recommend. Make it clear that you want a professional planner, not a broker or a money manager at this point.

How to Interview Them

When you have a short list of at least three prospects, set up an interview with each. Most planners provide an introductory consultation at no cost. This is your opportunity to ask questions about them. You approach it as if you're interested in hiring one of them for an important job working with you. You are. Don't be shy; they're accustomed to tough questions.

Here are some questions you'll want to ask:

➤ What credentials have you earned?

➤ What's your educational background? What colleges did you go to? What degrees do you have?

➤ How long have you been practicing?

➤ Can you provide a list of references?

➤ Do you have a typical plan that I can see?

➤ Are you licensed with the state securities division?

➤ Are you registered with the Securities and Exchange Commission?

You also want a copy of the adviser's Form ADV, Parts I and II. This is their registration form with the SEC—if they manage more than $25 million for clients—or your state's securities regulator if they're smaller or don't manage money. You should be able to get this form from the planner or adviser, but you can also get them from the regulators we just mentioned (see addresses and Web sites later in this chapter). Form ADV has two parts:

➤ Part I provides information about their education and their business. It also must identify if they've had problems with regulators or clients.

➤ Part II outlines their services, fees, and strategies. They're required to give you this part 48 hours before signing you as a client, but ask for both parts and read them carefully.

Next, you want to understand what services the planner can provide. Ask these questions:

➤ What types of services do you offer?

➤ Are you licensed to sell financial products?

➤ Do you sell financial products? What ones?

➤ Do you represent any companies?

➤ Do you manage investments for a fee?

➤ What is your client profile?

➤ How often do you talk with your clients?

➤ Are you the person who does the work?

Potholes

You may not be interested in any financial products that the planner has to sell, but you sure want to know if he does sell some. If you're interested in only planning help and the planner starts pitching products, you might question the objectivity of the advice.

How Do They Make Money?

Finally, you want to know how the planner gets paid. How does she support herself as a planner?

Remember, you're doing the interviewing and the hiring, and you want the financial arrangements made clear up front. So ask. A planner makes money in three basic ways:

Potholes

The cost of a fee-only planner limits the services to people who actually have several hundred thousand dollars to begin. If you're at or above that range, try to find one of them to interview as part of your search. The up-front fee to hire a fee-only planner may look steep, but you're buying unbiased advice. The commissions you'll pay over many years to the other types of planners may far exceed the fee-only planner's cost, and you'll never be sure if you got the best advice for you and your plan.

➤ **As a fee-only planner.** These planners charge an hourly fee ($75 to $250 an hour, depending on what part of the country they're in and how broad and deep their experience is); a flat fee of $1,000 to $5,000 for a comprehensive plan; or an annual retainer, often billed quarterly. The retainer may be a flat fee based on your assets. Extra work may be billed at an hourly rate. Fee-only planners are few in number.

➤ **As a commission-only planner.** These planners do basic financial plans, usually a canned, computer-generated one; offer advice; and sell products ranging from insurance and annuities to stocks and mutual funds. They earn a commission on the sale of products to clients.

➤ **As a fee-and-commission planner.** Often called fee-based planners, these planners charge hourly or flat fees for a financial plan and advice. They also sell financial products on commission to help you execute your plan. Make sure you understand what's what here. The plan may cost only several hundred dollars, but it isn't very personalized at that price.

Check Them Out

Following the interviews, use the information you received to verify credentials and check backgrounds. If you received referrals of current clients, call them to see how long they've worked with the planner and whether they're satisfied with the services.

Organizations

Contact the appropriate organizations on the following lists, depending on the type of professional you are interviewing, to check the planner's representations to you in the materials you received and from the Form ADV.

For a certified financial planner (CFP), contact

> The Certified Financial Planner Board of Standards
> 1700 Broadway, Suite 2100
> Denver, CO 80290-2101
> 1-888-CFP-MARK
>
> www.cfp-board.org

You want to know whether the planner is properly licensed and whether he has ever been disciplined by the board. Are there any complaints on file?

For a certified public accountant/personal financial specialist (CPA/PFP), contact

> American Institute of Certified Public Accountants
> Personal Financial Planning Division (AICPA-PFP Div.)
> 1211 Avenue of the Americas
> New York, NY 10036
> 1-800-862-4272
>
> www.aicpa.org

For a chartered financial consultant (ChFC) and chartered life underwriter (CLU), contact

> National Association of Insurance Commissioners (NAIC)
> 120 W. 12th St., Suite 1100
> Kansas City, MO 64105
> 816.842.3600
>
> www.naic.org

The NAIC can direct you to your state agency that regulates insurance. Check if the person is licensed to sell insurance and whether there are any violations on record.

For most financial professionals including planner, advisers, brokers, real estate agents, and mortgage brokers, contact

> National Fraud Exchange (NAFEX)
> 12020 Sunrise Valley Dr., Suite 360
> Reston, VA 20191
> 1-800-822-0416

You can request a background check for a fee of $39 for the first person and $20 per person for additional ones. The check will reveal whether the person has been subject to criminal, civil, or administrative action in the securities and financial services industry.

For anyone who sells securities, including a registered investment adviser (RIA), contact

North American Securities Administration Association
One Massachusetts Ave., Suite 310
Washington, DC 20001
202-737-0900

www.nasaa.org

Check with the preceding organization of state securities administrators to find out which agency in your state regulates securities-licensed financial planners with less than $25 million under management.

The National Association of Securities Dealers (NASD) is an association of companies that sell stocks, bonds, and other securities. If your planner or advisor sells any of these products, you can check out their disciplinary record in the central registration depository (CRD) file with the NASD.

NASD
1735 K St., NW
Washington, DC 20006
1-800-289-9999

www.nasdr.com

The Securities and Exchange Commission (SEC) is the federal agency that regulates the entire securities industry.

SEC
450 5th St., NW
Washington, DC 20549
1-800-732-0330

www.sec.gov

Registered investment advisers (RIA) who manage more than $25 million must be registered with the SEC.

Choose One

After you've interviewed all the candidates and checked out their backgrounds, choose the best qualified person with whom you feel most comfortable. Make an appointment and get started. Take what you have done on your plan with you. At a minimum, you'll be asked for your Net Worth and Cash Flow statements. If you are unable to complete these, tell the planner that's where you'll start working together.

It's Been Said

"Everyone is ignorant, only on different subjects."

—Will Rogers

If at any point during the relationship you become uncomfortable or have second thoughts about your choice, you should bring this up with the planner and discuss it. Perhaps the planner just didn't clearly understand what you want or need. If this discussion doesn't relieve your concern, you can fire the planner and get another one. You're in charge of your financial plan.

The Least You Need to Know

➤ If you think that you need help getting started with your financial plan, find a qualified professional financial planner you're comfortable with.

➤ A financial planner who can help you review your plan and discuss your finances is a valuable asset throughout your life.

➤ Don't just pick a planner from the Yellow Pages. Get referrals and check out her background before you hire one.

Part 3
Investing for Your Retirement

Becoming a successful investor means learning to think like one. It's a state of mind that you learn to cultivate. Despite attempts to reduce it to a numbers game, investing is more an art than a science. Practice and experience provide the best knowledge. Books and articles only provide ideas, and not all of them are good ideas in inexperienced hands.

How you manage your money over your lifetime is more important than what specific investments you use. You have a very long-term investing horizon with your retirement money. It has to keep working for you over 40 years, perhaps longer, after you retire early. What the markets do next week, next year, or even over the next 10 years isn't very important. What you do is.

Chapter 12

How to Pay for Your Goals

In This Chapter

➤ How to make your money work hard

➤ A basic investment strategy for each stage of life

➤ When and how to rebalance your basic portfolios

➤ Investing for intermediate-term goals

➤ Investing for short-term goals

Saving more than 20 percent of your gross income just doesn't float everyone's boat these days. But we never said that retiring early would be easy. So, if you're still with us, this is where the magic begins.

You're about to find out how Linda and George—and you, too—can make money work hard. From age 24 until they retire at age 50, Linda and George will save around $400,000. That, plus their employers' 401(k) contributions, totals less than half a million dollars. Yet their expenses and taxes due in just the year they're age 85 will be more than that!

Careful investment decisions combined with compounding returns will make the rabbit jump out of the hat for you. The basic investment strategies in this chapter are designed for people who …

➤ Know they need more than CDs.

➤ Aren't sure how to invest wisely.

➤ Are hesitant to invest in the stock market.

➤ Don't have the time to learn to manage stocks and mutual funds.

Potholes

For many current retirees, their money has run out and they live on a small Social Security check each month, plus the kindness of family. They can look forward to many years like this. They out-lived their money, and who knew people would live so long? Life expectancy has literally zoomed up in the last century, from 47 in 1900 to the mid–80s today. Has it stopped increasing? We don't think so. Medical science hopes to keep it going.

A Nugget of Gold

We talk a lot about average annual returns in this book, but the stock market hardly ever has an average year. The average annual return is a mathematical calculation of the average annual return on an investment compounded over a fixed period. Some years are better, and some are worse. Only by leaving the money invested do you enjoy the benefit of the compounding effect of the annual average rate.

The Way We Used to Retire

The old-fashioned retirement strategy was to invest strictly in income-producing stuff like CDs and bonds. You lived off the interest payments as long as possible. That worked better when inflation was less than 2 percent and people lived until an average of age 71.

For Linda and George to cover their expenses at age 51, when they begin retirement, they need an income of about $80,000. At 6 percent interest, they would need about $1.33 million to provide that $80,000. And they have more than that—about $1.47 million—in their taxable and retirement accounts. Great, right?

What happens at age 54 when their taxes and expenses are more than that 6 percent brings them? They'll take some of their investment money to cover the difference. Each year, they'll need to take more and more. At age 72, they're toast. All they'll have left is Social Security, and that covers only about one quarter of what they projected their expenses to be.

Unless you manage to save a lot more than our program suggests you need, the old way won't work any longer. Even if you work full-time until age 65, or whenever you can collect full Social Security benefits, you still need to save aggressively and invest in something that pays you more than 5 or 6 percent. At age 65, you have 20 to 30 years to pay expenses that are inflating every year.

The Way We Need to Invest Today

You're already (we hope) saving regularly in a tax-deferred retirement plan such as a 401(k) or IRA. You may also have begun a Roth IRA since they were introduced in 1998. Maybe you aren't saving enough, as you might have discovered in the preceding chapter, but you're working on that now.

The money that you put in these plans at age 30 compounds for 40 years. Then, when you begin withdrawing money, the balance continues compounding and actually growing as long as it's invested to earn more than you take out each year. The Roth IRA is even better. Not only do you not have to take it out after age 70, but when you do, there's no tax to pay.

The Basic Investment Strategy

You're working hard for your money today, and you may not have the time or interest to learn how to invest in stocks or figure out which of the more than 7,000 mutual funds are best for you. Not a problem. You can spend time on those things after you retire, if you want. In this book, we'll present you with a basic investment strategy characterized by the following:

➤ Stock market returns

➤ Very low costs

➤ Very low taxes

➤ Very low maintenance

➤ Safety over long periods

Some very bright people (not us—we're just smart enough to understand it) have spent a lot of time and computer power figuring out how to invest in such a way to accomplish all of this. By examining stock performance for the largest companies in the United States over 100 years, they found the way to invest to achieve all of those goals.

When you decide to retire early, you're taking a risk. By giving up 10 to 15 of your highest-earning years, you're betting that you won't need that money. The money that you saved, and its growth, must support you comfortably for many years. If it runs out early, you lose. So, it doesn't make sense to take too much risk with your money.

These bright people figured out that over long periods of time—30, 40, 50 years—you can invest 70 to 80 percent of your money in the stock market and have a great deal of confidence that you can withdraw money to live on for many years. It's not a guarantee. There are no guarantees in investing or in life (except for death and taxes, of course). But it's as good a strategy as very smart people can devise.

The basic investment strategy revolves around three main items: index funds, bond mutual funds, and money market mutual funds.

From the Hammock

When the stock market drops (as it did in 2000–2001), a whole new generation of investors gets an education in investing. At those times, it can be very difficult to maintain the long-term view. But having a well-built plan with a 50- or 60-year horizon gives you some perspective. It still takes going through a couple of major corrections to get (somewhat) used to it, but you will learn to ride the waves better in time while you keep the distant horizon in view.

139

Say What?

The **market cap,** short for market capitalization, is the value of all the outstanding shares of a company multiplied by the market price per share. The market cap may not be in proportion to the size of a company as measured by sales. In early 2000, many hot high-tech companies had huge market caps but low sales and no profits. But these companies aren't in the S&P 500 Index.

Index Funds

The core investment of the basic strategy is called an index mutual fund. The best known type is an *S&P Index* fund. When you invest in an S&P Index fund, you're investing in 500 of America's best companies. Over the last 75 years, the S&P 500 (or its equivalent before there was an S&P) has had an annual average return of just over 11 percent.

Over 10-year periods, any 10-year period, only 2 of every 10 stock mutual funds beat the S&P Index. And no one knows who those 20 percent will be ahead of time. Most of the winners don't beat the index by much. That's why our strategy uses an S&P Index fund.

You can substitute a Wilshire 5000 index fund, a Russell 3000 index fund, or a Total Market Index fund instead. They invest in nearly all the companies listed on the New York Stock Exchange and the NASDAQ. In all cases, the investments are based on the market value, called the *market cap* of each company. The larger the cap is, the more money is invested.

Say What?

An index is a specific group of stocks (or bonds) that represent the stock market or any imaginable slice of it. They serve as a benchmark against which the performance of mutual funds investing in that segment are measured. Standard & Poors creates and monitors a list, called the **S&P Index,** of 500 of the largest companies in the United States. S&P doesn't manage any of the funds or sell them. Most mutual fund companies have one of their own. Many professional money managers and mutual funds use the S&P 500 Index as their target for annual returns.

There are hundreds of index mutual funds that are designed to produce the same returns as their index. Usually, these funds hold all the stocks in their particular index in the same proportion as they exist in the index. They are not actively managed and, as a result, have very low expenses.

An index fund has many other advantages over other funds. There's no manager making investment decisions. A computer tracks the S&P, and when a company is added or subtracted a few times a year, the trade orders are issued. With few sales, there are almost no capital gains to distribute. The gains build up as long as the stocks are held. All this saves you money with regard to the following:

➤ Management fees

➤ Taxes on capital gain distributions

➤ Transaction costs

Each year the share price goes up by the percent that the companies in the fund collectively increase. When you finally sell shares, you owe capital gains tax on your share increase. Currently, capital gains are taxed at low rates compared to your earned income, interest, and dividends.

Can you do better than an index fund? If you have the time, interest, discipline, and talent, sure, it's possible. But 80 percent of professional money managers fail to do better over time, for one reason or another. You're investing for the long haul, so put the odds in your favor. We'll look at other investments anyway in Part 4, "A Safari on Wall Street," if you want to walk on the wild side.

Bond Mutual Funds

The second part of the basic investment strategy requires a fixed-income investment. A certificate of deposit (CD) at a bank is an example of a fixed-income investment. It pays you a fixed rate of interest on the money deposited. At the end of the term, you get your money back. Other fixed-income investments include these:

➤ Money market accounts and funds

➤ U.S. government debt securities

➤ Corporate debt securities, called bonds

➤ Bond mutual funds

The first three have a fixed rate of interest for a defined period. When that time is up, they mature; you get your money back. The interest rate is set when you purchase the investment (in reality, you're loaning your money to the issuer) based on the current market rate of interest for that specific type of security.

A bond mutual fund is a managed portfolio of bonds of different kinds, maturities, and, often, quality. The manager buys and sells them in an attempt to get a better *total return* than he would get by just collecting the interest. If the manager is right, the fund has a little higher return. We'll look closer at bonds and bond funds in Chapter 18, "A Zoo-ful of Bonds."

Every month, the fund makes a distribution consisting of the interest earned minus expenses incurred in managing the fund. If the manager also made money selling bonds at a higher price than they cost, the fund pays a capital gain dividend once or twice a year. But this amount usually isn't very much.

Your total annual return also includes the value of the bonds held in the portfolio. If the value increases, the fund share price goes up. If it decreases, the share price goes down. The bonds are valued every day, so the price is likely to change daily by a small amount. You don't get the benefit of any increase until you sell your shares.

Because a bond fund never matures, the only way you get your money out is to sell shares. When you sell, you will realize a capital gain or loss, depending on what your cost per share is at the time you sell compared to the share price when you sell. When you reinvest the dividends each month, you buy more shares at the going price. This changes your average cost per share.

In our basic investment strategy, we'll use a U.S. government bond fund that invests in *U.S. Treasury notes.* They're guaranteed by the U.S. government, and that's as safe as investments can get.

U.S. Treasury notes generally pay more than shorter-maturity bills and less than longer-maturity bonds— not always, but that's the norm. Because they mature in less than 10 years, their value doesn't jump around as much as that of longer-term bonds when market rates of interest change. They're less volatile. But over the long term, that stability overcomes the slightly lower interest rate. Intermediate-term Treasury notes show a little better total return than either bills or bonds.

Money Market Mutual Funds

The remaining component of the basic investment strategy is a money market mutual fund. Note that this is different from a money market account at a bank. Money market mutual funds pay distributions from net interest earned by the fund at a rate at least twice as high as the interest earned in most bank money market accounts. Money market mutual funds aren't guaranteed by the U.S. government, but no retail investor (you and me) has ever lost a penny in a money market mutual fund.

Say What?

To determine true investment performance, you want to know how much an investment has grown in value. The **total return** adds the change in value of the fund's holdings to the dividends that the fund pays. This may be more or less than the yield represented by the dividends.

Say What?

The U.S. Treasury issues Treasury bills, which mature in a year or less; Treasury bonds, which mature in 30 years; and **Treasury notes,** which mature in 2, 5, and 10 years. This 2-to-10-year period makes them intermediate-term debt.

Money market mutual funds pay monthly distributions at rates not too far below our U.S. government fund most years. But they pay no capital gain dividends, nor does their price vary from $1 per share. The dividend rate changes faster than the bond fund because money market funds hold short-term securities with an average maturity of 50 to 90 days, but not over one year. As the securities mature, the manager buys new ones at current rates.

The Portfolio Strategy

We'll use the basic investment strategy to create three basic portfolios: the Wealth Builder portfolio, the Wealth Maintenance portfolio, and the Wealth Preservation portfolio. The Wealth Builder portfolio is recommended while you're working and regularly adding new money to your investments as well as for your retirement plan money in early retirement. We suggest the Wealth Maintenance portfolio for taxable accounts when you retire early and during your middle retirement years, from around age 70 through 80 to 85 in your retirement accounts. The Wealth Preservation portfolio is for late retirement, after age 80 or 85, when you want to be sure your money will last as long as you do.

A Nugget of Gold

The distributions made by a money market mutual fund are reported to the IRS as dividends, just like distributions from other mutual funds. Payments made by a bank from a money market account are reported as interest. You will get a 1099–DIV or 1099–INT form that allows you to identify how the income should be reported on your 1040.

Portfolio Strategies

Taxable Account Portfolio Strategy

Before Retirement	Retirement to age 65	Age 65 and beyond
Wealth Builder	Wealth Maintenance	Wealth Preservation

Retirement Account Portfolio Strategy

Before Retirement	Retirement to age 70	Age 70 to 80/85	Age 80/85 and beyond
Wealth Builder	Wealth Builder	Wealth Maintenance	Wealth Preservation

The Wealth Builder Portfolio

The Wealth Builder portfolio is used to build your wealth in both taxable and tax-deferred retirement accounts. It provides the maximum return with maximum safety (according to those very bright people) in your taxable accounts until you retire and in your retirement accounts until age 70. The Wealth Builder portfolio allocates money in this way:

➤ 80 percent of your money to an S&P Index fund

➤ 20 percent to a U.S. government intermediate-term bond fund

Wealth Builder portfolio.

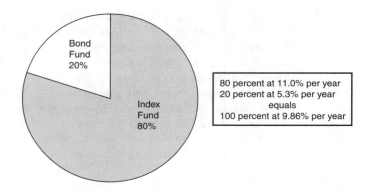

80 percent at 11.0% per year
20 percent at 5.3% per year
equals
100 percent at 9.86% per year

The Wealth Maintenance Portfolio

When you retire, you begin spending your taxable investments to pay your expenses. At age 70, you begin taking withdrawals from your retirement accounts. At these times, you modify the profile in the respective segments of your investments to the Wealth Maintenance portfolio, which allocates your money in these ways:

➤ 70 percent to an S&P Index fund

➤ 30 percent to a government bond fund

Wealth Maintenance portfolio.

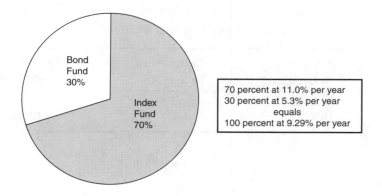

70 percent at 11.0% per year
30 percent at 5.3% per year
equals
100 percent at 9.29% per year

Because you're withdrawing money from these accounts to live on at these two junctures in your life (retirement and after age 70), changing the profile accomplishes two things:

➤ It makes the portfolio a little more stable.

➤ It allows for a substantial cash cushion against stock market declines.

There is one variation on the Wealth Maintenance portfolio for your taxable accounts when you retire. You put the money that you expect to draw for expenses for the coming year in a money market mutual fund at the beginning of the year. The balance of the 30 percent fixed-income allocation remains in the bond fund.

The Wealth Preservation Portfolio

At age 65, you switch your taxable account allocation one more time to 30 percent in the index fund. You still put the coming years' expenses in the money market fund and the balance in the bond fund. This further increases the stability of your portfolio and ensures that you'll have enough money to make it to age 70, when you begin retirement account withdrawals.

You make this same move in your retirement accounts at age 85 (age 80 for singles). That money will all be withdrawn in five years, so you want to protect it. A stock market crash when you're that age could be devastating to your finances. The 30 percent index fund portion still provides some growth in the last five years without exposing too much of your portfolio to the stock market.

A Nugget of Gold

The stock market has proven to be the best place to invest money for the long term. It's the only place you can earn a return that beats taxes and inflation over time. However, money that you need within five years needs to be protected from the possibility that the market has a bad year or two shortly before you need it. If that happens, it may take another year or two for the market to give you back your money. You can't afford that risk. Wise investing means that you protect the money you need in the short term.

Wealth Preservation portfolio.

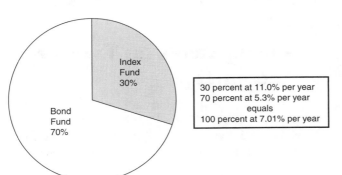

Index Fund 30%

Bond Fund 70%

30 percent at 11.0% per year
70 percent at 5.3% per year
equals
100 percent at 7.01% per year

Review and Rebalance

What could be simpler? Early in January each year after you retire, look at your account values from your statements from the end of the year. Figure the following amounts:

➤ The amount you need to withdraw from retirement accounts after age 70

➤ The amount you need to put in the money market fund in your taxable account

➤ How many shares of the index fund you need to sell to hit the 70 percent and 30 percent allocation in each

Potholes

If you were unable to make tax-deductible contributions to a regular IRA before 1998 and you made nondeductible contributions, you already paid taxes on that money. You should also have filed a Form 8606 for each year you did this and kept a copy for yourself. There's a $50 penalty for not filing this form.

When you withdraw from your IRA, the IRS provides a formula so that you don't pay tax on the amounts that you contributed on an after-tax basis. But, by age 70, this is a very small percent of your money, and the formula involves a lot of hassle. You probably need a professional tax preparer to help you. (See Chapter 21, "The IRA: Your Personal Tax Shelter," for more on IRAs.)

Most years, you can just sell index fund shares and put the money in the money market account. The bond fund serves as a buffer and a place to store money that you won't need in the money market account.

At age 70, you'll begin taking your minimum retirement plan withdrawals. Sell index fund shares to hit the 70 percent amount of your accounts' total value after you subtract the entire year's withdrawal. You don't have to take this money out all at once. Use a money market fund if you want to hold it in the account while you take it as you wish during the year. What you do take goes in your taxable money market account to pay the bills.

By rebalancing every year and changing the index fund percentage at ages 65, 70, and 85 (or 80), you always have at least three years' expense money not exposed to the market. If the stock market has a bad year (and it does, once in a while), you can hold off selling shares and rebalancing until it recovers (it always has). You have enough money to live on for several years. This way, you don't have to sell index fund shares when they're down.

Paying Taxes on Taxable Accounts

The three basic portfolios are low-tax portfolios. We say "low-tax portfolios" because an index fund pays very little dividends, and that means you don't pay much in the way of taxes. The gains build up in the share price. You do pay taxes on the bond fund and money market fund dividends in taxable accounts, but that is all the taxable income that you have in your portfolio (except part of your Social Security) until one of two things happens:

➤ You sell index fund shares in a taxable account.

➤ You take withdrawals from a retirement account (except a Roth IRA).

You sell index funds shares in a taxable account once a year after retirement. You'll probably be in the lowest tax bracket, currently 15 percent, during those years. Most of the sales proceeds are long-term capital gains. In 2001, they're taxed at 8 percent for people in the 15 percent tax bracket.

Your bond and money market dividends are taxed at 15 percent. However, you also have your standard deductions and personal exemptions, which shelter a large part of that income from tax. We'll look at the second case, taking distributions from your retirement accounts, in a bit.

From retirement to age 70, your taxes are low, unless you have lots more money than you'll need. The tax on the dividends has a small effect on your total portfolio return. Here's how taxes affect the total return for each portfolio before and after retirement.

Portfolio Returns and Taxes

| | | After-Tax Returns | |
Taxable Accounts	Total Return	Before Retirement	After Retirement
80%/20% portfolio	9.86%	9.30%	***
70%/30% portfolio	9.29%	***	8.95%
30%/70% portfolio	7.01%	***	6.41%
Capital gains tax	***	20%	8-10%

Taxes on Retirement Account Withdrawals

When you withdraw money from all retirement accounts (except a Roth IRA), it's taxable income unless you've made any nondeductible contributions to an IRA. Linda and George will still be in the lowest tax bracket when they begin withdrawals. They'll include all the money on their tax return and pay ordinary income tax on it, even if most of it was earned as capital gains. The IRS doesn't care how you earned it in tax-deferred accounts.

As Linda and George's required minimum withdrawals increase each year, some of their withdrawals will be taxed at the next-higher tax bracket. If their retirement accounts grew faster than the average market return over the last 75 years (they didn't just use an index fund, and they guessed right), their withdrawals may be much higher. So will their taxes. But keeping 72 percent of something extra is better than 85 percent of nothing more.

Don't complain about the taxes, as high as they are. The government wisely lets us compound our growth without taxes on untaxed income for many years. The government knows that it will get paid later while you build up your savings for retirement. The Roth IRA is an even better deal if you start it when you're young enough to contribute money to it for a number of years.

It's Been Said

When Joe Lewis was asked who had hit him the hardest during his boxing career, he replied, "That's easy—Uncle Sam!"

A Nugget of Gold

You don't pay for college all at once. Because it's one year at a time, you can adjust the short-term strategy over time. With five years to go, put 82 percent of the first year's money in the money market fund. It will grow, after taxes, to cover the payment in five years. Keep making the monthly payments to the index fund. After a year, transfer 82 percent of the second year's money to the money market fund. This gives you the opportunity to get maximum growth with maximum safety.

Investing for Intermediate-Term Goals

You have other goals that require a lump sum of cash to achieve. Perhaps the biggest one for many is the need or desire to pay for their kids' college educations. If that critical date is more than five years in the future, it's an intermediate- or even a long-term goal.

With more than five years to go, you can use an S&P 500 Index fund to build your savings. Even if the stock market has a rough year or two, you have time to let it recover and continue growing.

The following form and table allow you to determine how much you need to save each month for your goal. Until you are within five years of the goal, you can put all the money into the fund to get maximum growth. At five years, you follow the investment strategy for short-term goals (see the section "Saving for Short-Term Goals" later in this chapter). You sell the shares in the index fund and move the money to a money market fund or a short-term U.S. government bond fund.

You keep making the same payments to the new fund for the final five years. This change when you're within five years of your goal means that you're not really making much money after taxes. You are eliminating the risk of losing the money that you'll need while keeping up with inflation.

Because an index fund doesn't pay much at all in dividends, taxes aren't a factor until your sell shares. Then you'll owe capital gains tax on the profit. In addition, you'll pay taxes on the earnings for the final five years. The following Annual Savings Needed in Taxable Accounts form factors in the estimated tax effects for you.

For each of your intermediate-term goals, the following steps will allow you to find out how much you need to save and invest each month to achieve them.

1. Figure how much money you think you'll need in the future for your goal. Enter the amount on line 1 of the following form.

2. Find the savings factor in the table following the form that corresponds to the number of years to go before you need the money. Enter the factor on line 2.

3. Multiply the amount on line 1 by the factor on line 2. Enter the result on line 4.

4. Divide the amount on line 3 by 12 to get monthly savings needed to reach your financial goal.

Potholes

Don't forget inflation. If your goal requires $10,000 today, increase that by 4 percent a year. If you're saving for college, those costs have been increasing at 7 percent a year for the last couple of decades! You don't have to pay for all of it. Aim for 30 to 50 percent. Grants, loans, and scholarships can cover the rest.

For the example, the goal is $50,000 in 13 years.

Annual Savings Needed in Taxable Accounts

	Example	Yours
1. Need to save	*$50,000*	_____
2. Savings factor	× *.049*	×_____
3. Annual savings required	*$2,450*	_____
4. Divide by 12 = monthly savings	*$204.17*	_____

Annual Savings Factors

Years to Goal Minus 5	Intermediate Savings Factor
6	.146
7	.120
8	.101
9	.086
10	.074

continues

Annual Savings Factors (continued)

Years to Goal Minus 5	Intermediate Savings Factor
11	.064
12	.052
13	.049
14	.0462
15	.041

Don't be tempted to save less and go with the index fund longer than five years before you need the money. You want to have the best chance of reaching your goals on time. If the market does better than average, you'll get there quicker. You'll also get there quicker if you can manage to save even more. But you don't want to take unnecessary risks with your money and come up short. That's not part of your plan.

Saving for Short-Term Goals

You're looking at saving for a down payment on a house, or buying a car, a boat, or a vacation home. Or, maybe you want to redecorate and refurnish your living room. Whatever your goal is, it takes money and you don't have it. You want it sooner than later. If your time horizon is within five years, it's a short-term goal.

From the Hammock

Newspapers and magazines recently have been full of stories of people losing their fortunes in the stock market. Most of them have plenty of time to make another fortune, and maybe they've learned that fast money both comes and goes fast. The harder stories are those who had money they needed in a couple years for college educations, a downpayment on a house for a growing family, or other desired goal in high-tech stocks or funds. Now, most of that money has disappeared, and so has their short-term goal. It may take longer to save the money you need for a short-term goal, but you can't afford to gamble it away looking for a fast buck in the market.

We strongly suggested in Chapter 6, "Wealth: How to Get It and Keep It," that you not go into debt for anything that won't appreciate in value over time. This means saving money to purchase what you need. Because you can't finance a down payment on a house, that's included here, too.

Did you notice that we titled this section "Saving for Short-Term Goals"? Intermediate- and long-term goals are goals that you invest for over periods of longer than five years. Investing for short-term goals follows the philosophy that we suggested for your taxable money at age 65 and your retirement account money at age 85 earlier in this chapter. You want the money to be there when you need it. The saving part is much more important than the investing in the short term.

You can't pump what you have into the stock market hoping to increase it fast enough to get what you want sooner rather than later. This sounds like a great idea to some people, but not all of them get lucky. That's about what it is in the short term—gambler's luck. And if some gamblers didn't have bad luck, they wouldn't have any luck at all.

You can't count on the stock market in the short term. You're likely to make less than you would in a CD over a three-year period about 18 percent of the time. In the worst three-year period since 1945, you would have lost about 13.8 percent in an S&P Index fund from January 1, 1972, through December 31, 1974. You could have made over 25 percent in six-month CDs instead during that time. For the first two years in the fund, you would have lost 37.1 percent. Would you have stuck around to see what happened the third year? Probably not.

Within a three-year period, a money market mutual fund is the place for your money. Just keep adding money until you reach your goal. Here's a plan. If you have some money saved, start with Step 1. If not, skip to Step 2.

1. Shop around for the best CD rate for a CD that matures just before you need the money. Put the money you've already saved toward your goal in that. Tell the bank to reinvest your interest. The bank then can tell you how much you'll get at the end of the term.

2. Figure how much more you'll need. Enter that amount in the first line of the following Savings for Short-Term Goals form.

3. Find out the current rate that money market mutual funds are paying (check Sunday's business section in your paper, or call your mutual fund company). In the table following the Savings for Short-Term Goals form, find the row that is closest to that rate but not over it.

4. Find the column closest to the amount of time left until you want the full amount saved. Write the savings factor from your row and column on the second line of the form.

5. Multiply the amount on line 2 by the factor on line 2. Enter the result on the third line. This is your monthly saving required to reach your financial goal.

151

The example uses 5.5 percent over a 36-month period.

Savings for Short-Term Goals

	Example	Yours
How much you need	*$15,000*	_____
Savings factor	× *.0256*	×_____
Monthly savings	*$384*	_____

Short-Term Savings Factors

	Number of Months					
Rate	18	24	30	36	48	60
4.0%	.0540	.040	.0318	.0262	.0193	.0151
4.5%	.0538	.0399	.03155	.0260	.0191	.0149
5.0%	.0536	.0397	.0314	.0258	.0189	.0147
5.5%	.0534	.0395	.0312	.0256	.0187	.0145
6.0%	.0532	.0393	.0310	.0254	.0185	.0144
6.5%	.0530	.0391	.0308	.0252	.0183	.0142

If you have three to five years to go, you could put your money in a short- or intermediate-term U.S. government bond fund (which you now know invests in notes, not bonds). If your monthly payments are over $100, most funds will accept them. You can even set up an automatic monthly investment plan with many funds. You authorize the fund to take the money from a checking account on a certain day each month.

The risk is a little higher because interest rates can go up. That will reduce your share price a little because the values of the notes in the portfolio decline. However, the fund manager will buy higher-paying notes as time goes by, so your dividend will increase slightly.

Of course, interest rate could also decline. Then your share price goes up a little, but the dividend slowly decreases a bit. Either way, you're probably okay. Short-term bond funds aren't affected very much by interest rate changes unless the change is dramatic.

With a year to go, you should transfer the money to a money market fund and direct your remaining monthly payments there. That way, there's no surprise in the final year. Surprises are bad. No one ever got shocked or upset when they had more money than they needed. That's why the short-term investment program plays it safe.

For strictly short-term goals, whether you use a money market fund alone or in combination with a bond fund, you'll owe income taxes on the dividends. Pay the tax out of your other income and let the savings grow. For intermediate-term goals, the annual savings factor in the "Short-Term Savings Factors" table incorporated estimated taxes for both phases because the dollars are higher and so are the taxes in the last five years. You can pay the taxes as they're due from the money that you're saving and still reach your goal.

The Least You Need to Know

➤ You need to invest in the stock market to earn a return that allows you to retire early.

➤ Index funds offer a low-cost way to beat most actively managed mutual funds over time.

➤ Keep taxes on your investments low, and postpone them as long as possible.

➤ Long-term goals eventually become short-term goals. When you're within five years of reaching your long-term goal, you can't afford to take the chance that the money won't be there when you need it. The stock market isn't a place for short-term money.

Chapter 13

Keys to Successful Investing

In This Chapter

➤ How to overcome obstacles to investment success

➤ How inflation robs you

➤ Avoiding or postponing taxes

➤ Successful investors think about the long term

Once you begin investing, it becomes a lifetime pursuit. The fruits of your investments are what allow you to retire early and what support you for as much as half your adult life. How you behave as an investor is as important as what you invest in.

This doesn't mean that you need to take a lot of time learning the intricacies of investing if you don't want to. It doesn't have to become a hobby, and you don't want it to become an obsession. While you're working, the simpler you keep it, the better. When you retire, you'll have more time to delve into the intricacies of the stock market.

You can attend free seminars, read dozens of books, and sign up for classes on investing at your local high school or community college. Learning about economics and finance will give you more insight into the art of investing. But that's up to you. You don't have to know a lot about it to succeed. Just keep your investments within the limits of the understanding that you do have. That's your comfort level.

Be an Aggressive Saver

You can't invest money that you don't have (and we don't recommend investing borrowed money). The money that you save is the fuel that propels your investment portfolio. Once you've met all the basics that we talked about in Chapter 6, "Wealth:

How to Get It and Keep It," you're ready to begin investing your savings. You're ready if you meet these qualifications:

➤ You have no debt except a mortgage and school loans to finish paying off, and maybe your last car loan.

➤ You have three to six months' expenses in your 911 fund.

➤ You have sufficient disability insurance for both of you, if you both work.

➤ You have enough term life insurance (for both of you) to replace your income streams and the value of services provided.

➤ You have homeowner or renter insurance.

➤ You have health insurance.

Chapter 10, "Achieving Your Retirement Goals," showed you how much you need to save and invest each month to achieve your financial goals. It's a lot of money every month, maybe 20 percent or more of your income. That means you need to be an aggressive saver. The difference between low savings and aggressive savings is illustrated in the following chart.

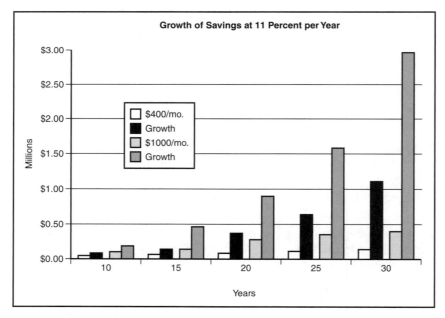

Saving a fixed amount every month really starts to pay off after 15 years.

This chart shows that while saving more doesn't make your money grow at a faster rate, your money does grow to become a much larger amount. This also illustrates that the earlier you begin, or the longer you save, the bigger the result is compared to how much you put in. It clearly pays to begin saving early.

It's better to be an aggressive saver than an aggressive investor. You can control how much you save, but the markets are not within your sphere of influence. When you save too little and too late, you feel compelled to invest too aggressively in hopes of catching up. This is risky business. You can lose money and end up farther away from your goal with no plan to recover.

Saving only $400 a month for 30 years gives you almost 30 percent more money than saving $1000 a month for 20 years. Even if you can't save as much in the early years as your plan calls for, you will benefit by saving as much as you can. Later, you'll be able to increase the amounts.

Beat Taxes and Inflation

These two bogeymen, taxes and inflation, are main obstacles to achieving your financial goals. Inflation relentlessly reduces the value, or buying power, of a dollar every year. And taxes are the price you pay for making money. Fortunately, the government lets you keep most of it. But, if you invest too conservatively, the growth of your investments, after taxes, may not stay far enough ahead of inflation to enable you to reach your goal.

> **From the Hammock**
>
> When Jim and his wife started saving, they didn't have a clue about how to invest it. As a result, they made a lot of mistakes and kept losing money on their investments. But they kept saving and slowly began to learn what investing was all about. They look upon the loses as the price of the education they received. And as long as they kept saving aggressively, their money would grow each year.

Contrary to what many people think, the return on your investment isn't the only thing inflation affects. The damage to the investment principle itself is far worse. Your return has to make up for this damage each year, too. One thousand dollars invested at 6 percent interest earns $60 in a year. If federal and state income taxes take 30 percent of that ($18), you have $1,042 left at the end of the year.

During the year, 4 percent inflation kept nipping away at both the interest and the $1,000 you invested. At the end of the year, the $42 in interest that you get to keep is worth 4 percent less, or $40.32. The tax hurt more than that. But your $1,000 is now worth only $960! Add the net value of the interest, and you now have a buying power of $1,000.32 compared to $1,000 the year before.

The taxes took only $18; inflation robbed you of $41.68. Sure, you still have $1,042 invested, but it buys only what $1,000 bought 12 months before. This is what you're up against.

You're taxed on investment income—interest, dividends, and capital gains—in taxable accounts. When a mutual fund sells stocks for net gains, it must pass that gain on to you as a capital gains dividend. And you owe capital gains tax on it. You're taxed on the growth of your investments in the shares only when the securities are sold. This growth is allowed to compound tax-deferred until you sell.

157

Potholes

There are two kinds of capital gains: short-term and long-term. Gains on securities held for exactly one year or less when sold are taxed as a short-term gain. Ordinary tax rates apply. When securities are held longer than a year, a long-term gain results. Capital gains tax rates of 10 percent for those in the 15 percent tax bracket, and 20 percent for those in higher brackets, apply under current law. No tax is due until after you sell the shares.

If you bought the security after January 1, 2001, and hold it for more than five years, the 20 percent rate falls to 18 percent. Taxpayers in the 15 percent bracket can sell a security they've held for five years and pay only 8 percent tax on the gain now.

Mutual funds will identify capital gains dividends as long-term or short-term for you. It's up to you to keep track of when you buy and sell shares. Your mutual fund statements will help you keep track of this and your cost. When you reinvest the dividends automatically, your cost per share changes.

Our basic investment strategy, outlined in Chapter 12, "How to Pay for Your Goals," is designed to translate aggressive saving into steady, long-term growth with a minimum of fuss and bother. It also avoids taxes on growth of your investments to permit the full amount of growth in the fund to compound over time.

It's Been Said

"When did taxes get started? Who started 'em? Noah must have taken into the ark two taxes, one male and one female. And did they multiply bountifully. Next to guinea pigs, taxes have been the most prolific animal."

—Will Rogers

Avoid Taxes

Tax evasion is illegal; tax avoidance isn't. Avoiding taxes on your taxable investments means investing in mutual funds that have a low turnover of stocks in the portfolio so that little or no gains are declared as dividends. If you own stocks directly, low turnover also means few capital gains. In both cases, long-term holding of stocks reduces the opportunity for the government to take a bite.

Eventually, most shares are sold and Uncle Sam gets paid. But until then, letting the full amount of annual growth compound safe from taxes is a winning strategy. If only 25 percent of each year's growth is exposed to taxes through capital gains dividends taxed at the 18 percent capital gains rate, after 20 years, the investment is about $8^1/_2$ percent smaller than if no growth was exposed to taxes. On a $100,000 investment, that's $68,941 less after 20 years.

Most mutual funds have a much higher turnover rate, and pay large capital gains dividends after good years. The index fund strategy is the simplest and best way to keep growth away from the tax man as long as possible. Very low turnover, especially in the S&P index and the total market index, means little or no capital gains dividend each year.

Beat Inflation

Inflation is impossible to avoid. The only solution is to invest your money so that it grows faster, after taxes, than the rate of inflation. Earlier in this chapter, you saw that 6 percent interest, after taxes and 4 percent inflation, resulted in no real growth. If you postpone the tax as long as possible, you're a little better off, but that's not the solution for inflation.

Investing to maximize your net gain while not taking unnecessary—and perhaps unwise—risks is the solution. The only rule here is to aim to grow your investments at least 3 percentage points a year more than inflation. You can't be sure of doing this every year; some years the stock market won't cooperate. But over time, it has.

Our basic investment strategy Wealth Builder portfolio in Chapter 12 looked like this:

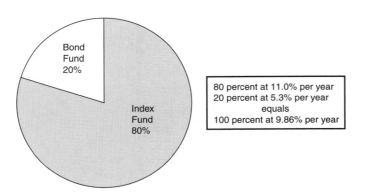

Bond Fund 20%

Index Fund 80%

80 percent at 11.0% per year
20 percent at 5.3% per year
equals
100 percent at 9.86% per year

For maximum steady growth and maximum safety, this portfolio allocation will beat inflation and minimize taxes over long periods of time.

On an after-tax basis, the average annual total return would be about 9.3 to 9.6 percent, depending on your tax bracket. There's virtually no tax on the index fund, and you pay regular taxes on the dividends from the government bond fund. At a 4 percent rate of inflation, your real return is as follows:

Total investment:	$1,000.00
Add total return:	+$98.60
Minus tax:	−$4.78
Total at end of year:	$1,093.82
Minus 4% inflation:	−$43.75
Net value:	$1,050.07

You would have a real return of about 5 percent, or $50. You're winning the battle. Putting 80 percent of your money in an index fund may look very aggressive to you. When you're building wealth for the long term, though, you need to be aggressive to combat inflation.

The 80/20 split in the Wealth Builder portfolio has proved in the past to be the safest mix that allows you to produce the kind of growth that you need over time. You'll need growth until you're in your 80s to cover inflating expenses. The risk that you'll outlive your money is much greater than any risk, over time, in the market.

In Chapter 12, we showed you how and when to reduce exposure to the stock market when you're no longer adding to or increasing your taxable and your tax-deferred investments. But, as long as you have many years to go and you're aggressively adding new money, you can afford to invest aggressively, too. If you want a financially comfortable early retirement, you can't afford not to.

Think Like a Long-Term Investor

How does an investor think? For that matter, what is an investor? The markets are a playground for all kinds of people who are trying to make money. There's no "one way," "right way," or "best way." Through experience, each person can learn what works best in his plan.

No two ways are identical because no two people are identical. It's not just differences in goals or finances—people differ in these areas, too:

➤ Wants and needs

➤ Short- and long-term goals

➤ Investing personalities

These are all different characteristics that each person must discover to find out what works best. For our purposes, an investor is one who endeavors to make a return on an investment over long periods that will beat holding money in the bank.

To help you achieve your goal of retiring early, you have one major ally—compound growth—and two dangerous enemies—fear and greed. When you understand how they can affect your investments, you're beginning to think like an investor.

Compound Growth

Here's our friend again, compound growth. You get a return on your returns every year that you leave your investments in the market. This is where aggressive

From the Hammock

When you invest for a goal with a far-off time horizon such as early retirement in 15, 20, or more years, you'll be growing your retirement account money for 40 years. In this case, Warren Buffet, the founder of the legendary Berkshire-Hathaway Company, counsels that you should consider your time horizon "forever."

saving pays off in the stock market. Over the long term, compound growth does most of the heavy lifting. Let's look at compound returns over 20 years, before and after 4 percent inflation on an annual investment of $10,000. The total investment is $200,000 over 20 years.

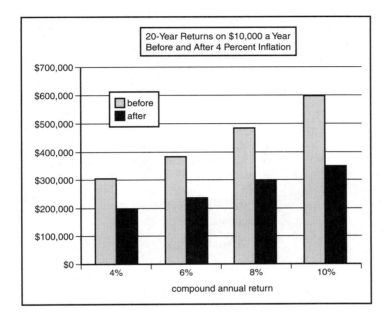

20-Year Returns on $10,000 a Year
Before and After 4 Percent Inflation

One percent more growth per year makes a differ-ence, but a four percent a year rate of inflation al-ways takes a big cut.

You lose money after inflation if you average only 4 percent a year. Each 2 percentage points that your annual return improves increase the ending value of your invest-ments by more than 20 percent. For periods of 20 years and longer, the extra annual compound return can make the difference between retiring early or not.

Beware Fear and Greed

The biggest obstacle to investing success isn't even inflation. We saw how to beat that. The problem is ourselves. We are our own worst enemies when it comes to making money in the market. The prime suspects are fear and greed. Fear keeps us out of the market, or drives us out when the market is falling. Fear keeps us out until we're sure that it has recovered—but how do we know when that is? By then, we have missed the rally.

Fear of losing money in the stock market makes us forget that we're investing for the long term. During those times when the market is dropping,

It's Been Said

"Experience is the name every-one gives to his mistakes."

—Woodrow Wilson

161

we need to remember that we don't need the money for many years, and that the market always recovers sooner or later and goes on to new highs.

Yes, the stock market goes down periodically, as we rediscovered in 2000. But you lose money, real money, only if you sell when it's down. Fear can make you do this. During such times you need to remember that you're a long-term investor. Historically, the market goes up three years for every one that it goes down. When you have an investment horizon longer than five years, you accept the down years because you need to be in the market when it goes up to reach your financial goals.

On the other hand, greed sucks us in when the market is booming, chasing hot stocks or hot funds that have probably already seen their best days, at least for a while. Greed lures us to change our investing plan to try to squeeze even more money out of the market. Then the fund, the stock, or the market can abruptly change direction. The stock market thrives on fear and greed, and usually at our expense.

The biggest risk that you face is not having enough money in retirement. The combination of too-conservative investing and inflation means that you're likely to outlive your money. That's a lot scarier than watching the stock market go down for 6 to 12 months every once in a while.

Over any 20-year period in the twentieth century, stocks as represented by the S&P 500 (or its equivalent, before the list was made) have never even lost 1 percent of their value. That's after inflation. But at 4 percent inflation, money left in the bank at 3 percent interest always loses a third of its value.

Potholes

Following markets closely while trying to understand what happens each day probably won't make you a better investor. The case can be made that it'll make you a worse one. You run the risk of getting emotionally involved with the day-to-day random gyration of stock and index prices. You're in danger of reacting emotionally, not rationally. Think long term, and try to ignore what the market is doing in any day, month, or year.

Characteristics of Successful Investors

You already know how to be a successful investor if you've followed us this far. Over the years, many people have closely studied successful stock market investors to find out how they did it. The answers always come down to how they think and act, not what they invested in.

Here are some of the traits and habits of successful investors that we've gleaned from the studies we've seen:

➤ They enjoy investing for its own sake, not just to make money.

➤ They are realistic about their abilities and about the returns they expect over long periods.

➤ The have a plan, a method for investing, that they're comfortable with. They stick to their plan through good times and bad in the market.

➤ They are patient, knowing that, over time, their plan will provide the return that they desire. They invest with a long-term view of the market.

➤ They accept their mistakes quickly and learn from them. They know that everyone makes mistakes.

➤ They think for themselves, which often means going against the crowd. They don't react to the noise and buzz that the markets generate.

If you stick to our basic investment strategy using index funds and a government bond fund, these habits are still important to you even though you are essentially a passive investor. You have a plan, and you need to stay with it; you're patient; and you're investing for the long term. You can be a successful passive investor without learning a whole lot more than what's in this book. It's a simple and effective strategy—if you stick with it.

Becoming a successful active investor takes years of experience and mistakes. Experience is often shorthand for, "I learned from my mistakes." There is no shortcut, no weekend seminar, and no book that makes you an overnight winner. Our basic strategy is a starting point for those who want to learn more about investing. It also serves as a benchmark against which you can measure your returns as an active investor.

The Least You Need to Know

➤ Save aggressively as early as possible to allow compound growth to do its work.

➤ The only safe investment is one that has a positive, long-term return after taxes and inflation.

➤ The stock market is not risky in the long term. True risk is outliving your money.

➤ Successful investors don't let fear and greed overcome their discipline to follow their plan patiently.

➤ You can be a successful investor without knowing a lot about the markets if you stay within your zone of comfort and understanding.

The Secret Techniques Laid Bare

There may be as many ways to invest as there are investors. The problem is that a lot of those ways don't work very well. They don't work because many investors lack a disciplined investing strategy. Even a relatively poor plan works better than no plan, as long as you stick to it. As you develop and then execute your financial plan to retire early, it will help you to learn how to think like a financial planner. The tools and techniques in this chapter provide a framework to guide you in learning that process.

The secret is to develop a strategy, a way to invest, that you understand and are comfortable following year in and year out. Our basic investment strategy in Chapter 12, "How to Pay for Your Goals," is part of such a plan—a very simple plan, but it works. If you want to create your own investing strategy, the next six chapters will acquaint you with the tools and types of investments that you can use to do so.

Several studies have shown that investors significantly cut their potential returns by not having or following a strategy. Without a strategy, you'll buy and sell funds and stocks depending on these factors:

➤ How you think the market is going

➤ What the talking heads on TV are saying today

➤ What the latest magazine tells you to do right now

➤ How you feel today

If the market wants to give you an average return of 11 percent a year just for showing up and staying in for a long time, why would you want to work hard to get 8 or 9 percent instead? Good question. But a lot of people do just that and may not even know that they are actually hurting their returns by their behavior.

Work with Your Money

A recent survey for United States Trust Co. discovered that the baby boomers surveyed had only 44 percent of their investable assets in stock or stock mutual funds. From 1993 through early 1999, they averaged 6.5 percent a year while the S&P 500 averaged more than 21 percent annually. Their money was taking a long nap. We may never see a long stretch in the market like that again in our lifetimes, but, over time, we suspect that 6.5 percent is beatable.

Lazy money is money that sits in a bank account or money market fund instead of earning two or three times more. We're not talking about your 911 fund, your auto fund, and other short-term savings that you have. They're doing their job by being there for you, not trying to grow too quickly. Once you have your basics in place, you should be investing 80 percent of the rest of your money in the stock market if you want to retire early.

Your money will work for you if you understand how to put it to work. You're the manager. That means it's your job to handle these things:

➤ To design a basic investment strategy that you're comfortable with

➤ To invest the money wisely according to your strategy

➤ To know when it's necessary to make changes in your portfolio

From the Hammock

During your first years of investing, it's natural to feel uncomfortable risking your hard-earned money in a confusing stock market. Don't let that stop you from doing it. As you get more experience, your comfort level will increase. You'll begin to develop and refine an investing strategy that feels right for you. Sure, you'll learn more about investing and the markets, but what you're really getting a better understanding of is yourself. Investing is a learning process over a lifetime.

It's Been Said

"Experience teaches slowly and at the cost of mistakes."

—J.A. Froude

This doesn't have to be complicated or difficult unless you want it to be. But it is a responsibility that you can't avoid; if you do, your money will get lazy. You can outsource only so much of the work to fund managers, advisers, and planners. The ultimate decisions are yours.

Keep Pumping It In

You save each pay period, month after month, year after year, to reach your financial goals. You're doing what many financial experts suggest is the best way to invest in the stock market over time. It's called *dollar-cost averaging*. You buy shares in your funds each month whether the market is going up or down.

But say that you receive a large sum of money—an inheritance, for instance—and you want to invest it (okay, not all of it, but most of it). Then you should forget dollar-cost averaging for that money as long as you know that you won't need it for at least five years. A 1993 study published in the *Journal of Financial Planning* reported that investing a lump sum all at once gives you a better return nearly two-thirds of the time after only one year than dollar-cost averaging.

A market decline in the very short term is the risk you take. But the market went up about three times more often than it went down during the last century. So keep the odds in your favor if you get a lump sum to invest, and put it in the market. The rest of the time, just keep pumping the money in, regardless of what the market is doing.

The Great Depression

Your grandparents lived through the Great Depression, from 1930 through 1941. The major market index then was the Dow Jones Average of 30 large companies. From September 3, 1929, through July 8, 1932, the Dow fell 89 percent and didn't recover to its previous level until 1954. Economists don't believe that all the circumstances

Say What?

Dollar-cost averaging calls for investing equal dollar amounts at regular intervals, regardless of prices. By doing this, you buy more shares at lower prices and fewer at higher prices, and thus your average cost per share is lower than the average price in the market over that time.

A Nugget of Gold

If you have 20 or more years before you plan to retire early, you should really want the stock market to go down for the next 10 to 15 years. You'll buy at lower and lower prices. Eventually, it will recover as it always has, and you'll enjoy huge gains. But this probably won't happen for you. To be honest, we won't be too unhappy for you, either. Each generation has experienced, and, we suspect, will continue to experience, major up and down trends in the market. We'll all take them as they come.

that created this difficult period will occur again, but what effect would this have on a portfolio? Ask Bert and Wilbur.

Bert put $2,000 a year of his hard-earned money in the market on January 1 of each year from 1929 through 1938. His rich cousin Wilbur saw how well the market had been doing in the late 1920s, and he plunked his $20,000 in on January 1, 1929.

| | BERT | | WILBUR | | Large Co. Stock |
Date	$ Invest	Total $	$ Invest	Total $	Total % Return/Year
Jan. 1, 1929	2,000	2,000	20,000	20,000	–8.42
Jan. 1, 1930	2,000	3,832	0	18,316	–24.90
Jan. 1, 1931	2,000	4,878	0	13,755	–43.34
Jan. 1, 1932	2,000	4,764	0	7,794	–8.19
Jan. 1, 1933	2,000	6,374	0	7,155	+53.99
Jan. 1, 1934	2,000	11,816	0	11,019	–1.44
Jan. 1, 1935	2,000	13,646	0	10,863	+47.67
Jan. 1, 1936	2,000	22,151	0	16,037	+33.92
Jan. 1, 1937	2,000	31,665	0	21,477	–35.03
Jan. 1, 1938	2,000	22,573	0	13,953	+31.12
Dec. 31, 1938		29,598		18,296	

Stock data from Ibbotson Associates Yearbook

Say What?

Deflation is a decline in the general price level of goods and services. It's the opposite of in-flation. From 1925 through 1932, prices dropped 26.6 percent. However, the last full calendar year that the United States saw any deflation at the retail level was 1954, when the Consumer Price Index fell .5 percent.

Bert used dollar-cost averaging in the teeth of the worst market we've ever seen and came out way ahead. He passed cousin Wilbur after four years, although he had invested only $8,000 at that point. After 10 years, he was 61.8 percent ahead of Wilbur.

By pumping in new money each year, Bert was buying low when the market was down. When the market rallied 372 percent from mid-1932 through early 1937, Bert made hay. The four years 1933 through 1936 were the best four calendar years ever for large company stocks.

And Wilbur? If he stuck it out, his stock declined an average of .89 percent per year during the worst 10-year period in the stock market. He came up $1,704 short, but his buying power increased to $22,345! Inflation averaged a negative 1.98 percent per year over that period, which is called *deflation*. The dollar gained in value as prices fell during the Great Depression.

If Wilbur had bailed out and taken what was left of his money after 1932, he would have lost a lot of money and buying power. By hanging in and waiting for the market to recover, he did okay. He just picked the worst 10 years to invest the lump sum.

We can learn two lessons from the story of Bert and Wilbur. In the first, Bert shows how dollar-cost averaging in a declining stock market pays off hugely in the long run. The second lesson, Wilbur's perseverance during the Great Depression, tells you that even if you invest at the peak of a market cycle, the odds are good that you will make money, not lose it, if you just hang in. Adopting a long-term perspective is very reassuring when stock prices are crumbling and show no signs of recovery soon.

How Many Baskets Do You Need?

Even if you didn't raise chickens, you might remember your parents telling you not to put all your eggs in one basket. When it comes to investing, this means spreading your money around in different types of investments. The question is, how much should you spread it and why?

Asset *allocation* is based on the observation that no one can predict what type of investment will do best over the short term. All investments don't go up or down together. The principle behind allocation is to protect your total portfolio from short-term volatility. Stocks may go down one year while bonds go up in value. That's what happened during 2000. Cash is cash, earning a steady rate of interest (but often losing to inflation and taxes). But what happens over the long term?

If you invested $10,000 at the beginning of 1971 in the S&P Index, at the end of 2000 you would have $414,113 (not accounting for taxes). If you allocated it one of the following ways, you would have less.

It's Been Said

"Money is like manure. If you spread it around, it does a lot of good, but if you pile it up in one place, it stinks like hell."

—Clint W. Murchison

Say What?

When you divide your money into different types of investments such as stocks, bonds, and cash, you **allocate** your assets. Within each type of investment, you diversify (see the section "Diversification" later in this chapter). This way, your stock money isn't concentrated in a few stocks, and your bonds aren't issued by only one borrower (except the U.S. government) or mature all at one time.

Over a 30-year period, the gain in a portfolio is likely to be the result of how much is allocated to stocks.

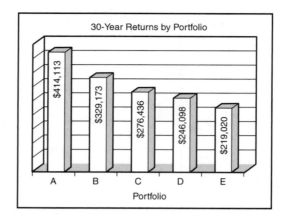

Portfolio	% Stock	% Long-Term U.S. Bonds	% Treasury Bills	Total Dollars End of 2000
A	100	0	0	$414,113
B	80	20	0	$329,173
C	70	20	10	$276,436
D	60	30	10	$246,098
E	50	40	10	$219,020

Allocation is a way to reduce volatility, but it also grows your portfolio at a slower rate in the long term. In this example, allocating money away from 100 percent stocks (represented by the S&P 500 Index) reduced the amount of money that you had after 30 years. The compound average annual return of Portfolio A was 13.215 percent. The return for Portfolio E was 10.837 percent, a difference of less than 2.5 percentage points. Yet Portfolio A ended up with 89 percent more, or $195,093, than Portfolio E. A small difference adds up when it compounds over a long period.

The annual fluctuation in value, or volatility, would have decreased the further away from 100 percent stocks you were. You would have made less in years that stocks went up a lot, but you would have lost less in the six years that stocks went down during this period.

Here's the basis for the question, "Do you want to eat well or sleep well?" If you can't shake your fear of a down market (and 1973 was down 14.7 percent, followed by 1974 down 26.5 percent), putting less money in stocks cushions the negative effect on your total portfolio in those years.

So, 6 out of these 30 years you would have lost less in your total portfolio than the S&P 500 Index if you weren't 100 percent in an S&P Index fund. Does that make you comfortable? As the graph and the chart show, in the other 24 years, you would have made less, and you ended up with less money.

When you're aggressively saving to retire early, you need as much growth as possible within the bounds of safety. Those very smart people we referred to in Chapter 12 found that having 80 percent in the S&P 500 was the optimum for growth plus safety over the long term.

When you're truly rich and you have enough money to live on forever, allocation away from stocks preserves wealth. It may not increase it after inflation and taxes, but the wealth isn't exposed to the chance of several bad years in the market.

You're not there yet, though. Your portfolio is likely to do best working hard for you over the next 30 or 40 years with 80 percent in stocks.

Diversification

Within each type of investment, you also want to diversify, or spread your money around. The risk of one company or industry going downhill fast when you've invested all your money in it is too great a risk to take. The risk of interest rates rising when your only bond matures in 10 years is also too great. Not only does your bond have a lower value until it matures and you get your money back, but you forgo the opportunity to earn the higher market rate of interest.

Until the 1990s, complex calculations indicated that owning 20 stocks in a variety of industries protected your portfolio against the chance that one company or industry would go in the tank. After the volatility of stocks in the 1990s and the effect of major changes in the business environment, it was recently suggested that you need 40 to 50 stocks to have the same protection that you used to get from 20.

That's a lot of stocks to manage. Mutual funds usually have more than 50 stocks (they're required to have at least 15) to get the benefit of diversification. Index funds have 400 to as many as 7,000, depending on the index they're matching. That's plenty of diversification.

Treasury bonds in your portfolio should have maturities spread over 1 to 10 years to protect the portfolio against interest rate changes. Corporate

From the Hammock

No one likes to lose money, but it's inevitable that the value of your investments will decline during some periods. The decline in the stock market that began in the Spring of 2000 hit those who were heavily in high tech stocks particularly hard. Diversification softened the blow to other portfolios. Meanwhile, investors had an opportunity to buy good companies or funds at lower prices. A steady dollar-cost averaging strategy during those periods is the silver lining to the dark cloud of severe market "corrections."

It's Been Said

"The first rule (of becoming wealthy) is not to lose money. The second rule is not to forget the first."

—Warren Buffett

bonds issued by companies also require diversification across many industries, just like stocks, plus diversified maturities as well.

You need a minimum of a couple hundred thousand dollars in your fixed-income allocation to efficiently buy a variety of bonds and obtain adequate diversification. (We look at this closer in Chapter 18, "A Zoo-ful of Bonds.") Until you reach that point, you can achieve sufficient diversification in an intermediate-term bond fund. It will cost you less this way, and you don't have to do the work to structure the portfolio.

Company Stock

Diversification in and of itself neither increases nor decreases your return. It protects your portfolio against the risk of one security blowing up. If something does blow up, you lose money, but the damage to your total portfolio is minor because it's just a small piece of it.

You should limit your holding of any one security, stock, or bond to less than 10 percent of your portfolio. The only exceptions are U.S. Treasury bills, notes, bonds, and insured bank deposits under $100,000 (the limit of the insurance guarantee by the Federal Deposit Insurance Company [FDIC]).

However, if you're enrolled in your company's 401(k), it may not be possible for you to stay under the 10 percent level. The company's matching contribution of company stock to a 401(k) is not salable until you leave the company, so your portfolio might wind up with a proportion of company stock greater than any of your other stocks. (Stock options are technically salable when you can exercise them, but that may be frowned upon at your company.) In this case, you have to live with the risk, but you can take other steps to protect your portfolio.

A Nugget of Gold

Structuring a Treasury bond portfolio over 10 years is called building a bond ladder. With five bonds, you buy them to mature every two years. When a bond matures, you buy a 10-year bond to replace it. This way, if rates go up, you have periodic opportunities to buy a bond that pays a higher rate of interest. If rates go down, yes, you buy a bond with a lower rate, but then most of your portfolio is paying interest at a rate higher than the current market rate.

If the total of stock or options hits 30 percent of your portfolio, you should take defensive measures. Keep your other stock and mutual fund investments as far away from your company and industry as you can. If your company is in high tech, even an S&P Index fund is too close; in early March 2000, when the technology industry began to decline, 44 percent of the value of the S&P 500 was in high-tech companies. (As of this writing, the S&P 500 is less than 25 percent in high-tech companies.) Most growth funds are well-invested in high tech also. In either case, that's too much risk to your portfolio.

In Part 4, "A Safari on Wall Street," we'll cover the kinds of stocks and funds that you can look at if this is your situation. They may not look as exciting as high tech, but anyone who had company stock and options in their high-tech employer in 2000, plus investments in other tech companies, may have seen his investments cut in half or more. If such a plunge would upset you, diversification would ease your worries and limit the damage.

Don't Panic

In the twentieth century, the U.S. stock market faced some serious crises:

➤ Two world wars

➤ Two wars in Asia (Korea and Vietnam)

➤ Forty-five years of nuclear-threatening cold war

➤ One great depression

➤ Two oil embargoes

➤ Two presidential assassinations (McKinley in 1901 and Kennedy in 1963)

➤ One presidential resignation (Nixon in 1973)

➤ Four years of double-digit inflation

The Dow Jones Industrial Average opened in 1901 at 70.44 and closed in 2000 at 10,786.85. That's growth of 5.2 percent a year, compounded. After inflation, it was a real return of 2 percent a year. This doesn't count the dividends that companies pay on their stock. Dividends added an average of about 4.5 percent a year for the century, although they've declined to less than 2 percent in the last few years.

Despite major crises in almost every decade and continuing political and economic stresses, the stock market managed to make forward progress. Stock prices always recovered as the economy of the United States and the world got back on the growth track. This growth, both here and especially around the world, will continue. Sure, they'll be more crises and setbacks, but an investor must approach the future with confidence and a long-term outlook.

The gyrations of the market are natural. Your job as a long-term investor is to make sure that you're in the market through thick and thin. The market will go down when some investors panic and sell, and it will go back up again and make new highs at some point after the panic subsides. You can't control the market, but you can control how you react to what it does in the short term.

Potholes

The stock market will go down 10, 20, or even 30 percent during your investing lifetime, taking your stock values down with it. It's guaranteed to happen sooner or later, and no one will know when ahead of time. The real risk is that you'll panic and sell when that happens. Not only do you lose your money, but you're not in the market when it inevitably recovers. In effect, you lose twice.

Time in the Market

Knowing that the market goes up and down like a yo-yo leads many people to try to get out at the top and back in at the bottom. Many try to make money doing this, but, so far, no one has succeeded in getting and staying wealthy this way.

An old Wall Street saying goes, "They don't ring a bell at the top or the bottom of the market." No one has a clue how high is too high or how low the bottom is. This doesn't stop people from trying to guess, but guessing does stop them from making money over time.

A Nugget of Gold

Your portfolio return over your lifetime will depend on how you answer two questions:

1. What percent of your investments were in the stock market?

2. What did you do when the market dropped 20 or 30 percent?

The correct answers, as we have already noted, are these:

1. About 80 percent until after I retire.

2. I kept buying, or I bought even more.

You have to guess correctly at both tops and bottoms time after time. Guess wrong, and you may miss the big moves. Some noted market timers got out of the market in 1993 because it had tripled in 10 years and stock prices were just too high. The Dow Jones Index proceeded to triple again over the next seven years while they waited on the sidelines. Time in the market, not timing the market, is how winners are made.

Chasing Winners

One of the main reasons why 80 percent of active fund managers fail to beat the S&P 500 Index over the long term is their unwillingness to stick to a disciplined strategy. Professional investors focus on the short term because their results are posted daily, weekly, quarterly, and yearly for all the world to see. If they don't keep up with their peers, they lose money, bonuses, and even jobs.

As a private investor, you're interested only in the long term. You want enough money to reach your financial goals in the future. Chasing after last quarter's or last year's winners is a recipe for failure. Those funds and stocks were usually the fashion or fad last season. The market is very fickle.

Investors who jump from fund to fund or stock to stock following what worked yesterday are often disappointed. They already missed the ride up, but they may get in just in time to ride the wave back down. They also risk paying taxes on last year's mutual fund capital gains, which are paid out late in the year or sometimes early the following year. Some of those gains are short-term and the taxes are paid at your regular rate, not the lower long-term gain tax rates.

Keep It Simple

Even if you don't go for our basic investment strategy in Chapter 12, following the secrets to successful investing outlined in this chapter will make your life easier. Whether it is also financially more rewarding depends on how well your investment choices perform.

Everyone wants to be able to predict the future. We have more information about companies, the markets, and the economy available to us today than the top professionals had as few as 10 years ago. The enormity and complexity of the world economic system and the quantity of information available is quite overwhelming. No one can make sense of it all and see the future more clearly.

Keeping it simple means sticking to your plan, your investment strategy, and not paying too much attention to the daily buzz in the markets and press. Buy and hold for the long term. Having a strategy prevents you from trying to outsmart yourself.

For the long-term investor, investing is a marathon. The goal is to cross the finish line. The lean, disciplined marathon runner who maintains a practiced running style and pace has a good chance. A sprinter, on the other hand, has an entirely different race to run, with a radically different style, pace, and strategy. A sprinter couldn't finish a marathon. While you aren't in a race, your strategy and discipline are just as important to achieving your long-term financial goals.

Keeping it simple also means that you don't need to overallocate or overdiversify your portfolio.

Potholes

"Past performance is no guarantee of future results." Every mutual fund is required to tell you that. Believe it. Morningstar ranks mutual funds based on past performance. When a fund earns four or five stars, the investor money rolls in. Everyone seems to want a piece of the action. But more than half of these top funds lose their ranking in less than three years. Their day in the sun has passed, at least temporarily.

It's Been Said

"Experience is not what happens to a man. It's what a man does with what happens to him."
—Aldous Huxley

Say What?

Morningstar (www.morningstar. com) uses **style** boxes to categorize the basic investing strategy of mutual funds in terms of the kinds of stocks that are in a fund portfolio at a given time. Funds may concentrate on large-cap, midcap, or small-cap stocks. Within each of these, they may lean toward growth stocks—companies recently growing faster than the average company—or value stocks—companies that haven't been growing fast but that may do so in the near future. A mix of these two kinds of stocks labels the fund as a blend fund.

Some advisers recommend holding one mutual fund in every *style*. Over long periods, all the styles converge toward the same return, the market average. Each style may have its day, but, in the end, they all get pretty much what the market gets; they are the market.

Holding a variety of actively managed mutual funds greatly increases your costs. Managed fund fees are 3 to 10 times more than those for an S&P Index fund. These fees are paid out of the funds' returns and reduce your growth each year. Managed funds also have a much higher turnover of stocks each year, leading to capital gain dividends. That means taxes in taxable accounts.

Investing in actively managed funds means that you begin with a disadvantage compared to index funds. The active funds managers must overcome the additional expenses and the taxes that you pay on the gains just to catch up to index funds. The Securities and Exchange Commission recently ordered funds to include their after-tax returns for the previous 10 years in their literature.

Keep your costs and expenses low, defer taxes on the growth of your investments as long as possible, and accept what the market gives you for being there rather than chasing last month's winners. This will keep your portfolio moving ahead with a minimum of time and trouble.

The Least You Need to Know

➤ It's your responsibility to supervise your money and keep it working hard for you.

➤ You need to steadily invest in the stock market when it's going down as well as when it's going up.

➤ Spreading your money around in different investments protects you against one big investment blowing up your portfolio.

➤ The market will take care of itself, and it will take care of you over time, if you let it.

➤ Your investing strategy can be as complicated as you want to make it—or, it can be simple and still do the job.

Chapter 15

You're the Boss

In This Chapter

➤ How to manage your portfolio

➤ Actively managed mutual funds

➤ Should you invest in international funds?

➤ Researching companies to buy stock in

➤ When to sell funds and stocks

You're the manager of your investment portfolio for the simple reason that it's your money. No one cares as much about it as you do. Lots of people are more than happy to help you manage your money—for a price. And you can let them. It's as simple as using no-load mutual funds or delegating it all to a money manager, financial adviser, or a broker. Mutual funds are the most popular way of doing this. A no-load mutual fund allows investors to buy and sell shares without paying a fee up front. We'll examine mutual funds in Chapter 17, "Herds of Stocks: Mutual Funds."

Whatever you do, and you may do it more than one way over the course of your life, the final responsibility for all the decisions and for the outcome remains with you. You're the boss. You hire the help, supervise and review their performance, and fire them, if they're not performing up to snuff. Your financial plan and your disciplined investment strategy provide the guideline.

How you choose to manage your portfolio depends on how you answer the following questions:

➤ How much time do you have to research, read about, and become familiar with investment options, risks, markets, industries, and companies?

➤ How much do you enjoy researching, monitoring, and evaluating the components of your portfolio?

➤ How confident are you in your ability to make investment decisions based on the information that you dig up?

➤ How comfortable are you at deciding when to sell either for a gain or a loss, and accepting your mistakes?

➤ How willing are you to learn how to do all these things, to make mistakes, and possibly to lose some money in the process?

How you answer these questions today determines where and how you begin executing your plan. Every investor was once completely ignorant of how to manage a portfolio. Some are willing to make the time to learn, while others choose not to. Either way works, as long as you know what responsibilities come with the choice you accept.

Paint, Wallpaper, and Trim

Our basic investment strategy in Chapter 12, "How to Pay for Your Goals," uses only an S&P Index fund, an intermediate-term U.S. Treasury bond fund, and a money market mutual fund. It's a simple, effective, time-tested way to reach your financial goals. As a low-cost, tax-efficient, and low-maintenance portfolio, it requires as little as a few hours of your time every year.

But is an S&P Index fund the best vehicle for your investment strategy? We don't know. That's a decision that only you can make. Do you know how to make that decision? If you do, and you determine that an index fund is not right for you, then look at other investments. Or, perhaps you want additional investments, such as managed funds or individual stocks with an index fund as a core investment.

As long as the annual return on your equity portfolio meets or beats the S&P 500 Index after taxes most years, you're doing great. After two or three years of underperforming the S&P Index, you should reevaluate your decision. You don't have to beat it every year—few managers do—but three out of five is the target to keep you on track to reach your goals.

If you don't know how to make that decision today, the S&P Index fund is the place to start. Call it the "earn while you learn" program. While you educate yourself on other types of funds and how the markets work, your money is working hard for you. When you feel more confident in your ability to make additional investments, you can begin the "learn by experience" program.

Everything Has an Index

There are many ways to slice and dice the stock market into discrete segments and create an index. Some of the major stock indexes serve as *benchmarks* for active fund managers to measure their performance against. Some key indexes are these:

➤ **S&P 500:** Four hundred and ninety-nine large-cap U.S. companies, plus Nestle.

➤ **Russell 1000:** The 1,000 largest U.S. companies.

➤ **Russell 2000:** The next 2,000 companies.

➤ **Wilshire 5000:** All New York Stock Exchange (NYSE) and National Association of Securities Dealers Automated Quotation (NASDAQ) stocks.

➤ **NASDAQ:** All companies meeting certain minimum size requirements not listed on the NYSE.

➤ **Morgan Stanley EAFE:** Index of Europe, Australasia, and Far East companies.

More than 20 indexes are reported daily in *The Wall Street Journal*.

Lipper Analytics tracks 25 equity indexes and 36 fixed-income indexes. These indexes are reported weekly in the mutual fund section of *Barron's Magazine*. Another 40 indexes are listed in the "Market Week" section of *Barron's*. These indexes are often sliced even more to fit the major styles of mutual funds marketed by fund companies and other financial institutions.

Obviously, such slicing and dicing amounts to overkill. Only a handful of these indexes are required for you to diversify your portfolio. You may want to put some money into midcap or small-cap index funds in addition to an S&P Index fund. The market periodically rotates and will favor one group over the others. Large-cap stocks dominated for much of the 1990s, midcap stocks outperformed in 2000, and small-cap stocks often do best coming out of an economic downturn.

Say What?

You measure the performance of a mutual fund against an index that matches that fund's particular style. The specific index is the **benchmark** that the fund manager tries to beat. If no index is appropriate, the benchmark is the average of all other funds managed in that style. If no specific benchmark can be identified, use the S&P 500.

Potholes

There's no hard-and-fast rule separating large-, mid-, and small-cap stocks. As the market goes up, the blurry lines between them also move up. Stocks also migrate from one group to another all the time, but the indexes are adjusted only at varying intervals. Many large-cap technology stocks in early 2000 were technically midcap or even small-cap by the end of the year. The indexes don't always reflect these rapid changes, whether up or down.

Sector Funds

You could also complement an index fund strategy by diversifying into *sector funds*. Many industry groups, such as transportation, insurance, multimedia, and retail, are available as sector funds. These managed funds concentrate on companies related to a particular type of business or industry.

Say What?

In investing, a sector is a distinct area of the economy or an industry such as telecommunications or autos. **Sector funds** invest primarily in stocks of one sector. The fund managers try to pick what they hope will be the best-performing companies in the sector. The funds generally rise and fall with the fortunes of their sector, but a good manager can make a difference in the performance when compared to other funds in the same sector.

It's Been Said

"You only have to do a very few things right in your life so long as you don't do too many things wrong."

—Warren Buffett

We don't suggest putting more than 10 percent of your equity allocation in any one sector if you maintain a core position of 50 percent in an S&P 500 Index fund. Most sectors are already well represented in this index, so this would give you overlapping coverage. This is particularly true for sectors such as technology and telecommunications, financial services, and healthcare.

Stay away from any sector in which you work, especially if you have company stock or options. Your paycheck, your company stock, and the S&P index fund already give you too much exposure to that sector.

High tech, healthcare, and financial services have been the top-performing sectors for the last 5, 10, and 15 years. They are the only sectors in which the average fund has beaten the S&P 500 Index over those time frames. Remember, however, that past performance is no guarantee of future results.

Over 10 years, 7 of the top 10 funds were technology and telecommunications funds. The other three were financial services funds. Over 15 years, 5 of the top 10 were technology and communications funds, while the other 5 were healthcare or biotechnology funds.

If technology and telecommunications still have a promising future ahead, it's possible that this performance may continue. Similarly, if medical and healthcare advances continue at a healthy pace—and 76 million aging baby boomers want the best care that money can provide (think rising health insurance premiums)—healthcare and biotech sectors may continue their performance.

Financial service businesses such as banks, insurance companies, brokerages, and mutual fund companies grow as more people earn and save more money. Many of them seek financial services to help them manage their growing wealth. The U.S. economy probably won't stop growing, at least for long, any time soon.

Adding a small piece of any or all of these sectors may improve your total portfolio return over time. We suggest that you not invest more than 10 percent of your equity money in any one sector. Keep in mind that the technology, biotech, and healthcare sectors are much more volatile than an index fund. They are also likely to pay significant capital gains dividends if they continue to do well. These dividends are taxable in your taxable accounts.

Other sectors may also outperform the indexes in future years. As someone once said, "The future is the hardest thing to predict." If you know something about a sector and feel confident that it's a growth area, you might consider it for a 5 or 10 percent slice of your money.

Other Managed Funds

There are some 6,600 domestic equity mutual funds, more than 1,850 world equity funds, and more than 2,200 fixed-income funds. The basic way to classify equity funds is through Morningstar's style box (see www.morningstar.com for more information on using style boxes).

Equity Style Box

	Value	Blend	Growth
Large-cap	Large-cap Value	Large-cap Blend	Large-cap Growth
Mid-cap	Mid-cap Value	Mid-cap Blend	Mid-cap Growth
Small-cap	Small-cap Value	Small-cap Blend	Small-cap Growth

☐ Low risk ☐ Moderate risk ☐ High risk

The style box allows you to identify what a fund's recent style of investing has been.

Morningstar and other companies such as Lipper Analytics attempt to classify mutual funds based on a combination of their last-known holdings and their recent performance in one of the nine style boxes. This is far from an exact science, and many funds frequently migrate from box to box as the managers try to keep their fund in the sweet spot of the market. Other managers try to stick with one style, even when it's temporarily out of favor.

181

If you decide to use general equity funds, here are several suggestions that you should consider:

➤ Four to six funds are enough, including any foreign or global funds.

➤ Each fund should be in a different style box to minimize overlapping stock ownership.

➤ Look for funds that have performed in the top quarter of their peers—funds of the same style and type.

➤ Funds with low fees and expenses and low turnover usually perform better because you keep more of the return.

➤ Plan on holding your funds for many years, unless they underperform their benchmark for two or three years in a row.

Non–U.S. Funds

Of the more than 1,850 world equity funds, about 370 can buy stocks in any country, including the United States. The rest buy only non–U.S. companies' stocks. Most advisers recommend putting 10 to 20 percent of an equity portfolio in foreign companies through mutual funds. More than half of the world's stock market value is outside the United States. Many countries' economies are growing much faster than the U.S. economy over time.

We're not opposed to this idea, but there are several arguments on the other side of the issue that have merit:

➤ About 42 percent of the profits of the S&P 500 companies come from sales *in* foreign countries. Many U.S. companies are significantly participating in foreign countries.

➤ Even larger portions of European companies' revenues come from sales *in* the United States.

➤ Foreign markets used to move at differing rates and sometimes even in a different direction than the U.S. market. This is much less the case in recent years.

We're not talking about exports in the first two points. These sales are sales in Europe by U.S. company divisions in Europe, and sales in the United States by European company divisions in the United States.

A Nugget of Gold

The world is a much smaller place today, and it's growing smaller. Large investors and institutions trade 24 hours a day as markets open and close around the world. When major economic news breaks and the "home" market is closed, traders immediately buy or sell on markets elsewhere. The global economy has reduced any potential advantage from diversifying a portfolio internationally, if not eliminated it altogether. You're an international investor by default.

They're here and we're there. These mutual "in-country sales" were five times the value of U.S. and European exports to each other in 1998, according to a recent article in *Business Week*.

If you do decide to use international funds, don't use a global fund. They often hold 30 to 60 percent of their portfolio in U.S. stocks, and you already have this exposure. Also, do not use a foreign index fund. Active managers in foreign market funds beat their indexes more often than they do in the U.S. market. No one is sure why, but the speculation is that foreign markets are smaller and less efficient. Information about many foreign companies is harder to get—and sometimes harder to trust.

You should select a fund and manager with at least 10 years of experience in foreign markets. Experience counts heavily when you're dealing in dozens of countries, languages, accounting practices, and laws. Beware of emerging market funds—they're extremely volatile and have been poor performers over the long run. That may change someday in the future, but it's a risky bet that you don't need to consider now. Check back in 5 or 10 years when these countries may be more mature economically.

Stocks

Keeping in mind that sufficient diversification for a significant stock portfolio requires at least 20, and maybe 40 or more, companies in a variety of industries, stocks still may be one of your choices. Even if you want to buy only a handful of different companies as a small part of your portfolio, the following suggestions will be useful.

Investing in stocks is very different from buying shares in mutual funds. First, there's a lot more research you should do:

➤ Read annual reports, and analyze the *10-Q* (quarterly) and *10-K* (annual) financial reports.

➤ Find out what articles in trade publications and investor magazines (*Fortune, Forbes, Barron's, Business Week, The Wall Street Journal, Kiplinger's, Smart Money, Worth,* and others) have to say about the company and industry.

➤ Find out what brokerage analysts are saying in their research reports, if you can get them (ignore the recommendations and the target prices—just read the analysis).

Say What?

Following every quarter, all publicly traded companies are required to submit a detailed financial report with the Securities and Exchange Commission. These quarterly reports are called **10-Q** reports. Following the end of their fiscal year (which may be at the end of any month, not just December), the report is called a **10-K.** In addition to financial details, these reports contain an extensive discussion of the company, its business, markets, risks, and any issues or problems that investors should know.

10-Q financial reports should be available within 45 days following the close of a company's quarter and 10-K reports within 90 days after the end of a company's year on the following Web sites:

➤ The Securities and Exchange, at www.sec.gov

➤ www.freedgar.com

➤ www.10Kwizard.com

Many financial Web sites such as www.moneycentral.com, www.quicken.com, www.finance.yahoo.com, and www.hoovers.com have news reports and links to the financial reports sites as well as to the companies' Web sites.

You can often request an investor information package to be mailed to you at the companies' sites, and you can always call or write their investor relations department to request this information. Be sure to specifically request the latest 10-Q and 10-K reports. Otherwise, you may get only a glossy annual report and a packet of press releases.

There's no such thing as too much good information on a company before and after you buy the stock. What does the company do? How well is it doing compared to its competitors? What does it plan to do in the next 12 to 24 months to grow and increase profits? Is management experienced and stable, or have there been major changes recently? Is the business the company is in growing and expected to keep growing?

You want answers to these questions, as a start. It's relatively easy to find out from the financial reports what a company has done in the past. But that's only a clue to what it expects to do or is expected to do by other knowledgeable observers in the future. Because no one can accurately predict the future, you need as many clues and opinions as you can get. Then you have to sort out and evaluate all the information to guide you in making your decision.

Analysis of a company's financial statements—balance sheet (similar to your Net Worth statement), income statement (profit or loss), and statement of cash flow—tells you how well the company has performed and how healthy it is financially as of the date it closed the books for the quarter or year. But things change, so that's only a starting point. You have to keep an eye on the company and review its quarterly financial reports and management discussion sections in the 10-Q and 10-K reports as they come out every three months.

We'll look more at stocks as well as mutual funds in Part 4, "A Safari on Wall Street." As you can see, investing in individual stocks takes a lot of research before you truly understand what you're buying and why. Otherwise, you have no idea whether the current price is too high, whether the stock should go up over time, and whether you should sell or hold in the future. If all this seems overwhelming or a lot of work to you, perhaps you're not ready to buy individual stocks yet.

Do all stock investors do this? Of course not. Those who do are much more likely to be successful at investing over the long run. The rest are speculating, relying on tips and luck to make money. That strategy doesn't work very well in the long run *or* the short run. If you don't have the time or the inclination, let the mutual fund professionals do the work for you. Then you need to learn to select a few good funds.

To be good at investing in stocks requires a passion for it. The hours spent every week researching and reading reports and articles should not feel like a chore. An understanding of how business in general works, and how the industries that your stocks are in work, is crucial to your evaluation process. Knowing how to read and analyze financial statements and the accompanying information allows you to understand and track the health and progress of the companies.

Mutual funds hire trained analysts to do nothing but research companies before and after adding them to their portfolios. All that work, and still 80 percent don't beat the S&P 500 Index over long periods.

When to Redecorate

In Chapter 12, we outlined how to change your taxable and retirement portfolios when you retire, when you turn age 70 and begin withdrawals, and, finally, when you turn 85 (80, for singles). These basic moves, combined with the annual rebalancing to maintain your target allocation, apply whether you use an index fund strategy or not. They're designed to allow your money to have the best chance for maximum growth while maintaining stability. As you grow older, the strategy also protects the money that you'll need within three years while allowing the rest to grow.

With actively managed funds or stocks, the equity percentages can remain the same as with the index fund discussed in Chapter 12. However, you need to take more time to monitor the performance of your funds and stocks each year.

Nonindexed Funds

When you use a variety of managed mutual funds instead of, or in addition to, index funds, when do you redecorate your portfolio? Managed funds must be monitored to make sure that they're still the same funds that they were when you bought them:

➤ Has the style changed?

➤ Has the manager left and been replaced?

➤ Has the performance fallen off for a couple of years?

If the style has changed, does the fund belong in your portfolio any longer? You picked that style for a good reason originally, so it probably doesn't belong now. Perhaps you already have a fund in that style. Pick one, usually the one that remained true to its style, and sell the other one. Then buy another fund in the original style to replace it.

185

If the manager has changed and the fund had been performing well under the old manager, keep a closer eye on the performance and style with the new manager each quarter for the next year. A manager's leaving is usually not a reason to change funds by itself. If the fund underperforms over the following three or four quarters, though, it may be wise to change. If the style changes under the new manager, it's time to sell and replace it.

The most important thing to look at is whether the fund failed to meet or beat its benchmark or the average of its peer group of funds. Be sure you have the proper benchmark for each fund before you buy it. If the fund lags for a full two or three years, give it the boot. Research similar style funds, and replace it immediately with a new one.

You don't need to measure fund performance every month—every six months will do. With a variety of managed funds, you can expect some to be doing well while others aren't at any given time. That's why you have the variety. If all your funds are doing well the same year, either the market is really on a tear, or you may have less variety than you think. If so, they could all do poorly together, too. Check the styles and make any necessary changes to diversify your portfolio better.

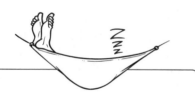

From the Hammock

We've not been too enthusiastic about recommending a portfolio of individual stocks as your main investment strategy. We hope that we've made our reasons clear along the way. We personally believe that it is possible for individual investors to beat the stock indexes with a portfolio of stocks. Many investors do, including ourselves. But from what we see and hear, most don't. That's usually because they aren't following a patient, disciplined program within a financial plan, or they aren't doing enough research.

Stocks

When you buy a stock, you should plan to hold it for at least three years. Give the company a fair chance to execute its plan. But if you find bad news particular to the company—not just a lower-than-expected earnings report for a quarter or two (find out why)—then you should reconsider holding it. More research is in order.

As long as the company is executing its plan, sales and profits are growing, and the stock price is increasing faster than the relevant market index, there's no reason to sell. If the price gets too far ahead of where you think it should be based on your ongoing analysis, you might want to sell some or all of it before it falls back. That's often called taking some money off the table.

How do you know when the price is too high? Again, analysis and experience help here. What is too high for one investor may be comfortable for another. But many investors sell too soon and leave a lot of money on the table. One recent study showed that the stocks that investors sold at a profit went up more than the ones that they subsequently bought. It's definitely an art, not a science, and experience is the only teacher.

We can't give you any hard-and-fast rules here. We wish that we could. There are many styles and strategies for investing in stocks, each with its own set of "rules." The "rules" also depend on the stock, the industry, the tone of the markets, and the condition of the economy.

Buy and hold, whether a mutual fund or a stock, is the ideal practice. In the real world, you need to monitor your portfolio and each part that contributes to its growth. Things change, and you have to learn when to change with them. The patient investor allows funds or stocks ample time to prove themselves. But after two or three years of subpar performance and no convincing reason to expect that an improvement is coming, this investor then makes the changes that must be made.

So, while you occasionally have to make changes to the composition of your portfolio to keep it on track, there's no need to act in haste. And at the same time you sell something, you need to have another fund or stock that you believe will do better to replace it. You need to maintain your exposure to the market.

Active management of a portfolio of nonindex funds and stocks is necessary. You can farm out the job to money managers, advisers, planners, or brokers for 1 to 2 percent of your assets per year, plus fees and expenses of the funds, or commissions on stock transactions. But you're still the boss. The final responsibility for the performance of your portfolio is yours. It's your money.

Potholes

The North American Securities Administrators Association estimates that Americans lose about $1 million dollars an hour to securities fraud. Always request the latest annual report and 10-Q for any stock, or the prospectus for a mutual fund or other type of investment. If you receive these, then fraud is not likely going to be a problem. This doesn't mean that these are good investments, however. That's up to you to research and determine before you invest any money.

The Least You Need to Know

➤ Going beyond investing in index funds requires active management of your portfolio. Experience is the best teacher.

➤ You may already be investing internationally, and you didn't know it.

➤ Buying and managing individual stocks requires a lot of time to properly research and evaluate the companies. It's not for everyone.

➤ Give your funds and stocks at least two to three years to prove themselves.

Part 4

A Safari on Wall Street

Millions of new investors piled into the stock market during the 1990s. Mutual funds grew large and plentiful as the new money poured in. Stocks went on a tear. But not everyone in the market made piles of money before the party ended in 2000. And then, many of those who did make money saw their pile get smaller.

The stock and bond markets are unpredictable. But venturing out in the jungle of stocks, bonds, and actively managed mutual funds doesn't have to be a gamble. There are proven, fundamental ways to invest over long periods. You can learn how to do it, if you want. Or, you can stick to index funds and beat most of the pros in the long run.

Chapter 16

Stocking Wild Game

In This Chapter

➤ What the stock market really is

➤ Fundamental analysis of companies

➤ Understanding a company's earnings

➤ How to use common ratios such as PE and ROI

It's a jungle out there! The process of buying and selling stocks—and the stock market itself—can be mysterious to the individual investor. Many kinds of players are invested in the stock market. They have different strategies, time horizons, and goals. Together, they—and you—make for a huge, wild spectacle that drives stock prices to and fro. It is the greatest example of a true, free-market, capitalist economy at work.

In the short term, markets trade on emotions and very short-term expectations more than on value and earnings. In much longer time frames, expectations collide with reality and good companies rise to the top. You, the long term investor, face the challenge of trying to identify who those good companies are today and are likely to be tomorrow.

Where Is the Jungle?

The "stock market" refers to a variety of places and ways that stocks are bought and sold today. Most of the action takes place in New York City, but the Internet increasingly makes location irrelevant.

A Nugget of Gold

The stock market isn't the biggest game in town. Currency markets, in which the dollar and other countries' currency change value from minute to minute against each other, trade $1.5 trillion per day, more value than the U.S. stock markets trade in a month. The dollar value of futures and options traded on the Chicago Mercantile Exchange averages 20 times the dollar volume in the stock markets each year.

A stock exchange is a physical location where orders are placed and filled by people. The exchanges—the New York Stock Exchange (NYSE) is the dominant one—feature a *specialist* for each of the listed stocks. All trades on the exchange for that stock go through the specialist, who fills orders out of his inventory.

The National Association of Securities Dealers Automated Quotation (NASDAQ) system is an electronic network linking market makers for stocks not listed on the NYSE. One stock may have a number of market makers competing to fill orders. They post the prices at which they're willing to buy (the bid price) or sell (the ask price) on the electronic network. The difference between the bid price and the ask price is called the spread. Access to these prices is available to anyone, for a fee.

What happens after you give your broker an order on the phone or hit the Buy or Sell button on your computer screen isn't too important, as long as you get what you want at the price that you wanted within a reasonable time frame. The truly important stuff is what you do before you buy a stock.

Tracking Trophy Stock

When you buy shares in a company, you become an owner of that company, often one among millions. Your shares are stored on a computer somewhere rather than being represented as a paper stock certificate (unless you request one and, maybe, are willing to pay a small fee for it). But never confuse the stock

Say What?

The **specialist** provides an orderly market for a stock. He buys when others want to sell, and he sells when others want to buy. He constantly sets prices to try to balance the supply and demand. He makes money by maintaining a small margin, often only a couple pennies per share, between the price at which he buys and sells.

with the company. You're not giving your money to the company to use in its operation unless you buy the stock at an *initial public offering,* or a secondary offering. You're buying it from the specialist, a market maker, or another investor.

Will Rogers was quoted as saying, "Only buy stocks that go up. If they don't go up, don't buy 'em." Unfortunately, there's no way—repeat, no way—to know that a stock will go up. Investors have put considerable effort into trying to determine whether a stock is likely to go up. These efforts have produced thousands of books and articles, and hundreds of strategies, formulas, and programs. Some of them work, some of the time.

The Hunt

We're not able to tell you everything you need to know to pick a good company and a good stock. We'll focus on a few key elements that will get you started on the process of evaluating companies.

No one method (or even several methods) of valuing companies comes close to being foolproof. All the mathematical tools available are simply that: tools to analyze the past. They have no real predictive value. Despite all the analysis that can be done, ultimately an investor must take a leap of faith into the future.

The purpose of fundamental analysis is to try to determine a reasonable value for a share of stock in a particular company at a point in time. By comparing that rough estimate to the current market price, an investor can decide whether to buy, to sell, or to hold. The focus of analysis is on these considerations:

➤ The business

➤ The products and service

➤ The market a company operates in

➤ The management of the company

➤ The earnings—profit after taxes

➤ The asset values—what the company owns and is owed

➤ The cash flow

➤ The dividends, and whatever else the company chooses to do with the earnings

Say What?

When a company first sells shares to the public, it has an **initial public offering (IPO)**. Usually, only a small percent of the total shares are sold at this point. The rest are held by founding investors, venture capitalists, and management. Occasionally, a company may have a secondary offering and offer additional new shares to raise more money. A secondary offering may also sell shares owned by key investors.

It's Been Said

"In the short run, the market is a voting machine; in the long run, it's a weighing machine."

—Benjamin Graham

193

Say What?

Ratio analysis uses simple mathematical expressions of the relationship of one financial element to another. If a company sells $1 million of its product and has a net income of $50,000, the ratio of net income to sales is $50,000 \div 1,000,000 = .05$. Tracking ratios over five or more preceding years assists an investor in judging whether a company is improving in the areas analyzed.

From the Hammock

When you place an order "at the market," you don't know the price at which your order will be filled. In a fast-moving market, it could be a price very different from the bid or ask price that you saw only a few minutes ago. Put a specific price on your order. This is called a "limit order." The market may have moved away from your price, even if you placed it at the bid or ask price or within the spread. You can always change your order, but this way, you control the price you pay or receive.

The last four areas employ *ratio analysis* to determine the health and direction of the company based on its present condition and recent track record. These ratios directly indicate the effectiveness of management's on-going decisions in combining cash, other assets, and people to attempt to produce and sell a product at a profit.

What You're Looking For

The first step is to learn enough about a company to decide whether it's in a business that looks promising and whether it knows what it's doing. You don't want to invest your money in a company until you have a good idea of what it does and why the stock price should go up in the future. You need to know the following:

➤ What the company is up to

➤ Where it plans to go

➤ Whether it's doing the right things to get there

➤ What's happening in its industry

➤ What its competitors are doing

➤ What the long-term prospects are for growth in sales and earnings

Some of this information is in a company's 10-K report as well as the chief executive officer's letter to shareholders in the glossy annual report (which isn't available for about three months after the close of the company's year). The following Web sites report news on companies and industries:

➤ www.moneycentral.com

➤ www.quicken.com

➤ www.finance.yahoo.com

➤ www.hoovers.com

➤ www.investor.cnet.com

➤ www.marketguide.com

➤ www.cbs.marketwatch.com

➤ www.forbes.com

Brokerage houses issue analysts' reports for clients on many companies. Even discount and online brokers have reports for clients now, often from a regular brokerage. You can also access many of these reports at www.multex.com. Some are available to read or download for free, while others require a payment.

The Tracks

The most prominent tracks that a company leaves are what it reports as earnings—profits after taxes—which are reported every three months. Reported earnings are a result of management and outside auditors interpreting a lengthy list of accounting conventions and rules known as Generally Accepted Accounting Principles, or GAAP. Because the rules are subject to various interpretations (and, occasionally, violation), reported earnings are not as meaningful as investors would like them to be.

The Financial Accounting Standards Board (FASB) consists of seven independent members appointed by a Board of Trustees to establish principles and standards of accounting for accountants to follow. The board also provides interpretations and guidelines to assist accountants in implementing these rules. FASB is the authority for the practice of accounting in the U.S. Foreign companies that want to have their stocks traded in U.S. markets must also use GAAP and FASB rules to present their financial statements for U.S. investors.

To add to the confusion, there are alternate ways to define and present earnings which companies are allowed to use in addition to earnings according to GAAP. Many companies will present "pro forma" statements that report earnings before accounting for *amortization* of the value and costs of certain acquisitions of other companies or products, and write-offs against earnings of a variety of unusual or "one-time" events. This is designed to highlight the true net operating income after taxes. But you also need to understand those deductions that were left out.

A second method, called "earnings before interest, taxes, *depreciation*, and amortization" (EBITDA),

Say What?

When a company makes a large capital investment in a building or equipment, it pays cash. GAAP doesn't allow this amount to be deducted from earnings all at once. It must be deducted over time as the value of the investment declines. This is called **depreciation.** Until July 1, 2001, when a company bought another company using its stock to pay for the purchases rather than cash, the value of the purchase usually was greater than the value of the purchased company on its balance sheet. The difference, called goodwill in accountant-speak, had to be deducted over time from the earnings of the purchasing company. This is called **amortization.**

represents straight operating cash earnings. Some companies would never have any "earnings" to report unless they used EBITDA. Interest, taxes, and depreciation always represent real cash expenses paid out at some time.

In January 2001, the FASB announced that, as of July 1, 2001, companies would no longer be required to amortize goodwill. This will create large increases in reported earnings under GAAP for many companies that have made big acquisitions in recent years. Reported earnings under GAAP should be a lot closer to pro forma earnings and cash flow. The same may be true for EBITDA if amortization played a big role in reducing reported earnings in the past.

Unfortunately, this may take extra work to distinguish between reported earnings before July 1, 2001, and earnings after that date. Companies may elect to report two sets of historical earnings numbers, one as originally reported, and another with the new rule factored in over past years. If they don't, the comparison process will get more difficult.

EBITDA and pro forma reporting methods have valid uses in analyzing companies. However, they can also cause confusion, and they are often reported by the media or used by stock analysts to support their recommendations.

No one method is correct, or even accurate by itself. Be sure you know which one you are using and what it means. Periodically, the GAAP rules change because the SEC or the FASB issues a new ruling. This is often an attempt to adapt to, or to control, the ongoing dance between management, the auditors, and the SEC around how to report "earnings" accurately.

Interpreting the Tracks

Earnings are what frequently drive stock prices—but not earnings as an absolute number. Many fine companies with good earnings elicit only a yawn from investors. It's the rate of increase in earnings and sales that floats (or sinks) a stock's price. Investors often project the rate of increase into the future and bid up the price. If they believe that the rate of increase won't last long, though, they abandon ship in droves.

The price of a stock on a given day, divided by the earnings reported over the previous 12 months, makes

It's Been Said

"Humans must breathe, but companies must make money."

—Alice Embree

Potholes

The PE reported in your newspaper may be quite different from the PE reported in another paper. The major reporting services, such as Dow Jones and *The New York Times*, use different "earnings" in their formulas. You need to find the explanation of how the particular "earnings" are calculated to understand what you have. There's usually a key that defines terms used at the beginning of the stock listings.

up the famous PE, or price to earnings, ratio. In light of the preceding discussion on earnings, you need to know which earnings are used before that PE has any meaning.

The stock price is the multiple of annual earnings that the market is willing to pay for a share of a company. The market expects earnings to rise fast enough to make the price a bargain. The market values a $60 stock with $2 per share earnings as worth 30 years of earnings (60 ÷ 2). Earning $2 a year on a $60 investment is an earnings yield of only 3.33 percent (2 ÷ 60), often half of what a CD earns. Hope and greed can propel a stock's price to exalted levels based on little more than a Ouija board's projection of earnings.

Many investors favor using something called forward PE to value a stock. This is based on someone's projection of "earnings" over the next 12 months. Projecting earnings is a popular sport among analysts, and they get paid millions to play this game. These projections are just educated guesses, and their accuracy is usually much worse than that of your local weather forecaster.

Fortunately, a few people are keeping score on how accurate the analysts' projections have been. Two Web sites rate and rank analysts' earnings projections and then present the estimates from analysts with the best records in the recent past. Both www.starmine.com and www.bulldogresearch.com are free. Their data comes from I/B/E/S, a leading compiler of earnings projections.

First, settle on what "E" you will consistently use for a PE ratio in your ongoing analysis. The most valid use of the PE is to measure a stock's PE within its historical range of PE ratios. This range, of course, must be plotted using the same "earnings" numbers you are using. Either you plot the range over the last 10 years your way, or you accept someone else's earnings and use that range.

Value Line Investment Survey includes historic PE ratios, updated every three months, for many stocks. A subscription runs $570 a year (or $55 for a 10-week trial offer), but most libraries have a subscription. Each page on a company is jammed with a wealth of useful information, as well as an analyst's take on the company and its stock price. Check with the reference librarian at your local library.

It's Been Said

"It's not the bulls or the bears you need to avoid—it's the bum steers."

—Chuck Hillis

A Nugget of Gold

It's difficult to make any meaningful comparison between the PEs of companies, even within the same business. They're all very different companies. All this relative PE analysis is saying is that, today, the market likes the company with the higher PE. Investors may change their collective minds next week, and they may be wrong both times!

If a stock is trading at the high end of its PE range, it may be overpriced. It's possible that it could break out and establish a new, higher range because the market—the majority of investors—thinks that the company now has greater promise and will do much better in the future. It could happen, but it doesn't very often.

If a stock is trading low in its historic range, it may be a good value. Or, it may be breaking down. It's up to you to find out which you think it is. That means more research again. When used in this kind of range analysis, the PE is still only a single, simple tool that you use to help make decisions.

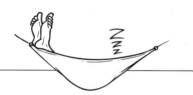

From the Hammock

Buy at a PEG of 1.0 or less if everything else seems good. You may want to take your profits when the PEG gets to 2.0 or more. Sure, it can go even higher, but why? Only due to the emotions of investors, not any fundamental values in the company. If you're patient, you'll usually get the opportunity to buy it back sometime in the future at 1.0 or less. Meanwhile, find another company with a promising future and a reasonable PEG.

Which Way Do the Tracks Go?

You can compare the PE ratio to the growth in a company's earnings over the last five years. Let's say that the current PE ratio is 10, and earnings are growing at 10 percent a year on average. The PEG (PE ÷ Growth) is 1.0 (10 ÷ 10). If earnings have been growing at 20 percent, then the PEG ratio is .5 (10 ÷ 20). This company is growing at twice its PE ratio and may be a great buy. You need to look closer to find out.

When the sales and earnings of a company have been growing at very high rates, investors are willing to put a high PE ratio on a stock and feel comfortable. You'll see PE ratios in the high double digits, or even triple digits for market darlings. Growth is projected to continue at this rate forever, and it would sometimes take that much growth to rationally justify the price today.

PEG ratios of 3.0 or more are common when markets are overpriced. At these times, you'll often see articles suggesting that any company selling at a PEG of less than 2.0 is worth buying. We're not sure why a company priced at nearly twice its rate of growth is a good deal. But when markets are slow, you'll see reports that a company selling at a PEG ratio of less than 1.0 is a good deal. That makes more sense, but you still have do more homework to find out why this may be true.

It's Been Said

"You can't buy what's popular and do well."

—Warren Buffett

Another Way to Track 'Em

Many analysts and investors prefer to use cash flow as a measure of a company's real earnings. This isn't the quite the same as "cash earnings" from EBITDA. Cash is the lifeblood of a company, just as in your house.

Companies have had reported earnings yet have gone out of business because cash flow remained negative for too long.

A company's statement of cash flows uses information from both the balance sheet and the income statement to define cash flow from the following areas:

➤ Operations—what the business activity generates

➤ Investing activities, including investing in plant and equipment

➤ Financing activities, such as borrowing money or selling new stock

Cash flow should be positive most of the time, of course. Cash flow from operations must support the investing activities that pay for the new facilities to allow the company to grow. Cash flow from operations also pays the interest on loans, as well as eventually paying back the money borrowed. When cash flow from operations gets stuck in reverse, you can expect bad news from the company sooner rather than later.

If cash from operations is close to reported earnings under GAAP, the earnings are considered high quality. If both cash flow and reported earnings are growing at about the same rate, that's a healthy sign. If cash flow from operations is declining, or negative, while reported earnings are not, there are problems that will become public soon and affect the stock price.

Dividends

Some companies pay a cash dividend each quarter. If the business is doing well, the board of directors may raise the dividend. Occasionally, to conserve cash during a particularly difficult period, the dividend may get lowered or even eliminated. That's usually not good news.

Historically, dividends made up a significant portion of many stocks' total returns. As noted in Chapter 14, "The Secret Techniques Laid Bare," the Dow Jones Industrial Average increased at an average rate of 5.2 percent per year through the twentieth century. In addition, the stocks in the Dow paid dividends that added about 4.5 percent to this. Almost half the historical annual total return came from dividends.

The dividend yield on a stock is the annual dividend amount divided by the stock price. These days, the dividend yield on the Dow is about one third of the historical average, and the dividend yield on the S&P 500 is even less. Many companies don't pay any dividends at all. Banks and utilities, on the other hand, still pay dividends in the 2 to 4 percent range. For the most part, dividend yield is no longer a productive way to evaluate stocks.

Dividends are out of favor with many investors for two reasons. A company pays dividends from after-tax profits (unless it doesn't have profits to be taxed). The stockholders pay taxes on the dividend again at ordinary income tax rates. It's a very inefficient way to share wealth when you give the tax man two bites.

The second reason for low—or no—dividends is that companies need to use the cash to reinvest in their business. Growth takes cash to buy new plants and equipment, to invest in research and development, and to hire new people. Many companies pay dividends and then borrow money to invest in growth. You, as an investor, might question the logic and wisdom of that practice. But many older companies still do it, even though it often limits their growth.

An old retirement strategy called for living off the income from dividends and hoping for a little increase in the stock price over time. This strategy has faded with the dwindling of high dividends. Today, a high dividend is often the sign of an unhealthy company. It may recover, or it may cut the dividend and hope to restore it in the future, if it has one. In the modern market, companies hope to reward stockowners with growth of earnings leading to an increase in the stock price.

Other Ways to Find Big Game

You can calculate dozens of other ratios from the information in a company's financial statements. They measure the following:

➤ **Profitability:** Earnings-to-sales ratio

➤ **Use of assets:** Return on assets, assets to liabilities, and turnover of certain types of assets such as inventory

➤ **Use of debt:** Ratio of debt to equity, ratio of debt to assets, and return on cost of debt

Some of the ratios that investors use to evaluate companies are listed here:

➤ **Gross profit ratio:** Gross profit (after cost of materials, labor, and factory expenses) divided by sales. This ratio measures the cost of producing what the company sells.

➤ **Operating ratio:** Total expenses for sales, management, and research and development, divided by sales. This indicates how well management is controlling expenses.

➤ **Equity ratio:** Stockholders' equity, divided by total assets. This shows the proportion of the company that is financed by the stockholders.

➤ **Asset turnover ratio:** Sales divided by total assets. This ratio tracks how efficiently assets are used.

➤ **Current ratio:** Current assets divided by current liabilities. This indicates how well the company can pay what it owes.

➤ **Quick ratio:** Cash, marketable securities, and accounts receivable divided by current liabilities. This shows whether a company can pay bills due within 60 days.

➤ **Accounts receivable turnover ratio:** Three hundred and sixty-five days divided by accounts receivable, divided by sales. This shows how many days it takes to collect money after sales are made.

All these ratios (and there are many others) are used to measure one or more aspects of the health of a company and the effectiveness of management in the past. An investor hopes that a healthy trend, as demonstrated through ratio analysis, may continue in the future. Good—and improving—ratios give an investor a greater confidence to invest in the stock.

Ratio analysis also aids in determining whether you think the market is fairly valuing a company. Different investors and investment strategies focus on those ratios that give them a warm, fuzzy feeling about the company. What works for one may not work for another. Therefore, there are no "right" answers or absolutely good ratios.

Different types of businesses and industries generate their own healthy range of ratios. These ranges depend on the industry's requirements for capital, competition levels, and the long-term growth prospects for the industry. You need to know the company and its industry well to properly interpret ratios for a company in context.

If you really want to learn more about ratios and financial analysis, the granddaddy of investment analysis books is *The Intelligent Investor,* by Benjamin Graham and David Dodd. It's worth reading to see how a great analyst's mind works. But for a more up-to-date take on the subject, look for a college textbook on financial analysis and accounting, or sign up for an evening course at a local college. Many offer such courses at reasonable prices. If there's a university nearby, find a second-hand textbook store for a used text at an affordable price.

Get a Closer Look at It

Whether or not a company pays dividends, you want to know what happens with the money that is reinvested in the company. The rate of return on stockholders' *equity* (ROE) over time is the best measure of whether management is reinvesting earnings well.

It's Been Said

"I never attempt to make money in the stock market. I buy on the presumption that they could close the market the next day and not reopen it for five years."

—Warren Buffett

Say What?

A stock is called an **equity** because it represents ownership of a piece of the company. The total stockholder's equity, or ownership interest, on the balance sheet is determined by subtracting all the liabilities of the company from its assets, just like your Net Worth statement. The stock price is usually greater than the equity divided by shares outstanding.

Reported earnings at the end of the year, divided by the stockholders' equity at the beginning of the year, gives you the return on equity as a percent. Use historical numbers over the last five or more years to get a feel for what the company earns on its equity. If there was a major management change, watch for a change in this ratio in the following years to see whether new management did better or worse.

All other things being equal (and, of course, they're not), you want to see a real return on equity—real after subtracting inflation from the return—of 7 percent or more over time. Less than that means that the company is not investing wisely. Sales and earnings are not growing enough to justify the investment. This will be reflected in the stock price. If you can make 3 or 4 percent real return after inflation on government bonds, you want your investment in something that's not guaranteed to earn a lot more than that.

There are two additional factors to consider when calculating ROE. First, if the company has a lot of cash (more than 50 percent) as a percent of its equity, that will depress ROE. Having cash is good, naturally. It allows a company to invest its own money for growth or acquisitions. It also provides a cushion during lean times. If cash is more than half of equity, subtract 75 percent of the cash from equity and recalculate ROE. This will give you a truer picture of what the assets employed in the business earn.

The second factor is debt. Companies may borrow long-term to invest in operations or buy other companies. If a company shows long-term debt on the balance sheet, add this to equity and calculate return on total investment (ROI) over the last five years. Return on equity may be very high if a lot of debt is used. Real return on investment (ROI) should remain a respectable 7 percent over time also. If not, the debt isn't being invested wisely.

When you have the trend numbers for ROE or ROI, you can use them to evaluate future years' returns. You can do your ROE or ROI analysis using reported earnings or any of the other earnings numbers we discussed earlier. Whatever you use, be consistent. Cash flow may be the most accurate and useful, but it's the most difficult to determine. You can visit www.holtvalue.com to find more information on using cash flow in your analyses.

We strongly suggest that you use some ratio analysis as part of your investing process to become familiar with how it is used. Then you'll understand what professional analysts and the business media are talking about when they use these ratios and terms. You *can* become too reliant on ratio analysis. Remember, it has only limited ability, at best, to suggest what may happen in the future.

Potholes

If debt is equal to or greater than equity, the company is highly leveraged. Interest costs cut into earnings, and debt repayment and interest consume cash flow. In most types of businesses, a company with more debt than equity is at risk if sales and earnings hit a downdraft. ROI and cash flow need to be very good to cover the interest on the debt and repayment of the debt at this level.

Hiring a Tracker

Fundamental analysis is a lot of work. You have to enjoy playing with numbers. Chartered financial analysts and MBAs get paid well to do it. Brokerage houses and mutual funds hire these people by the trainload. It takes years of practice to develop the skills to make any real sense of ratio analysis, and it takes a lot of experience to do fundamental analysis well.

Investing in a managed mutual fund is the easiest way to hire this kind of help. (We'll look at how to analyze mutual funds in the next chapter.) Funds are often the least expensive way to hire a manager for your money if you buy funds with expenses that are lower than average.

Many investors begin as do-it-yourself types, picking funds or stocks on their own. Of course, this is the best way to learn. But you may also learn some other things:

➤ You don't have enough time.

➤ You don't like doing it.

➤ It causes you too much anxiety.

➤ You're not particularly good at it.

➤ You'd rather go fishing or read a book.

These are all very good reasons to look for someone to manage your stocks or funds for you. Follow the guidelines in Chapter 11, "Finding and Using a Financial Planner," to hire someone. These are also very good reasons to use our basic investment strategy in Chapter 12, "How to Pay for Your Goals." You won't do worse than the market, and you're likely to do better than the majority of your fellow investors over time.

The Least You Need to Know

➤ You're buying and selling stocks against traders and investors who know more than you. Do your research on companies as a long-term investor to give yourself some advantage.

➤ You can apply and analyze dozens of ratios when studying financial reports to help you evaluate companies and their stock prices.

➤ Understand what "earnings" are being used and how you can use them in your analysis.

➤ Everything you learn about a company tells you where it came from and how healthy is today. But all that information provides only small clues to where it will be in the future.

Chapter 17

Herds of Stocks: Mutual Funds

In This Chapter

➤ Index funds and managed funds

➤ Mutual funds come in many styles

➤ Fees, expenses, and loads explained

➤ How to use past performance figures

➤ Beta, standard deviation, and Sharpe ratio

Investors have been flocking to mutual funds for the last 10 years. Many people automatically invest in mutual funds through a 401(k) plan at work. At the end of 2000, there was $3.96 trillion invested in equity mutual funds, up from $246 billion at the end of 1990.

Mutual funds are organized as *trusts*, which subjects them to strict legal requirements to protect investors. They are regulated by the SEC, which has been working hard to make them consumer-friendly over the last several years.

There are many reasons for the popularity of mutual funds. The first is they give investors the ability to invest in the stock market with professional management. Many investors want to let the pros do the stock picking and then make the difficult buy and sell decisions for those stocks on their behalf.

A second reason is safety. The securities owned in a fund are held by a custodian, often a bank trust department. Your investment in a mutual fund is insured up to $500,000 against theft or fraud by the Securities Investor Protection Corporation (SIPC). This is a nonprofit organization chartered by the U.S. Congress for this purpose. In addition, most fund companies and brokerage houses carry insurance well above this amount to protect your investment.

Say What?

A business **trust** is a legal entity set up to hold and manage property including cash for the benefit of another under a formal arrangement determined by the laws in each state. The trustee is held to high standards in the management and administration of the trust assets.

A mutual fund also gives you a good level of diversification because it's composed of a lot of stocks. Some funds are much less diversified than others, however. For this reason, you want to have more than one fund unless you use a total market index fund. Such a fund offers maximum diversification, but it primarily invests in U.S. companies. While there are hundreds of foreign companies that trade in U.S. markets, they're only a small part of the more than 7,000 stocks.

The final major reason to use mutual funds is the ease of buying and selling shares. All you need to do is mail in a check and a deposit form every month once you open a fund account. Your fund company may have an automatic withdrawal program to make this easier for you. The only danger is that it's too easy to sell. All it takes usually is a phone call. But, if you do a good job selecting your funds, there's not much reason to sell except to rebalance your portfolio every year or two.

From the Hammock

The volume of shares traded on the stock market has mushroomed in the last five years. A major reason for this is the ease of buying and selling stocks over the Internet at lower and lower costs. When we had to call a broker to place a trade and pay over $100 each time, we thought more about it, and maybe the broker would present reasons to reconsider rash actions. Now, a couple of mouse clicks and we can make a trade without a second thought.

For many, their emotions and the excitement of the action lead them to buy or sell without much rational thought. To achieve consistent success in investing is challenging enough when you have a well-defined plan and execute it thoughtfully. The ease of fast trading is a constant threat to undermine the best laid plan.

Identifying Herds of Stocks

For individual investors, investing is not the competitive sport that it is for professionals. This is a great advantage for you. You don't have the pressure that the professionals feel to beat the market every month and year. Beating the market isn't even the point as far as you're concerned, despite what you may hear and read. You want to give yourself the best chance to achieve your financial goals. Constantly striving to beat the market isn't necessarily the best way to do that. It often means that you fall below the market as you move from fund to fund trying to catch the hot ones.

The 6,600 domestic equity funds come in all shapes, sizes, and styles. They are roughly broken down into four basic kinds:

➤ Index funds

➤ Diversified funds

➤ Sector funds

➤ International funds

With so many funds to choose from, you need a disciplined procedure to whittle down the number you can choose from. This chapter will help you do just that.

Index Funds

An index fund is composed of all the stocks in its benchmark index. It isn't actively managed to attempt to pick the best-performing stocks in the future. Stocks are bought and sold to match the companies and their relative market-cap weighting in the specific index. This keeps buying and selling to a minimum.

You can choose from many indexes, based on style and market cap. You can also buy an index fund that essentially indexes the entire U.S. market. Either a Wilshire 5,000 fund, a total market index fund, or a Russell 3,000 fund will do this for you. The same level of diversification can be achieved with an S&P 500 Index fund, a midcap index fund, and a small-cap index fund. These three types of

Potholes

One thing that the SIPC and other insurance don't cover is loss of value of your investment due to a drop in the value of the stocks in the portfolio. This market risk is the one that you can't insure against except by allocating some of your portfolio to fixed-income investments such as bonds. Of course, then you face other risks, such as inflation, interest rate changes, and not having enough money to retire comfortably.

It's Been Said

"Never invest your money in anything that eats or needs repairing."

—Billy Rose

funds will perform differently in most periods, but your portfolio will perform like a total market index fund. The advantages to index funds in addition to the diversification are as follows:

➤ Very low expense ratios (.26 percent or less)

➤ Low turnover and, therefore, low trading costs

➤ Low annual tax impact due to low turnover

➤ No sales charge (unless you try really hard)

Managed Funds

Most mutual funds are actively managed by either a single manager or a team of managers. They're usually supported by analysts who research companies and make recommendations to the manager. The objective of a managed fund is to beat its benchmark index. Why else would you invest your money with a manager if you weren't going to get a better return than an index fund would earn for you?

Style

The style box created by Morningstar (www.morningstar.com) is an attempt to classify funds as having a strategy leaning toward one particular style. This is important for some investors and professional money managers of pensions and endowments who direct large amounts of money through professional managers. They want to diversify a portfolio across several styles of funds, primarily to meet a short-term objective of reducing volatility in their total portfolio.

The style box allows you to easily identify a fund's recent style of investing so you can compare it's performance to other funds in the same style.

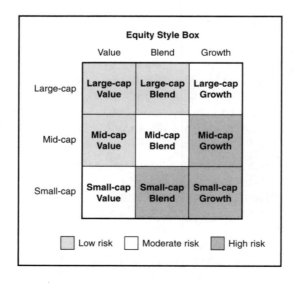

Say What?

Growth fund managers seek to own stocks that are increasing in price faster than the market. Turnover tends to be high as stocks take turns leading the pack, while others falter and stop growing or decline. **Value** fund managers look for stocks of good companies with lower PE ratios than the market. They patiently wait for the market to recognize the potential or the real value of these companies.

True value managers will sell stocks that have increased to where they're no longer considered a bargain. These stocks are often bought by growth managers by the time value managers are selling them. In the long run, these approaches tend to even out in returns. A "blend" fund combines both of these strategies about evenly.

Because the market favors different styles of investing at varying times, putting your money in a variety of styles means that some funds may be going up while others are not. The portfolio value remains more stable. Balancing *growth* with *value*, large-cap with small-cap and midcap, and combinations of these, tends to dampen the degree of ups and downs.

The result is similar to owning a total market index fund, but you pay more in fees and expenses when you spread your money around to actively managed funds. And you have to monitor the performance of the various funds to make sure that each is meeting or beating its benchmark.

Many fund managers don't consciously attempt to invest in a certain style. They follow their research on companies and use their experience to try to own stocks of any style that they believe will do well. Consequently, in any given quarter, their fund may be changed from one style to another by Morningstar and Lipper Analytics. If a fund name has a particular style in it, the manager is obliged to invest predominantly in that style.

Say What?

Every mutual fund is required to give you a **prospectus,** a document that lays out how the fund is operated; who the manager is; its financial history, including returns and all expenses; and any other information that the SEC thinks you should know before investing. It's a good idea to read a prospectus. They're written in English these days, not the lawyerese used in the past.

209

One difficulty with trying to maintain a style is that companies' stock prices go up and down. This moves a company from small-cap to midcap or from midcap to large cap, and changes its designation from value to growth. And it all works in reverse when the price goes down a lot. In the first few pages of a fund's *prospectus,* you can find a general statement of the fund's objective, along with its history.

As an investor in actively managed funds, if that is your choice, you have only one style concern: The three or four funds that you own should rarely overlap in style. If the only purpose for using style to select funds is to reduce volatility (and we argue that it is), you need to diversify your fund styles. If you notice that two of your funds are operating in the same style for two or more quarters, is this long enough? One of them should be replaced. They overlap too much and will perform similarly in both up and down markets.

Over periods of 10 or more years, the styles tend to have similar returns. A *Consumer Reports* study of 78 top U.S. mutual funds in their respective styles showed the following average annual returns for the 10 years through 1997:

Cap Size	Return	Style	Return
Large-cap	17.27%	Growth	16.77%
Midcap	17.60%	Value	16.80%
Small-cap	16.30%	Blend	17.63%

We previously pointed out that a small difference in annual returns adds up over long periods. But there is no way to predict which style will have that 1-percent-a-year better return over the 10 years.

It is telling that, of the three different cap-size combinations over periods of 1, 3, 5, and 10 years, the blend funds outperformed 8 out of 12 times. They also had the best overall returns. Style is of little importance to you as a long-term investor. It makes no difference to your return over time.

Types of Managed Funds

The most common type of mutual fund is a diversified fund. The fund manager consciously tries to invest in a variety of industries, market caps, and, in the case of international funds, different countries. By spreading the money around in this way, the manager hopes to reduce the damage that may occur when one industry or sector of the economy stumbles. With so many industries and companies from which to choose, the manager must rely on a stable of anaysts and years of experience to be successful over time.

Sector funds are managed funds that concentrate up to 80 percent of their shareholders' money in a specific industry. That may be as broad as a technology fund or as narrow as a fund that focuses only on wireless communications. When the targeted sector does well, it can be a real rocket ride up. Not all sectors are as volatile as technology, but they are largely at the mercy of the broad market and economic forces. When the sector goes down, there's no place to hide.

From the Hammock

In 1999, several technology sector funds gained over 200 percent, and over 100 funds exceeded 100 percent. Since March of 2000, some of these moon shots cratered, down as much as 72 percent a year later. Even if you believe as we do that technology is the growth engine for the future, the ride will continue to be extremely volatile. You'll need a strong stomach if you expect to make money in this area. Fortunately, almost every company that hopes to grow and profit will need to make use of various technologies to do so. In this sense, every company is a technology play, but most of them won't experience such thrills and spills.

International funds come in three basic flavors. Global funds will buy stocks of companies anywhere in the world, including in the United States. Some may decide to invest up to half of their portfolio in the United States if they believe this is where the best returns will be. Foreign funds only invest outside of their home country. This permits investors to diversify away from their domestic holdings without worrying that the manager may decide to invest in some of the same companies they already own as stocks or in their domestic funds. Finally, there are funds that invest only in a specific geographic region, such as Europe, or only in a specific country. The focus is clearly spelled out in the name of these funds. As with sector funds, when the local or regional economy declines, there's no place for the manager to hide. The fund's charter requires that the fund only invest in that geographic region. We suggest that you only use regional or country funds if you have a good understanding of the economy and politics of the area.

What About Fees and Expenses?

Perhaps the main reason why so few actively managed funds manage to beat their benchmark index (and the index funds that match it) over time is the fees and expenses they carry. With an average of about 1.2 percent per year, plus expenses for trading and marketing, the average actively managed mutual fund has to do almost 3 percent a year better than its index to give you, the investor, the net return of the index. And that's before any taxes that you may owe on distributions.

Three percent a year is a tough nut to crack. The average diversified U.S. equity fund returned 15.95 percent a year from 1991 through 2000. Add the 3 percent in fees and expenses, and it had to earn almost 19 percent while the market (the S&P 500) returned 17.5 percent. The average fund cannot, by definition, beat the average; the average fund, weighed down by those expenses, does worse than the market.

If you select actively managed funds for your portfolio, be aware that those fees and expenses will cost you. You pay them out of the gross return of the fund, and the fund reports only the net return. The annual and semiannual mutual fund issues of personal finance and business magazines occasionally run articles showing how low-cost funds generally outperform high-cost funds.

All reported fund returns assume reinvestment of dividends. Reinvesting your dividends is how you use the power of compounding to achieve a much higher return. If you take the distributions out each year, your long term return will be much lower than the reported average annual returns. Let's look at the returns on $100,000 for three funds that average a gross return of 15 percent over a 20-year period.

➤ Fund A is an index fund with an expense ratio of .25 percent.

➤ Fund B has an expense ratio of 1.00 percent.

➤ Fund C has an expense ratio of 1.5 percent.

After 20 years, the index fund has 24.5 percent more money than Fund C, and 14 percent more than Fund B. The extra $308,260 in Fund A over Fund C will make retirement either earlier or better—or both.

Mutual fund expenses can reduce your long-term returns by as much as 20 percent over long periods even if the funds had identical returns before expenses.

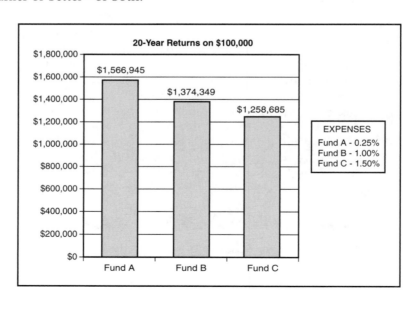

Pay close attention to fees and expenses when picking funds for your portfolio. The 1.5 percent expense ratio doesn't look like much in a year when the fund makes 25 percent. But when it makes only 4 percent or loses money, 1.5 percent becomes a big factor.

In your taxable accounts, you also need to look at the tax efficiency of a fund. If you have to pay taxes on large, annual capital gain dividends, that also cuts into your long-term return. You may not pay the tax from the fund money itself to allow it to compound, but the taxes come out of your cash flow somewhere. That means that you have less money to invest.

A fund's published fees aren't the only expense that a fund deducts from gross returns before you get credited with the rest. The buying and selling of shares adds transaction expenses. The greater the percentage of a fund's assets (stock shares) that are sold, the higher the turnover, and the more expenses the fund pays. The high turnover is supposed to increase the fund's returns and cover these expenses. It doesn't always work this way for many funds.

In recent years, average turnover of actively managed funds has been around 90 percent. In 2000, it was 108 percent. Some funds still buy for the long term, but more funds are actively trading their portfolios to time the market as it moves from favoring one style to another and from sector to sector. This 108 percent turnover means that a fund holds a stock for an average of 11 months (12 months ÷ 1.08 = 11.11 months).

A Nugget of Gold

Starting in mid-2001, the SEC required mutual funds to show after-tax returns over 1-, 5-, and 10-year periods. You can compare these returns with their pre-tax returns to gauge the tax efficiency of a fund. Beware that the tax rate the SEC requires funds to use here is the highest federal tax rate (currently 39.6 percent). Chances are, your rate is lower. In addition, much of the distributions made by equity funds are long-term capital gains, which are currently taxed at only 20 or 8 percent, depending on your ordinary income tax rate. However, the after-tax return calculations won't count any state taxes.

Picking the Right Herd

So how do you select a portfolio of mutual funds? It's easier than picking stocks, but there's still some work involved researching funds to help you make good choices. First, let's get a couple of confusing questions out of the way: Should you go with load funds or no-load funds? And what's with all those different classes of funds?

The Lowdown on Loads

Funds may be no-load, low-load, front-end load, back-end load, or just plain load. The load, in all cases, refers to a transaction fee that you pay (or don't pay, in the case

Say What?

The **expense ratio** of a mutual fund is the percentage of its average total assets spent for the management and operation of the fund during the preceding year. The annual return of a fund as reported to shareholders and the press is what is left after expenses are deducted from the fund's total return.

Potholes

One of the extra fees allowed in the annual expense must be identified as a 12b-1 fee if it is charged. This fee may run from .25 percent to as much as 1.0 percent a year. It's designed to compensate your adviser for the advice and service that you receive after you own the shares. Don't buy a no-load fund on your own that charges a 12b-1 fee for advice and service that you give yourself. The fund uses it to advertise for new shareholders, not to help you in any way.

of no-load funds) when you buy or sell shares. Each fund has its own unique load and fee structure. It's up to you to understand the options and select the one you want. The different types of load are marked as different classes of shares such as A, B, and C. We'll investigate these for you in a few paragraphs.

A no-load fund charges no up-front or redemption fee. A true no-load fund has only one class of shares with one *expense ratio*. No-load funds are ideal for the do-it-yourself investor who is willing to learn how to design and manage a portfolio of funds. There's plenty of information available on mutual funds for those who don't feel the need to pay for guidance.

Low-load funds charge upfront fees equal to 1 to 3 percent of the amount of money that you invest. A 3 percent load on a $10,000 investment is $300, leaving $9,700 to put to work in the fund. There are several reasons a fund might charge a small load in this range:

➤ To discourage in and out trading of the shares

➤ To cover marketing costs or other expenses

➤ Because they have a good fund and they think people will pay to get in

The load fund may have two fees—one to buy shares, or a lower one to sell shares, called a back-end fee or redemption fee. Typical front-end loads usually start at 5.75 percent. They may decline based on how much you commit to invest over a 12-month period. A $50,000 commitment is usually the first step on this ladder. That may reduce the load by 1 to 1.25 percentage points.

The main purpose of the load is to compensate your broker or advisor for putting you in the fund. If you want and need advice, you should get it and this is a small price to pay for good advice. There's also a small ongoing fee paid to your adviser as long as you remain in the fund. This is to compensate your adviser to assist you in evaluating your investment in the fund and answering your questions. By all means pay the load if you want the assistance. Just be sure that the advice is good and that the adviser continues to help you later on.

Load funds may give you the option of paying the load in a variety of ways. A typical program might look like this:

Class	Load	Annual Fee
Class A (or I) shares	5.75% up front	1.10%
Class B (or II)	3–6% back-end	2.00%
Class C (or III)	Maybe 1% front- or back-end	2.00%
Class D (or IV)	Variations on all these	

The back-end fee on Class B (or II) shares may decline to zero after six years or so. The annual fee may also be reduced to the 1.10 percent level then or a couple years later.

A back-end load or redemption fee may disappear after a few months. That's designed to discourage in-and-out trading in the fund, or market-timing. Other back-end or redemption fees stay for years, although they may come down the longer you hold the fund. If the fee never goes away, the dollar amount of the fee increases as the value of your fund holding grows. It becomes much larger than the front-end load, and it may discourage you from selling even when your portfolio strategy or analysis says that you should.

Loading Up

More fund families are switching to load funds or are adding load funds to their stable of no-load funds. The load gives them money to pay a commission to a broker or agent to sell the fund. No-load funds rely on advertising to attract your interest. In a highly competitive fund world, having hundreds of thousands of brokers, advisers, and planners actively selling their funds can increase the amount of money that the funds manage. That, in turn, increases the amount of fee income that the fund collects each year.

The majority of fund investments every year are made into one form of load fund or another. Many people prefer to get advice on selecting and managing their funds. The loads or higher expenses provide compensation to the person who sells the fund and continues to monitor its performance with you.

From the Hammock

If you plan to stay in the fund for six or more years, pay the load up-front. That's the cheapest option in the long run. The higher expenses for the other classes cost you dearly year after year. If you don't plan to hold the fund for at least that long, why are you buying it?

In the long run, there is little or no difference between paying the upfront load (to avoid the higher annual expenses) and buying a similar no-load fun. A 1995 Morningstar study found that, after 10 years, the load funds they tracked had caught up to no-load funds in total return, despite the load cost and higher annual expenses. Buy your funds the way you feel most comfortable, and get the funds that you want to own over the long haul.

Using Past Performance

We finally get to the good part. Isn't performance what it's all about? Well, yes. The performance of your funds in the *future*. Remember "Past performance is no guarantee of future results"? It turns out that past performance lends nothing more than hopes for future performance.

One-year, three-year, or five-year performance records of a fund or a manager have zero predictive value. None. Ignore one-year performance records altogether. A fund in the lowest quarter of performance in one year has a better chance of being in the top quarter the following year than a fund in the top quarter the first year has of being in the top quarter the next year.

On average, only 26 percent of funds in the top quarter one year are in the top quarter the following year. Most often, the funds with the biggest gains one year show the biggest losses the next. So pay no attention to one-year performance except to stay away from last year's top performers.

Longer Periods

What about a fund manager's performance over three-year, five-year, or longer periods? Statisticians, who use complex mathematical formulas to try to ferret out a cause-and-effect relationship between two variables, disagree. Some say that a 20-year performance record is required to conclude that the results are due to anything other than chance and random distribution. Another group holds out for 40 years, and a few conservatives insist 70 years is the minimum.

Few fund managers have managed any fund, let alone the same fund, for 20 years. So past performance as an absolute number is not helpful in picking funds that will do well in the future. Past performance isn't totally useless, however, and it's all we really have to work with. Here's how to use it:

➤ Compare funds that are classified in the same style box or sector for five years and that have had the same manager the whole time.

➤ Match these funds' performance against each other for the five preceding years, one year at a time.

➤ If the fund has no consistent style, match it against the S&P 500 Index each year.

Now you can pick the fund that has consistently performed above the average of its peers year after year. This way, you're not investing just because the manager had one good (possibly lucky) year out of five that pushed the five-year total return or average annual return to the top. The consistent performer just might have something going for him or her. You'll wait another 15 years to find out, as long as the performance stays above average.

The Stars

Morningstar ranks funds on 1-year, 3-year, 5-year, and 10-year performance, changing each quarter, when necessary. Five stars is the top rating using its risk-adjusted performance formula against all other funds (not just funds of a similar style, unfortunately). So what does this mean?

Again, not much. You already know to avoid star ratings or any other kind of rating for one-year performances. Morningstar was forced to give one-year ratings by the NASD under pressure from mutual funds eager to show off hot, one-year performances. However, Morningstar calls this "data pollution." And Morningstar will be the first to tell you that none of its star ratings have any predictive value.

Here's the record we found on star ratings:

➤ The majority of five-star funds in a year performed below average in each of the following four years, according to a 1994 study by Lipper Analytics.

➤ On average, three-star funds outperformed five-star funds in 1995, 1996, and 1997, based on a study by Financial Research Corp.

➤ Four-star funds, as a group, performed the best.

This doesn't mean that you should buy only four-star funds. Use that as a starting point, along with three-star funds. Examine their annual performance against that of their peers, other funds of the same style, on a year-to-year basis over at least five years.

Then, after you buy a fund based on this research, continue this same analysis once or twice a year to make sure that the fund is still doing well. If it falls below the average of its peers for two years, it may be time to replace it with a better-performing fund in a similar style.

Morningstar has a subscription service that you can purchase by mail or receive online at www.morningstar.com. Check to see if your local library has a subscription.

A Nugget of Gold

The top 10 percent of funds in a category—equity, hybrid (stock and bond), taxable bond, and tax-free bond—over the period measured receive five stars. The next 22.5 percent get four stars. Then the next 35 percent earn three stars. The rest, the bottom third, get one or two stars. The average five-star fund loses one or more stars after six months.

217

Other Tools

You'll often see mysterious names and numbers applied to mutual funds in Morningstar's reports and elsewhere. The common ones are statistical measurements:

➤ Beta

➤ Standard deviation

➤ Sharpe ratio

Beta

Beta compares the volatility of a fund over the last 12 months to the S&P index. The index, regardless of what its performance was, is 1.0. A fund that went up and down more than the S&P scores a beta of over 1.0. The higher the score is, the more volatile the fund was in the short term. Less volatile funds than the S&P Index score less than 1.0.

Beta is not a very useful tool for the long-term investor. Some of your funds may have a higher beta at times than other funds. If your portfolio is well diversified, the total beta will be around 1.0. All that beta measures is how rough or smooth the ride was during the previous year compared to the market. It says nothing about past or future performance, or even about the future beta of the fund.

Standard Deviation

Standard deviation measures the degree that a fund has varied from its own average return over the past three years. The higher the value is, the more the fund's return has fluctuated around its average return. This is just another way of measuring volatility.

Say that a fund has a three-year annual average return of 10 percent and a standard deviation of 15 percent. This means that over the past three years, about two thirds of the annual returns fell within the range of –5 percent and +25 percent. You add and subtract the standard deviation to and from the average return to get this range (10 – 15 = –5; 10 + 15 = 25). So, one third of the time, the annual return was expected to be less than –5 percent or greater than +25 percent.

It's Been Said

"There are three kinds of lies: lies, damned lies, and statistics."

—Benjamin Disraeli

As in all other cases measuring past performance, there's no prediction involved. If a fund is managed in the same way and the market behaves the same way over the following three years, the standard deviation may be similar. The manager may be consistent, but you can count on the market being very inconsistent. Standard deviation says nothing about a fund's absolute performance, either past or future.

Sharpe Ratio

The Sharpe ratio is the product of Stanford University professor and Nobel Prize–winner William Sharpe. Morningstar mutual fund reports list the Sharpe ratio for the preceding period.

The Sharpe ratio is called a reward to variability ratio. That means that it measures past performance against the volatility that the stock or fund experienced in the past as it gained the performance.

First, how much better than Treasury bills did the fund perform over the period? That is the reward component. Then this "excess" return is divided by the standard deviation over the same period. The result measures whether you were adequately rewarded for experiencing that degree of volatility. The higher the number is, the better the volatility-adjusted performance was. In other words, you got more reward for the volatility the fund experienced.

The Sharpe ratio, too, measures past performance. Professor Sharpe recommends that you use low expenses first, low turnover second, and then the Sharpe ratio as the tie-breaker between two essentially identical funds in your selection process. However, he personally prefers index funds.

Now you see that picking mutual funds for the long haul, while easier than picking stocks, isn't a walk in the park, either. Three cautionary reports underscore this:

➤ A Financial Research Corp. study for Phoenix Investment Partners looked at mutual fund investors' behavior from 1990 through March 2000. The average fund investor reduced his 3-year returns by 20 percent, on average, because he consistently got in the hot funds too late and out of other funds too early.

➤ A Morningstar study covering the 1988–1997 period looked at the funds that investors took the most money out of each year because they did so poorly. It found that 78 percent of those funds went on to beat the average equity fund over the next one, two, and three years. These funds also outperformed the funds that took in the most investor money (five-star funds usually) 89 percent of the time.

A Nugget of Gold

Professor Sharpe's latest offering is available through his Web site, www.financialengines.com. This process analyzes a portfolio against all periods in market history to determine the odds that you'll reach your financial goals given the amount of money that you invest, the time frame, the investments that you use, and the goal.

The process is called Monte Carlo analysis. The result will say something like, "You have a 79 percent chance of reaching your goal," given the variables that you plugged in. By changing the variables, you can see if you get a better (or worse) chance. It's all based on historical market returns, however, and even Sharpe has no idea what the market or a fund will do in the future.

219

➤ Also from Morningstar, investors in growth funds that averaged 12 percent annual return for five years ending in May 1994 lost an average of 2 percent a year during that period! How? The investors kept switching funds to buy the latest top performers. They bought high and sold when the fund dropped. Then they put their money in the next latest hot fund, only to ride it down, too.

These reports and others like them tell us that many investors experience difficulty in making as much money as the market is willing to give them just for being in a passive index fund. We'll hope that you'll conclude from this list of surveys and our discussion of mutual funds that picking actively managed mutual funds takes some research and ongoing homework on your part.

Researching and buying mutual funds may be easier than picking individual stocks, but you still need to create a strategy to guide you in the design of your portfolio and to select the funds that will work together over the long haul toward your goals. Until you feel you're ready to do this, we suggest that you keep your money in index funds so you can earn while you learn.

The Least You Need to Know

➤ The only reason to buy and hold actively managed mutual funds instead of index funds is because they consistently outperform their benchmark index. If they can't do that, don't buy them or hold them.

➤ Loads, high fees, and high expenses are difficult for active managers to make up and still give shareholders a return that beats the fund's benchmark index.

➤ Take your time selecting mutual funds, and choose those that have consistently superior year-to-year performance against their peers, that have low expenses, and that have low turnover.

➤ Check your funds once every six months using the same evaluation method used when you bought them. Keep them as long as they perform better than the average of their peers most years.

➤ Past performance is no guarantee of future results. It might not even be a clue.

Chapter 18

A Zoo-ful of Bonds

> ## In This Chapter
>
> ➤ Bonds: more complex than CDs
>
> ➤ The value of a bond varies before maturity
>
> ➤ How bond funds differ from bonds
>
> ➤ Various types of bonds and funds
>
> ➤ When and how to own bonds directly

Did you ever go to the zoo and visit the apes and monkeys? Such variety: gorillas, chimps, orangutans, and little monkeys of many kinds. They are fascinating and entertaining, and, although they are different sizes, they all look somewhat alike.

The bond market reminds us of this collection of simians, except that it's not fascinating or entertaining to most people. It looks very boring. Fixed income—yawn. But inside the cages is a very complex and complicated world. The bond market is much bigger than the stock market—and more difficult to understand.

Most sectors of the bond market are dominated by large, institutional players. One group—mutual funds, pension funds, and endowment funds—buys huge chunks of bonds primarily for the income. The other group is composed of traders. They have no desire for income. They buy and sell even larger chunks of bonds for very short-term gains (they hope), using borrowed money. This activity drives the bond market on a minute-to-minute basis.

Individual investors usually buy only two types of bonds—U.S. Treasuries and municipal bonds issued by state and local governments. They buy them as long-term investments, not to trade.

Are Bonds Tame?

A bond indenture is a legal contract between the borrower, who issues the bond, and the creditor, who loans the money to the issuer.

➤ A bond usually pays a specified rate of interest, known as the coupon rate, for a specified period.

➤ A bond legally obligates the issuer to pay the interest as well as return the face value amount of the bond to the bondholder when the period is up. This period is known as maturity.

➤ A bond may be sold on the market before maturity at a market value that may be more or less than the face value.

Potholes

A bond's yield is the annual interest paid as a percent on the current market value. When issued, the yield is close to the coupon rate, but it changes as the market value changes. The yield on a bond fund is more complex. The SEC requires that funds must state the true yield to maturity of the bonds in the portfolio over the past 30 days, adjusted for expenses. It's based on the fund's offering price per share, which is usually the market value of the bonds and cash in the fund, plus any load to buy the shares. Make sure that you get the SEC yield, not the "distributed yield," which is based on the distributions that a fund makes. These two yields can be very different.

Let's say that you purchase a bond from the issuer. You contract to loan $10,000, the face value of the bond, at 6 percent annual interest for five years. Every six months, you receive a check for $300. After five years, you get your $10,000 back. Sounds just like a bank CD. What's the big deal?

A bank may allow you to withdraw your CD money before maturity and will charge you a penalty as specified in the contract. A bond must be sold on the market if you don't hold it to maturity. The price that you get depends on the current rate of interest, the current quality rating of the issuer, and how long before the bond matures. This is where bonds get more complicated.

A Nugget of Gold

U.S. government Treasury notes and bonds are considered the "gold standard" of the bond world; they're guaranteed by the U.S. government. Almost every other issuer applies to Moody's or Standard & Poors to get a quality rating. These companies closely investigate the finances of the issuer. Then they assign a rating based on the likelihood that the issuer will be able to pay interest and redeem the bond at maturity. The better the rating is, the lower the rate of interest is that the issuer must pay. Any rating below BBB (Standard & Poors) or Baa (Moody's) is considered noninvestment grade, or speculative. AAA is considered the best grade, except for Treasuries.

If the market rate of interest for similar bonds has increased to 7 percent since you bought your bond a year ago, your bond is now worth about $9,600. Why would someone want to give you $10,000 for a bond that pays only 6 percent when that person could buy one that pays 7 percent? No reason at all. You take a haircut on the bond if you want to sell.

On the other hand, if rates drop to 5 percent, your bond is now worth around $10,400. You could theoretically sell it for a $400 capital gain. (Buying and selling bonds on the market comes with a hidden cost. There's a bid and ask spread, just like with stocks, except that this spread isn't public knowledge.) Even if you managed to make a small gain, you wouldn't really come out ahead in the long run. You gave up your 6 percent bond, and you can replace it only with one paying 5 percent. The bond market constantly balances everything out this way.

The longer the maturity is, the greater the change in the value is when market rates change. The measure of this is called a bond's *duration*. The lower the duration is, the less the value changes, or the less volatile it is. The following graph shows roughly how this works.

It's Been Said

"An economist is a man who can tell you anything—he'll tell you what can happen under any given conditions, and his guess is liable to be just as good as anybody else's."

—Will Rogers

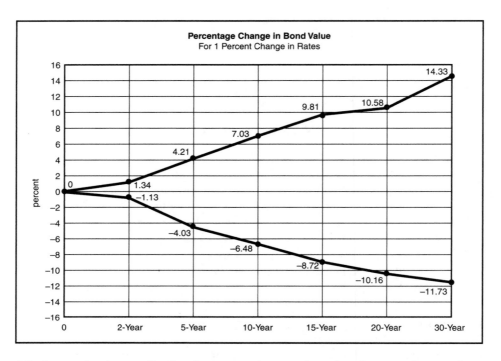

Percentage Change in Bond Value
For 1 Percent Change in Rates

The longer the time until a bond matures, the more its value changes when market rates change.

Say What?

Duration of a bond, or a portfolio of bonds, really is a complex formula that uses the price, the maturity, the income payments, and the timing of all these cash flows to determine how long it would take to recover your original investment. The result is also the approximate percent that the market price will move when rates increase or decrease.

What you need to know from this is this: The duration of a bond is likely to be greater the farther out the maturity of the bond is. When rates move, the longer-duration bonds change more in value. And the change is *opposite* the direction of the rate change. Interest rates go up, and bond prices down; interest rates go down, and bond prices up.

This interest rate risk is important for two reasons. First, if you need to sell before maturity, you may not get the face value for your bond. Second, if rates go up and stay up, you're stuck holding the lower-rate bond until maturity. There's rarely any net gain by selling at a loss to buy the higher-yielding bond, unless you still have many years to go until maturity. Rates will go up and down over that time, so you may actually gain nothing at all by swapping. The bond market is very efficient.

Bond Language

Any thorough discussion of the bond market is a vocabulary exercise. Bonds have their own special language. Here are a few of the key terms that will help you understand the world of bonds:

➤ **Basis point:** The basis point is one-hundredth ($^1/_{100}$) of 1 percent (.01%). Yield is expressed in basis points by the market pros.

➤ **Total return:** This is the interest paid, plus or minus the change in value of a bond, or a portfolio of bonds, over a year.

➤ **Prices:** Bonds are actually are quoted in increments of $^1/_{32}$. A price of 100:10 means a price of 100 and $^{10}/_{32}$.

➤ **Par:** This is the face value of a bond—how much you get when it matures. A bond trading at a price of 100 is trading at par.

➤ **Premium:** If a bond's price is over 100, it is trading at a premium to par.

➤ **Discount:** If the price is less than 100, it's trading at a discount to par.

➤ **Yield to maturity:** This is the total annual return on a bond, including interest plus or minus any premium or discount, amortized annually to maturity.

➤ **Yield to call:** Some bonds can be redeemed or called at a specified price (usually a premium to par) before maturity. This will change the annualized yield to the call date.

A Nugget of Gold

For more information on the bond zoo and the language, you can visit www.investinginbonds. com and www.bondtalk.com.

A bond may be issued for any length of time. Several companies issued 100-year bonds a few years ago. There's a species of government bonds in England, called "gilts," that have no maturity. Some banks issue securities with no maturity, but the rates change to match market rates. They're called floating or adjustable-rate securities. Money market funds buy them.

Why Rates Change

Interest is the price that a borrower pays to rent money. The lender wants to get the money, the principal, back and also collect the interest along the way. The lender also wants the value of the total amount received, interest and principal, to be worth at least as much as the principal was the day it was borrowed—preferably more.

A-ha! Inflation strikes again. Inflation relentlessly reduces the value of a dollar, as we showed in Chapter 8, "Estimating Your Retirement Costs." The lender is willing to lend money only if the interest rate anticipates an expected rate of inflation plus several percent more. The real rate of interest is the difference between the interest rate and the rate of inflation.

But no one knows what the rate of inflation will be next year, let alone over 20 or 30 years in the future. Lending money becomes a bet that, after future inflation, the real rate of return will be greater than zero. That's a scary bet.

Look back at the chart of inflation over the last 50 years in Chapter 8. What was the effect of inflation over 12 percent in 1974, 1979, and 1980 on the value of a 20-year U.S. Treasury bond bought in December of 1971 and paying 6 percent interest? Inflation increased at an average rate of 6.25 percent each year for the next 20 years. The rate of interest was less than the rate of inflation! Therefore, the real rate of return was negative. And the bondholder owed taxes on the amount of interest received each year. At the end of 20 years, the lender got the $10,000 back, but it was worth only $2,748 in 1970 dollars.

But, if you bought a 20-year Treasury bond in August 1981 with an interest rate of 14.5 percent, you did great. Inflation averaged only 3.3 percent, so the average real rate of return was 11.2 percent per year. That more than made up for the fact that, at maturity in 2001, the $10,000 was worth $5,111 in 1981 dollars.

Clearly, inflation affects the market rate of interest. Lenders want 2 to 4 percent real return (depending on the quality of the issuer) over time. Even the threat or fear of inflation will spook the bond market. But if inflation doesn't increase soon, rates will drift back down. Inflation drives interest rates for intermediate- and long-term bonds.

From the Hammock

The daily dollar volume of trading in U.S. Treasuries is much larger than the volume in the stock market. But the heavy hitters in the bond market use mostly borrowed money. They can make a good, quick profit if the market moves their way by a handful of basis points (a basis point is $^1/_{100}$ of 1 percent). A rumor, a raised eyebrow by a governor of the Federal Reserve, or a hint that the inflation rate might be increasing a tad is all it takes to set off a flurry of trading and a quick move in market interest rates.

When Bill Clinton took office as President, he was warned to keep the bond market happy or the big traders could raise havoc with interest rates and squeeze the economy. That could upset whatever plans he had for his presidency. Remember his campaign slogan, "It's the economy, stupid"? He found out that it was true, and the bond market had a lot to say about it.

No one knows what inflation will be. That's inflation risk, and, in the bond market, it translates to interest rate risk. The safest bet to make is the 5-year maturity bond. The yield is usually almost as high as that of longer-term bonds, but you get your money back a lot sooner. Near-term maturity bonds fluctuate less in value when interest rates change because their duration is shorter.

The total return of intermediate-term Treasury bonds (such as the 5-year notes) exceeded inflation in 36 of the last 46 five-year periods since 1950. The total return was positive before inflation in 86 percent of those years, and positive after inflation in 60 percent of the years.

You don't invest in bonds to make money so much as to preserve money. As long as you reinvest the interest payments (or dividends from a bond fund), you have a good chance to maintain, or possibly increase, the value of your investment after taxes. A bond component stabilizes your portfolio, while the stock market usually has a more volatile effect. And, in about 30 percent of the years since 1950, the total return on intermediate-term Treasuries has beaten the S&P 500.

Hiring a Zookeeper: Bond Funds

You can't get adequate diversification of maturities at a reasonable cost with less than $100,000 to invest in the fixed-income allocation of your portfolio. Our Wealth Builder Portfolio in Chapter 12, "How to Pay for Your Goals," has a 20 percent allocation to fixed income. Therefore, until your total investment portfolio reaches $500,000, we suggest that a bond mutual fund is the only way to go. We also strongly suggest that you focus on U.S. Treasury intermediate-term funds. You can get slightly higher yields on other good-quality funds, but we're not sure that the small reward is worth the extra risk.

The amount of fees and expenses is critical with bond funds, even more so than with equity funds. Bond funds rarely have double-digit returns that make up for high fees and expenses. Look for funds with expense ratios under 1.00 percent. They go as low as .25 percent or less. The extra expenses don't buy better performance.

Bond funds are different from bonds in three major ways:

➤ They never mature. Except for a few targeted maturity funds, managers buy and sell bonds to stay within a maturity and duration range. You get your money only when you sell shares, and it may be more or less than your cost per share.

➤ There's no fixed yield. The yield on bond funds will follow market yields with a lag time, depending on the average maturity of the holdings and the manager's trading.

➤ The distributions consist of interest payments minus expenses, some return of principal in certain types of funds, and occasional capital gain distributions, if the manager was a net seller of bonds above cost.

The biggest advantages of mutual funds are the fund managers' experience in picking good credit risks (not an issue with Treasury bonds), and their knowledge of the ins and outs of a complex market and economy. You can also easily buy (and sell) shares in small amounts, which you can't do with bonds.

Putting a Ladder in the Monkey Cage

When you have more than $100,000 in your fixed-income allocation in either your taxable accounts or your retirement accounts, you can save the mutual fund fees and set up your own mini-fund. It's called a *bond ladder*. We estimate the cost at between $1/2$ and 1 percent of your investment when you buy a $25,000 bond, but that's it. You save good money in the long run.

We suggest that you use only Treasury bonds to build your ladder. Stick with safety all the way, and don't buy a bond with a maturity longer than 10 years. With $100,000, have a broker (discount or regular) buy four bonds each with a face value of $25,000 along these lines:

➤ Three-year note
➤ Five-year note
➤ Seven-year note
➤ Nine-year note

Some of these may actually be long-term bonds with some age on them. As long as they're under 10 years to go until they mature, that's fine. In your taxable account, try to find ones selling near face value. The discount or premium becomes a tax headache. If you can't get one near par, don't change the spacing on your ladder; just buy what's available, and deal with the tax issue after it matures.

Put the six-month interest payments in a short- or intermediate-term U.S. Treasury fund, or in a money market fund set up for this purpose. When a bond matures, buy another bond in the most distant slot in your original ladder (nine years, in our example) with the proceeds plus the accumulated interest money. There's no need to go beyond five rungs on your ladder. Keep the maturity at 10 years, maximum, with 2-year spacing.

The interest from your mini-fund will remain fairly stable over the years, slowly following the long-term trend in market rates. You'll buy some bonds at a higher rate and others at a lower rate as these rates shift. A ladder protects your portfolio as best as possible from inflation with a minimum of effort.

Different Species of Bonds

The major types of bonds and bond funds available are as follows:

➤ U.S Treasury (Treasuries)

➤ Government bonds

➤ Municipal bonds (munis)

➤ Corporate bonds

Because we're not advocating that you buy individual bonds in most cases, we'll only point out key characteristics of each type. You can buy mutual funds for each, sliced and diced into subcategories based on maturity and credit quality. In the case of municipals, you can buy funds that concentrate on specific states, too.

U.S. Treasuries

Don't confuse Treasuries with *U.S. savings bonds;* they're in another part of the zoo altogether. Treasuries are sold in 2-, 3-, 5-, and 10-year notes, and 30-year bonds. They are fully guaranteed by the U.S. government. Notes and bonds are sold at special auctions during the year, where authorized dealers bid for a quantity at a specific yield.

Individual investors can participate in the auctions on a no-bid basis in increments of $1,000 at www. publicdebt.treas.gov. Your order is automatically filled at the winning bid. You can get a "Treasury Direct" information package from the Web site or the Bureau of Public Debt at this address:

> Bureau of Public Debt
> Division of Consumer Services
> Washington, DC 20239
> 202-874-4000

Say What?

U.S. savings bonds don't have much of a role in a long-term investing program when you have the ability to invest in a U.S. Treasury mutual fund or buy Treasury bonds yourself. For more information on the varieties of U.S. savings bonds and how they work, contact this office:

> Bureau of Public Debt
> Savings Bond Operations Office
> 200 Third St.
> Parkersburg, WV 26106–1328
> 304–480–6112

Or, visit
www.savingsbonds.gov.

Treasuries are actively traded. Any broker will sell you a Treasury, and you can usually pick a maturity in many months of any year. Interest on Treasuries is not taxed by state or local governments, but it is subject to federal tax at ordinary income rates. The drawback is the spread, or markup. This markup is still a mystery. Bond pricing is slowly being dragged, kicking and screaming, out of a dark closet by the Internet. If you're not buying at least a $25,000 bond, the markup that you pay is too much of a hit to your return.

The reason for this mystery over the spread between the bid and ask prices on bonds is rooted in history. The exclusive club of bond dealers on Wall Street has been able to keep buyers and sellers from making a market in bonds without going through a dealer by never publishing a price at which they'll buy and sell. So investors don't know what the market price is. Even big institutional bond holders had to call dealers to get a price and that price was only good at that moment.

This is slowly changing. Some Internet sites available at a price to big bond holders (mutual funds, banks, pension funds and the like) post actual transaction prices soon after a purchase or sale is made for bonds with an active market. Trading through the Internet rather than by phone occurs at some brokerages now, but you still won't see a bid and ask spread so you know how much of a markup you're paying. Eventually, this information will be available, just like it is in the stock market. Then the dealers will have to compete on the basis of the spread and that will ruin their margins.

A Nugget of Gold

The U.S. Treasury started selling 10-year and 30-year inflation-adjusted bonds in 1997. The coupon rate is much lower than that of regular Treasuries because the principal is adjusted each year for inflation. Interest is paid every six months on the new principal amount. When the bond matures, you get the inflation-adjusted amount. The market prices these bonds to yield between 3 and 4 percent. However, you have to pay income taxes each year on the interest plus the adjustment to the principal.

Government Bonds

Two types of agencies issue government bonds. The government-sponsored agencies (GSEs), such as the Federal Home Loan Mortgage Corporation (known as "Freddie Mac"), and the Federal National Mortgage Association ("Fannie Mae"), are stockholder-owned. They buy mortgages from banks and repackage them as "pass-through" bonds. Your mortgage may be in there somewhere.

The "pass-through" means that the monthly mortgage payments and prepayments pass through to the bondholders each month, minus a small fee. The payments differ every month because you get varying amounts of your principal back. Usually, these bonds are paid off long before their actual maturity because of the prepayments. You get your money back a little at a time.

Bonds also are issued by full government agencies with authority to raise money for their public purpose. These bonds are fully guaranteed by the U.S. government and, like Treasuries, are usually exempt from state income taxes. Most states tax the interest from GSE bonds.

Both kinds of government bonds pay a rate of interest slightly higher than that of Treasuries of similar stated maturities. They're not usually bought by individual investors. The best way to participate is through a government bond mutual fund. The fund automatically reinvests your interest and any pass-through payments so that you can keep compounding the return on your investment.

Municipal Bonds

State and local governments, and local authorities created to build and maintain projects to serve a public purpose, issue municipal bonds (munis). They can have maturities of up to 40 years, and they are often issued in multiple maturities.

General obligation (GO) munis are backed by the power to raise taxes, if necessary, to pay them. They are rated by Moody's or Standard & Poors based on the financial health of the issuing government. They may also be insured by an independent agency, which guarantees payment if the issuing government unit *defaults* or files for bankruptcy.

Potholes

Government mortgage bonds and funds don't always trade in the same pattern as Treasuries. They're more sensitive to the economy as well as politics. The independent agencies, especially Fannie Mae, periodically come under attack in Congress. It's the 800-pound gorilla in this market with nonprofit status and political clout. Congress created it, and Congress can regulate, restrict, or restrain it, if it chooses.

Say What?

When a government, or any other issuer, is unable to pay interest and principal on its debt, it is in **default.** The lawyers, and sometimes the courts, go to work to salvage the situation. Rating agencies continually review the finances of bond issuers to try to detect when things are deteriorating. Then they downgrade the bond rating. This reduces their market value. When an issuer defaults, it's difficult to know what, if anything, you'll get if the bond isn't insured.

From the Hammock

Each state has its own rules concerning municipal bonds.

Interest on all munis from any state is exempt from state tax in Alaska, D.C., Indiana, Nevada, South Dakota, Texas, Utah, Washington, and Wyoming.

Interest from certain types of in-state bonds is free from state tax in Illinois, Iowa, Kansas, Oklahoma, and Wisconsin.

Florida taxes out-of-state munis held on January 1 of each year at 0.1 to 0.15 percent of their value.

All the rest of the states exempt interest from in-state munis only.

A Nugget of Gold

To figure out the tax-equivalent yield on a muni bond or fund, first subtract your personal highest tax bracket from 1.0. For the 28 percent bracket: $1.0 - .28 = .72$. Then divide the muni yield by this result: $5.00 \div .72 = 6.94$.

If this rate exceeds the rate on a similar Treasury bond or fund, it's a better deal, tax-wise. For comparison to a rate where the interest is also taxed in your state, add your state tax rate to your federal tax rate in the preceding formula.

Revenue bonds are issued for a specific purpose such as the construction of a hospital, toll highway, bridge, or power plant. The interest and principal are backed by the revenue stream from the project. These munis pay a higher rate of interest than GO bonds because of the risk that the revenue won't be as high as projected and the issuer could default.

Municipal bonds are usually free from federal tax, but more federally taxable munis have been issued in recent years. They're also usually free from state tax to residents of the state in which they are issued. This tax-free status allows issuers to pay lower interest rates. Muni rates typically range from 70 to 90 percent of Treasury rates for similar maturities.

Depending on the rate difference, you may get a higher after-tax yield with municipals than with other bonds. A 5 percent coupon on a muni is equal to a 6.94 percent taxable yield if you're in the 28 percent federal tax bracket. Interest on private activity bonds issued through a state government, local government, or a government-created authority may be federally taxable.

Say What?

The **Alternative Minimum Tax (AMT)** was designed to ensure that wealthy people didn't escape paying taxes through various legal tax shelters. It's a separate tax calculation with its own complex rules, deductions, and form. Because the levels at which it kicks in were set years ago and were not indexed to rise with inflation, more middle-class taxpayers are getting hit with the AMT. Congress may do something about this problem soon, we hope.

Some municipal bonds are issued for more of a private purpose than a public purpose. A major industrial development is one example. A private corporation backs the payment of interest and principal. Therefore, the bonds are more risky than straight municipals. The interest is generally free from federal tax, but not always; you have to ask, or read the indenture (the legal document that creates the conditions under which the debt is issued). The big risk is if it is tax-free and you fall into the *Alternative Minimum Tax* hole. Then the interest becomes taxable at the federal level.

Municipal bonds often can be called back by the issuer after a period of years. When interest rates drop, they can issue new bonds at lower rates. This practice cuts the debt service cost for local governments. The call date and the price at which it may be called are known when the bond is issued. But it can still be a shock when your 8 percent tax-free bond is called and you can get only 5 percent in the market when you reinvest.

From the Hammock

While corporate bonds pay a higher rate of interest than government bonds of similar maturities, that's because corporations can go bankrupt much easier than governments. We suggest that you leave picking corporate bonds to the pros if you want a higher return. Buy a top quality corporate bond fund, but remember that you'll pay the fund's expenses and you'll pay both federal and state taxes on the interest.

Corporate Bonds

Major companies borrow money by issuing bonds for as long as 100 years, but usually for 30 years or less. The interest rates are higher than that of Treasuries and government bonds and are fully taxable at both the federal and state levels. Rating agencies also scrutinize the companies' financial statements for any potential weakness. Corporate bonds are often upgraded or downgraded as a company's fortunes change.

Interest paid to corporate bondholders has priority over dividends paid to stockholders. When a company is liquidated in Chapter 7 bankruptcy, bondholders may get a reduced payment of principal, while shareholders frequently get nothing.

There are several subspecies of corporate bonds. Convertible bonds may be exchanged for stock at a predetermined conversion ratio at some future date. For this privilege, convertible bonds pay a lower rate of interest than a straight bond. But they can also appreciate in value if the company's stock price shoots higher. Mutual funds usually corner the market on these bonds if they're any good.

When a company with a weak financial history issues a bond, or when a financially strong company hits the skids, its bonds are downgraded to below BBB or Baa. Then they're called high-coupon bonds, or often junk bonds. The company's ability to pay the interest and redeem the bond at maturity may be in doubt.

These bonds may not be junk, but they can be dangerous. There were 99 defaults in 1999, and the number has been increasing since then. Several mutual funds specialize in these bonds, and the funds' yields can be in the teens. The default rate can go over 5 percent, and it's the funds' job to try to pick the safer bonds. The junk bond market gets very messy when the economy is weak.

Zeros and STRIPS

State and local governments as well as corporations may issue zero-coupon bonds (zeros). Dealers who buy Treasuries can create a STRIP (Separate Trading of Registered Interest and Principal). Both types of bonds sell at a steep discount to face value. The interest is automatically reinvested over the life of the bond. At maturity, the bondholder receives the full face value. The difference represents the interest.

The interest rate is generally higher than that of a regular bond of similar maturity. This delayed cash flow nature makes a zero a long-duration bond. The market value will rise and fall more than the market value of a regular bond. A zero allows an investor to make a small investment with a known payoff at a specific date in the future. But, unless it's a municipal zero or it's held in a tax-sheltered retirement account, the annual accrued interest is taxable each year.

Zeros and STRIPS trade on the market, but, again, the markup can be mysterious. When you buy or sell one of these in the market, the accrued interest to date is automatically figured in the price. You need to get several quotes on identical bonds before you buy or sell either of these.

Off to the Zoo

Our suggestion is to start with an intermediate-term Treasury fund with low expenses. It's simple and easy, and the safety is guaranteed. Just keep automatically reinvesting dividends and adding 20 percent of your long-term savings to the fund each year. If you want to create your own mini-fund using a Treasury note ladder when you have enough money to diversify maturity dates over 10 years or so, go ahead.

If you're in the 28 percent or higher federal tax bracket, you might add an intermediate-term municipal bond fund in your taxable account. Unless you live in a high-tax state such as New York or California, a general muni fund is best. Single-state funds work for residents in these high tax states, but there's a risk due to lack of diversification. If your state's economy and finances suffer for one reason or another, the share value of your fund will be depressed. In the long run, however, it should recover and you'll collect higher dividends while you wait.

The Least You Need to Know

➤ Don't confuse the interest rate, the yield, and the total return of a bond or bond fund. They mean different things.

➤ Intermediate-term U.S. Treasuries are usually your best fixed-income investment. Longer-term bonds don't offer enough reward for the extra volatility and interest rate risk.

➤ When market interest rates go up, bond prices go down, and vice versa.

➤ The real return of a bond, after inflation, is what counts.

➤ Tax-free municipal bonds may be a good alternative if you're in one of the higher tax brackets.

Tough call!

Chapter 19

Risk Your Money or Your Retirement

In This Chapter

➤ What risks you face

➤ The long-term view changes risk

➤ Your biggest risk is outliving your money

➤ Most risks can be managed

➤ The risk of too much information

You hate to lose money, right? Studies show that most people aren't averse to taking risks with their money. But they hate losing money even more than they enjoy making money. When it comes to investing, the fear of losing money is often the dominant emotion.

On Monday, October 19, 1987, the Dow Jones Industrial Average of 30 large companies fell 508 points, or 22.6 percent. The Dow had returned to its level of 19 months earlier. Panic had been building during the previous week, but when it hit Monday morning, no one was prepared for what happened. The market was in freefall, breaking all records for percentage drop in a day, points lost, and shares traded.

This was the dramatic conclusion of a longer slide in the market that had begun at the end of August. By the close of the market on October 19, the Dow had given up more than 36 percent in two months. It didn't actually hit bottom until November. Yet, the long-term investor who was in the market all year didn't lose money by the time December 31 rolled around. The Dow was up 2.26 percent, and the S&P 500 was up 2.03 percent for the year.

A Nugget of Gold

It doesn't take a lot of selling to drive down the prices of stocks. The stock market is a great example of the interaction between supply and demand. If potential buyers decide, for whatever reasons, to sit on the sidelines for a while, the sellers are providing the supply, but there's little demand until prices come down far enough to get buyers interested again. This can take 30 minutes or as long as several years. When the sellers are done selling, prices stabilize. At some point, the buyers decide to become active again, and demand takes control.

Those who bailed out in panic on that Monday were the ones who lost money. Most of them also missed the biggest one-day percent gain of 10.15 percent in the Dow two days later, on Wednesday the 21st. However, it did take almost two more years for the market indexes to recover and pass their August 1987 highs.

From July 1989, the Dow increased by 312 percent and the S&P 500 increased by 325 percent over the following 10 years. Some investors who panicked in 1987 may still be waiting until it's "safe" to go back in the market.

What Is Risk?

The learned academics who study the markets define risk as volatility, the amount of up-and-down movement in the markets over short periods. We looked at some of these measurements of volatility, called beta and standard deviation, in Chapter 17, "Herds of Stocks: Mutual Funds." These definitions are used because they can be measured mathematically and precisely. But they measure only what happened in the past. They're history.

Other, more useful, definitions of risk are these:

➤ The possibility that you'll lose money

➤ The chance that you'll earn less than you could investing in U.S. Treasury bills

➤ The possibility that you won't beat inflation and taxes

➤ The possibility that you'll outlive your money

➤ The chance that your emotions will cause you to behave in a way that blows up your investment strategy and undermines your plan

These definitions of risk are also easier to understand than mathematical formulations. That's good because they are the true risks that you face as you build and execute your financial plan. These are the risks that we show you how to manage in this chapter and throughout most of this book.

No measure of past volatility or past performance in the markets can shed any light on the future. We don't know how to see the future or measure its uncertainty. But we do know that volatility is no risk to a long-term investor who doesn't react as markets gyrate.

Invest for the Long Term

Investing is what we do with money over the long term—periods of five years or more. In the short term, the stock market has proven too volatile to entrust it with money that we need soon. That money in the market might not be there when we need it if the market drops 20 or 30 percent and doesn't recover in time. In the short term, volatility is, indeed, risk.

Beyond five years, the volatility in the markets is our friend. It gives long-term investors periodic opportunities to buy at lower prices. Everyone likes a sale, right? The steady, dollar-cost–averaging investor automatically benefits when the markets drop and stock and fund shares go on sale.

Say What?

"For true long-term investors ... volatility represents opportunity rather than risk, at least to the extent that volatile securities tend to provide higher returns than more placid securities."

—Peter L. Bernstein

From the Hammock

Value-oriented stock buyers are the bargain hunters of the market. They're willing to wait patiently until a stock's price comes down to a price they consider cheap. But not all cheap stocks are values. It requires ongoing research to determine when the price really is cheap and to have a rational expectation that it eventually will recover.

Some stocks prices decline steeply for good reason, and remain there for years. When you can get it right most of the time, there's good money to be made. When you're wrong, you have what is called dead money, or even no money, invested after several years.

Over the last 75 years, the S&P 500, or an equivalent group of large company stocks, was up 72 percent of the time. Over any five-year period, it was up 90 percent of the time (100 percent since 1933) and up 97 percent of any 10-year period.

When you understand that you aren't likely to lose money over the longer term, you can learn to accept short-term volatility in the markets. That's the price for the increasing returns that the stock market has offered investors for 200 years. Your emotional fear is checked by rational understanding and the knowledge that you can invest in the stock market to maximize returns and achieve your financial goals.

The Short Term Can Be Scary

When markets are going up, about three quarters of all stocks rise. When markets fall, 90 percent of stocks go down. This is called market risk. It often makes little difference how well the companies are doing when the market is heading in one direction under a full head of steam.

Between early 2000 and mid-April 2001, the following 12 companies saw their stock prices decline an average of 76 percent from their highs. These are not just giants of the technology sector; they're dominant companies in the S&P 500 and the Dow indexes. While we expect their prices to rise from their current low levels in the next year or two, a drop of this magnitude may happen again. You need to know that your portfolio will survive it as long as you don't panic at times like that.

Company	High	Low	Drop
AT&T	61.00	16.50	−73.0%
Cisco Systems	82.00	13.19	−83.9%
Compaq Computer	35.00	14.30	−59.1%
Dell Computer	59.69	16.25	−72.8%
Hewlett-Packard	68.09	26.00	−61.8%
Intel Corp.	75.81	22.25	−70.7%
Lucent Tech.	75.38	5.50	−92.7%
Microsoft Corp.	115.00	40.25	−65.0%
Motorola Corp.	61.50	10.50	−82.9%
Nortel Networks	89.00	12.50	−86.0%
Sun Microsystems	64.66	12.85	−80.1%
Worldcom Inc.	52.50	6.69	−87.3%

Many other profitable technology companies fell much more during this period, and a number of dot.com companies fell all the way to 0. The NASDAQ index, with a large number of technology companies of all sizes, fell about 63 percent from its high. Although this is market risk in the extreme, it happens periodically. During the same period, the Dow declined only about 8 percent, and the S&P 500 fell 20 percent from a high the previous year.

A Risk-Free Investment?

Most discussions of risk rely on some definition that measures it against a "risk-free" investment. The "risk-free" investment most often used is U.S. Treasury bills. These are short-term (less than one-year maturity) debt issued by the Treasury Department. They are called risk-free because they are guaranteed by the U.S. government.

Are they truly risk-free? No. You now know what the effect of inflation is on low interest-rate investments. For the 40 years ending in 2000, T-bills had an average annual compound return of 6.06 percent. During this period, inflation averaged 4.5 percent a year. That's about a 1.5 percent real return—before taxes. If you paid 25 percent in taxes annually on the interest, your total real return for 40 years is 0.

You're never going to retire if you manage to earn nothing on your investments after inflation and taxes. Earlier in this book, we pointed out that your biggest risk was outliving your money in retirement. That's true whether you retire at 45 or at 65.

If you retire early, whether at age 45 or at age 55, the number of years that you may have to support yourself in retirement is obviously greater than that for someone who retires at 65 or later. Therefore, your risk is higher. The only way you can manage that risk is to invest where you have the best opportunity to beat inflation and taxes, and still grow your money at an average annual rate of 3 percent or better per year.

Time and Risk

In his book, *Against the Gods: The Remarkable Story of Risk* (John Wiley & Sons, 1996), author Peter L. Bernstein writes, "Once we introduce the element of time, the linkage between risk and volatility begins to diminish. Time changes risk in many ways …."

Any number of statistical analyses of investment performance over the last 100 years will show stocks as the only consistent way to beat those twin demons, inflation and taxes, over long periods. By our definition of the real investment risks you face, stocks—in the form of an S&P 500 fund or a total market index fund—are the best game in town.

There's no guarantee that this winning scenario will occur in the future. "The future is the hardest thing to predict," says Woody Allen. And we can find no evidence that historical market returns contain any clue to future market returns and behavior.

Potholes

The stock market can be quiet for long stretches of time. On February 2, 1964, the Dow-Jones average was 766.08. On August 12, 1982, 18½ years later, the Dow stood at 776.92, only 10.84 points higher. During that period, the high point was on April 27, 1981 at 1024.05. That represented an annual average gain of 1.7 percent per year for just over 17 years! And that's before factoring some horrendous inflation. Over the ensuing 15 months, the Dow gained 65.7 percent to maintain the 20-year period record of never losing money.

All market strategies, including our basic investment strategy, are based on historical market behavior. It's all that any of us have to work with, and it isn't much. There are no risk-free investments where you can be sure to get a real return after inflation and taxes.

History tells us only that stocks have always outperformed any other investment for 50 overlapping 20-year periods since 1932, and almost all 10-year periods. We don't know whether this record will continue. An optimistic, long-term view of the U.S. economy and the world economy underlies a belief that it will. We also believe that a patient and disciplined approach to the stock market provides the best chance for you to have a long and comfortable retirement—perhaps your only choice.

Making Changes as Time Passes

We have seen how time reduces the risk of losing money in the stock market (at least, in the past) for long-term investors. Your short-term money, the cash that you'll need within three years, should be in short- to intermediate-term U.S. Treasury investments and money market funds.

You will become, but only in part, a short-term investor after you retire. Our basic investment strategy in Chapter 12, "How to Pay for Your Goals," outlined a way to reduce your equity exposure as you enter various stages in your life. The following table presents a quick review of this progressive reduction of funds in the stock market.

| | Equity Exposure in | |
Stage	Taxable Accounts	Retirement Accounts
Before retirement	80%	80%
At retirement	70%	80%
At age 65	30%*	80%
At age 70	30%*	70%
At age 85 (singles, 80)	*	30%

Up to 30 percent equity as long as you have at least two years of expense money in fixed-income investments.

The reason for changing your equity exposure is this: Say that you've been cruising along in the market making an average of 12 percent a year for the past 10 years in your retirement account. Your million dollars has grown to $3.1 million. Life couldn't be better. You're 70 years old, and you plan to start withdrawals at the end of the year.

In the eleventh year, the market gets clobbered by a 17 percent loss. The following year, there's a 30 percent loss. (These were about the percentage drops in the S&P 500 Index in 1973 and 1974.) Your pile is reduced to only $1.6 million while you were withdrawing $200,000 a year to pay the bills. Instead of $3 million growing at $360,000 a year, you have $1.6 million, and it's shrinking fast. At $200,000 a year, you're in danger of running out of money, and the market might not bail you out in time.

If you had 30 percent of your retirement account in fixed income at the beginning of the year in which you turned 70, that $930,000 would provide you with five years of withdrawals without disturbing your equity money. The $2.17 million balance kept in equities would shrink to $1.26 million if you had two lousy years like 1973 and 1974 back to back. But you wouldn't have to sell any equity shares to make withdrawals. You would be able to wait until the market recovered.

The market did recover in 1975 and 1976, with the S&P 500 Index climbing 56.6 percent, not including dividends. You would be back to $2 million. Then you could rebalance and put $660,000 in fixed-income investments (30 percent of the current total in the account). You'd still have more than $1.5 million in the market to hopefully continue growing.

Your increased fixed-income allocation protected you for several years. This allowed the market a chance to recover. Nine times since 1950, the S&P 500 Index has fallen about 20 percent or more. The average time to recover to the previous high was 32 months. The 1973–1974 market drop took 95 months to make it back. Since then, the average recovery period has been only 16.8 months.

Keep time on your side, both as a long-term investor and when you need a specific sum within three to five years. Protect your short-term money and allow your longer-term money to keep working hard for you.

Still Can't Take Volatility?

If you conclude that you just can't take the extreme volatility in the markets that comes with equity investing and that your emotions are putting your investments at risk, you have two choices:

➤ Make and save a lot of money. Two million dollars in U.S. Treasury notes may earn $100,000 to $120,000 a year. That will cover $50,000 or so in today's expenses 20 years from now. Eventually, you'll have to sell the Treasuries to live, too. That means saving more than $60,000 a year in Treasuries for the next 20 years to get to that position.

➤ Plan on living on a lower income in retirement. Whatever you can save, plus Social Security, will be all you have. It won't be enough to live anywhere near the style to which you have become accustomed while you're working.

If you save $600 a month ($7,200 a year) for 30 years, and earn 4 percent a year after taxes on the savings, you'll have enough to make $25,000 a year in today's dollars ($81,000 in 30 years at 4 percent inflation)—for about four years. Then, you're out of money. If you make the same annual investment in the stock market at 10 percent a year, after tax, what then? That would allow you to withdraw 10 percent a year (about $80,000 the first year) as long as you live.

243

Retirement is a high-risk proposition because you don't know how long you'll live or how well your investments will really do. Early retirement is even riskier. In either case, the best opportunity to have a financially successful retirement is to save early and often, and to put most of your long-term money in a diversified portfolio of good-quality stocks such as an index fund. Don't give up the income from your job until the numbers work for you.

Other Risks

All investors face a large number of identifiable risks. The good news is that they are manageable or controllable by you, the investor. This doesn't mean that the risks go away; it means that you can limit the damage that they may do to your portfolio through proper use of the following:

➤ Allocation

➤ Diversification

➤ A long-term horizon

➤ Your rational brain

➤ Prudent investing

From the Hammock

The stock and bond markets often breathlessly await the latest government statistics on everything from inflation to new housing starts. If the number isn't close to the forecast, the markets react, sometimes violently. Most of the key government statistics are of a preliminary nature. They are revised, often substantially, over the next month, quarter, and year. The market rarely reacts to these revisions despite their greater accuracy because that's history. Investors only want to know whether the next preliminary report agrees with their expectation or not. It's usually safe to ignore these market reactions and focus on the long term trends in the economy.

The following table identifies many of these risks and shows how to control them. Our basic investment strategy is also designed to control all these risks about as well as possible—and with little effort on your part other than just following it. If your investment strategy differs from our basic strategy, you must consider all these risks to give you the best opportunity to reach financial freedom.

Risk	Definition and Effect	Control Strategy
Outside Risks		
Economic	Major events: war; politics; recessions; cause volatility, lower prices	Seek long-term investment. horizon; diversification; patience
Inflation	General price level increases faster than the return on your portfolio	Seek higher total return by changing allocation to bonds
Deflation	The general price level declines; assets lose value; bankruptcies rise	Invest in companies with little debt; buy quality long bonds
Not enough income	In retirement, investment Income loses value	Diversify to include equities for growth
Natural disasters	Fire, earthquake, weather disrupts economy	Diversify geographically
False information	Rumor, opinion, and predictions disrupt markets	Think; ignore market noise and confusion
Emotions	Fear, greed, and insecurity—yours and others	Think long term; control your emotions
Market-Based Risks		
Market risk	Volatility due to money flows, investor psychology, news, rate changes	Use a long-term horizon and good allocation and diversification
Liquidity	Lack of buyers when you want to sell, or a limited market for the security	Go for long-term investments and avoid illiquid securities
Fads in market	Trends such as momentum investing, sector bubbles, "must-own" stocks	Diversify widely and invest prudently, not emotionally
Reinvestment risk	Inability to reinvest at the same rate of return	Diversify bond maturities-and plan ahead
Currency risk	When dollar rises, foreign investments decline in dollar value	Diversify internationally-when you invest abroad
Interest rate risk	Change in market rates can affect values of securities and market psychology	Allocate portfolio and diversify maturities of bonds
Industry risk	Industry sectors respond differently to economy	Diversify and understand the industry
Company risk	Company product cycles and competition affect prices	Diversify and understand the companies

continues

continued

Risk	Definition and Effect	Control Strategy
Market-Based Risks		
Management risk	Management strategy may not be effective	Diversify and pay attention to news
Credit risk	Danger of default or bankruptcy for bonds or stocks	Use high-rated bonds; diversify and watch
Opportunity risk	You don't have cash when a good opportunity appears	Allocate investments and keep cash on hand
Excessive costs	Ignoring high fees, loads, commissions, and expenses	Think, ask questions, plan ahead, and beware

Most of the strategies to manage these risks involve some of these components

➤ Investing with a long-term horizon

➤ Allocating your portfolio in equities and fixed income, including some cash in a money market fund

➤ Diversifying across industries

➤ Investing in a variety of companies as well as in different economies

➤ Using your brain to balance your emotions and think through your investments before making them

A financial plan and a well-designed investment strategy are your foundation to protect your assets and to build on for your future. The execution requires patience and discipline, acting and not reacting. Protecting your investments against these risks means using all the tools available to you.

Information Risk

The one risk that we left out of the preceding chart deserves special attention. This risk has increased tremendously over the last decade because the amount of information available has exploded. Nevertheless, it is at least as manageable as the others. The risk really isn't the huge amount of information on investing and investments; it's what you do with it and how you react.

A Nugget of Gold

As the flow of information has increased and the variety of media disseminating information has multiplied, accuracy seems to have deteriorated. We've learned that spin must be assumed and that accuracy must be questioned until proven otherwise. Get multiple confirmations or analyses of everything before you act. When in doubt, doing nothing is often safest. Act in haste, repent at leisure. It's better to say, "I wish I had ...," than to say, "I wish I hadn't ..." when it comes to investing.

Instant mass communication and the ability to trade at the push of a button from your home or office combine to increase the danger that you pose to your own portfolio. Information overload makes it more difficult to determine what's important and what's just noise or spin.

In this confusion, fear and greed can take the opportunity to cause damage. This is a good argument for using mutual funds, especially index funds, for your equity investments. An index fund doesn't buy or sell on the news of the moment. If you use actively managed funds, you let the pros sort out the information and make the decisions. However, if you choose to invest in individual stocks, you need to be cautious so that you don't get caught up in the emotions of the moment.

Regulation FD

On October 26, 2000, the SEC's Regulation Fair Disclosure (FD) became effective. Companies can no longer selectively disclose vital information to favored analysts and investors. When a company has something to say that could affect its stock or bond price, it must make a public announcement.

In practice, this means calling a news conference, issuing a press release, filing an *8-K form* with the SEC, and opening end-of-quarter conference calls to anyone who wants to listen by phone or Web cast. Any information accidentally revealed in private must be made public within 24 hours.

Regulation FD may level the playing field more, but most private investors aren't tuned into these Web sites all day. Neither do you have time to listen in on conference calls every morning and afternoon, or patrol the Internet for press releases. The pros are paid to do this, and they react immediately when news breaks.

Your Advantage

The increased flow of information may make the markets even more volatile until most market players adapt to them. When only a few favored people got the news early and relayed it to their clients, the stock would move perhaps more than usual. Others would wonder who knew what. Eventually, the news would filter out and the rest of us found out. Now, in theory, we all know good news or bad news at once.

Say What?

Companies must file an **8-K form** with the SEC when there are "unscheduled material events or corporate changes which could be of importance to the shareholders or the SEC." These filings are available on the Internet at www.edgaronline.com, and www.10kwizard.com, as well as through many financial sites with links to these.

It's Been Said

President Harry S Truman used to quip that he was looking for a one-armed economist, one who would never say, "On the one hand this, but on the other hand that."

Despite the ability to access breaking news, you still have to assume that by the time you hear or see it, everyone else saw it before you and acted on it. The stock price moved to reflect the news, and you're too late to take advantage of it. That's not at all bad from your perspective as a long-term investor.

You may decide, after reviewing the news and other information and analyses that you want to sell your stock in a company before things get worse. That's prudent investing. Do your homework first rather than reacting.

However, you may discover that the market has overreacted due to its short-term bias. You may decide that now is a good time to buy more of the stock instead. The long-term investor likes opportunities to buy good companies when everyone else is selling them. It takes solid fundamental analysis to be comfortable going against the market and be successful in the long run.

Potholes

Be wary of always believing that the consensus sentiment on the direction of the stock market. History suggests that this sentiment is usually accurate except when it isn't.

The private investor still has a huge advantage over professional money managers and fund managers. You can look at the long term. Your returns are not made public and judged daily. You have the leisure to review and act with thoughtful, rational balance. You can rise above the market noise, and the fear and greed that drives the markets on a daily basis.

This is truly a major advantage. The biggest risk that investors often face is their own emotions and their behavior based on these emotions. If you can control that much, the odds are in your favor. You can effectively execute a long-term investment strategy to reach your financial goals.

The Least You Need to Know

➤ There's no such thing as a risk-free investment.

➤ Short-term volatility is not risk for a long-term investor, unless your emotions cause you to act in fear or panic.

➤ The risk from not beating inflation and taxes over time is much greater than the risks in the market.

➤ A well-constructed portfolio and a willingness to be patient and follow your investment strategy is the best defense against the risks that you face in the markets.

➤ You, the private investor, have the advantage over the professionals because you can afford to take a long-term view and not react to short-term news.

Part 5
Tools You Should Use

We're firm believers that when the government gives you the opportunity to postpone or avoid taxes, you should take it. Tax-sheltered retirement plans of one kind or another are available to practically everyone with an earned income. Take advantage of all the ones you can.

The original, comprehensive government retirement program, Social Security, won't be a major contributor to your financial freedom, but it's a piece of your plan that may make a difference at key times during your retirement.

Your estate plan, including a will, is the ribbon on your financial planning package. The goal of estate planning is to ensure that your financial plan and your money continue to serve the purposes that you intended for them.

Chapter 20

Keep the Taxman Waiting While You Work

In This Chapter

➤ 401(k), 403(b), and 457 plans

➤ Small business and self–employed plans

➤ Pensions

➤ Getting your money out

Are you sleeping on the job? If your eyes are open, you should be participating in whatever retirement plan your employer offers. Even if your employer doesn't contribute anything to the plan (and shame on him), you should. The opportunity to put money in a tax-deferred retirement plan is just too good to pass up. You need to use every trick you can to retire early, and this is one of the biggies.

There are a variety of retirement plans around. In part, what you are offered is a function of what kind of employer you have. Private companies use 401(k) plans, pensions, and cash balance plans. Governments, including school districts and other nonprofit employers, may offer 403(b) or 457 plans. Small businesses may find it easier to offer SIMPLEIRAs, SEP-IRAs, or Keogh plans.

In many cases, both you and your employer contribute to the plan. When your employer wants to give you money if you sign up for the plan and contribute, don't hesitate. Money that can compound tax-deferred until, and beyond, age 70, is a key to your retirement plan.

401(k) Plans

The 401(k) plan is likely to be the option that you'll run across most often. More than 40 million workers are saving for retirement using a 401(k) plan. These plans are called defined-contribution plans, and they're set up by an employer. They allow employees to contribute to the plan through payroll deductions. The employer may also contribute to the account on behalf of the employee. The key is that it is an individual account, and it is portable. This means that if you leave that employer, the account can go with you in one way or another.

401(k) plans are self-directed plans in which the employee makes the investment decisions, choosing among options provided by the employer. As a qualified retirement plan, the contributions are permitted to grow tax-deferred until the proceeds are withdrawn. For that privilege, you normally don't have access to the money until you reach age $59^1/_2$. Pulling it out before then could trigger a 10 percent penalty tax by the IRS.

How much you can contribute to these plans is limited by the law and by your employer's plan. For 2001, the maximum contribution is usually the lesser of 15 percent of your income or $10,500. This $10,500 will be indexed to cost-of-living adjustments every year, but it must be made in increments of $500. Your employer may allow you to contribute more or less than the 15 percent.

That's your limit, but the IRS allows you and your employer a combined contribution limit of up to the lesser of $35,000 or 25 percent of your salary. Many employers offer a match to employees. A typical match is 3 percent of your pay, on a dollar-for-dollar match to your contribution. So, if you contribute 3 percent of your income, your employer will also contribute 3 percent. You may—and, in most cases, should— increase your contribution as far as you're allowed.

There are 401(k) regulations common to all plans. The regulations might state that your employer can allow you into the plan on the day you are hired, or they might require as much as a year's employment before you can enroll in the plan. If you have to wait, you can save money in an IRA or taxable savings account in the meantime.

Moving Money Out

Upon leaving your job, you do have access to the money in your 401(k):

It's Been Said

"The world is full of willing people; some are willing to work and the rest willing to let them."

—Robert Frost

A Nugget of Gold

Not all 401(k) plans are equally good. As with any investment, you want low fees and expenses to manage your plan as well as within your plan options. And you want a choice of good options for your money. You can research your plan provider at www. 401kexchange.com and www. search.com. You can analyze your portfolio at www.morningstar.com and www.financialengines.com, although there's a fee for all but the initial analysis. Some employers have signed up with a company that provides this service for employees.

➤ You can transfer it to a rollover IRA.

➤ You can transfer it to your new employer's plan, if transfers are allowed.

➤ You can do nothing and leave the money there to grow until you're $70^1/_2$ (if it's more than $5,000).

The transfers should be made within 60 days and should be made between the plan trustees. If you take possession of the money in order to make the transfer yourself, your old employer is required to withhold 20 percent for the IRS. You must replenish your account with the 20 percent that your employer took. (The money that your company withheld is considered regular payroll withholding, and it applies to your taxes due for that year on your Form 1040.) If you don't replace the 20 percent, the IRS considers it a taxable distribution. Then you owe regular income taxes on that 20 percent plus a 10 percent penalty tax to the IRS. If you don't roll over your money in 60 days, you'll owe regular taxes on the money you received, plus a tax on the 20 percent that your employer took, plus a 10 percent penalty tax on the full amount.

Your best option, when you leave the job, is to roll it over directly to an IRA. This gives you the most flexibility and choice. You fill out an application for a rollover IRA from the financial institution of your choice, and the new IRA custodian processes the transfer for you.

We suggest setting up an IRA brokerage account with a financial "supermarket" such as Fidelity or Schwab so that you can buy stocks as well as mutual funds from different fund families. You can self-direct this account by investing the money online, or you can do it the old-fashioned way and use the telephone to direct your trades. IRAs are covered in more detail in Chapter 21, "The IRA: Your Personal Tax Shelter."

Rolling it into your new employer's plan may be a bit tricky. Employers can make you wait a full year before allowing you to enroll in their 401(k) plan. While waiting, you can either leave the money with your former employer or roll it into an IRA. If you choose the IRA rollover, make sure that the

From the Hammock

If you're eligible for a 401(k) plan with a company match at work and are not utilizing it, you are leaving free money on the table. That's right—you're walking away and leaving money on the table, money that your employer won't make available to you in any other way.

A Nugget of Gold

No matter how you make the transfer, make copies of all the paperwork and use certified mail with return receipt requested. Then check the new statements closely to be sure that everything rolled over properly. Stuff happens. This is a fast-growing part of the IRA business, but neither side of the transaction (you're in the middle) may have all the kinks worked out yet.

Potholes

Some employer plans allow you to borrow from your account. You are permitted to borrow up to half of the amount in your account, to a limit of $50,000. You must pay interest on the money (even though it's your money!) at the rate set by the employer's plan. The interest does go in your account, but you're missing out on what that money could earn for your retirement if it were invested. The loan must be repaid within five years. If you lose your job, the loan amount is due and payable within 60 days or less. Ouch! So think before borrowing, and be sure that your job is secure.

It's Been Said

"I've been rich and I've been poor. Rich is better!"

—Sophie Tucker

401(k) money is not co-mingled with any other IRA funds, or it may be difficult, if not impossible, to roll it into your new employer's plan.

Your last option when you leave a job is to take the money and run! That's not a good idea. If you do, your employer is required to withhold 20 percent of the total for taxes. If you're in the 28 percent federal tax bracket and you live in a state where you will owe state income taxes on it, your tax liability could be close to 35 percent. Then there's that 10 percent penalty that just won't go away if you are under age 59^1/$_2$. So, you could lose almost half of your money to taxes and penalties. You're better off keeping those dollars working for you in a retirement plan.

Here's some incentive not to spend it: At age 30, if you have $5,000 in your account and you take it out, after the taxes and the penalty you'll have $2,750 to spend. Yes, that could pay for a nice vacation. But let's say that you leave the money there until you retire at age 60, and you add no more money to that particular account. If you're able to get the market average of 11 percent on your account for the next 30 years, you will have—drum roll, please—$115,000. If you spent the money instead, after 30 years you won't remember the vacation you took. And the T-shirts that you bought won't even be around to be used as rags to wash the car.

After You Retire

If you retire and leave your job at age 55 or older, you are allowed access to your 401(k) account before age 59^1/$_2$ without the 10 percent penalty—but don't forget that regular taxes are still due. Resist any pressure to *annuitize* your plan money. That's usually your worst option because the money can't grow. You expect to live for several decades in retirement, and a fixed income will get clobbered by inflation.

If you don't want to leave the money in the plan, do the direct custodian-to-custodian rollover to an IRA and manage the money yourself. If you can leave it in the plan or the rollover IRA until age 70, it will grow. At 10 percent a year, it will triple in 12 years and quadruple in 15 years! That's how you pay expenses in retirement.

A Nugget of Gold

Some companies match your 401(k) contributions with company stock, not cash. If you have employer stock in your 401(k) plan when you leave, you may be better off taking the stock directly. Roll over the rest of the investments into an IRA. You will pay taxes only on the cost of the shares when they were originally put into your account (plus the 10 percent penalty, if you're under 59$\frac{1}{2}$).

You can hold the shares in a regular brokerage account. Then, when you sell the shares, you'll owe taxes only at the capital gains rate, not at your regular income tax rate. And there's no requirement that you ever sell them. The shares will be part of your estate (and estate taxes may be due). Then they pass to your heirs with a new, higher cost basis at the price on the date of your death.

The rules require that mandatory distributions begin at age 70$\frac{1}{2}$, taxed as regular income. But if you are still working at age 70$\frac{1}{2}$, you will not be required to start mandatory withdrawals until you retire.

When You Inherit an Account

If you inherit your spouse's 401(k) or 403(b) account, you can leave it in your spouse's name or roll it into an IRA in your spouse's name with you as the beneficiary.

If you leave it in your spouse's name, you have access to it before you reach age 59$\frac{1}{2}$, without incurring the 10 percent penalty—and, as a widow or widower, you may need or want access to that money. You must begin withdrawals the year after your spouse would have turned age 70$\frac{1}{2}$. You can do the same if you inherit your spouse's IRA: Leave it in your spouse's name, and you have access to the account as the beneficiary.

Say What?

When you convert your plan to a fixed annuity, you **annuitize** it. A fixed annuity is a contract between you and an insurance company. In a 403(b) plan, you usually have a deferred annuity. In return for giving the insurance company your money, the company guarantees a series of regular payments for a specific period of time after you retire, usually the annuitant's (that's you) lifetime. Once again, you need to read the fine print carefully.

Potholes

The new distributions rules can also apply to 401(k) plan distributions only if your plan sponsor chooses to adopt them. There's no requirement that they do so, and the extra work involved for them if they do so may not make it attractive. If they don't change the plan rules, you should roll your 401(k) over to an IRA when you leave your job so you can take advantage of the new rules.

From the Hammock

The new IRA distribution rules that go into effect on January 1, 2002, represent a great break for owners, and beneficiaries. Not only can the distributions be stretched out and allowed to grow tax-deferred longer, the increased flexibility to name beneficiaries and how they can use the IRA are a welcome improvement. We'll look closer at these rules in Chapter 21 when we discuss IRAs.

You can also roll the 401(k) account into an IRA in your spouse's name, with you as the beneficiary, and have access to the money before reaching age $59\frac{1}{2}$ without incurring the 10 percent penalty. You do owe income taxes on the withdrawals; Uncle Sam still wants his share.

Under the new IRA distribution rules effective in 2002, your best option may be to then roll your spouse's IRA into an IRA of your own (assuming you were the primary beneficiary). Though you can't receive distributions without paying the penalty until you're $59\frac{1}{2}$ when you do this, you can take the distributions over your life expectancy rather than your spouse's. You can also name your own beneficiary who will be able to establish a new life expectancy distribution schedule upon receiving the IRA.

Before making any retirement decisions, check with your financial adviser to see what will work best for you. Equally important, you want to know well ahead of time if the IRA custodian will allow you to do things this way. If not, find one who will and then transfer the account.

403(b) Plans

403(b) plans are offered to employees of nonprofit institutions such as schools or hospitals. Less than 42 percent of those who are eligible utilize a 403(b) plan. You can't retire early unless you're stashing money away pretax somewhere.

These plans are also referred to as TSAs—tax-sheltered annuities. A 403(b) is an agreement between the employee and the 403(b) provider. All the employer does is withhold the contributions for the employee and forward them to the provider. The employer takes no responsibility except to transfer the employee's money to the chosen provider. There's no requirement that an employer contribute any money, so it's usually up to you, the employee, to fund the account.

Your employer's plan may allow you to contribute in one of two ways (check with your benefits administrator about this):

➤ Under a salary reduction agreement whereby you elect to defer up to $13,500 of your pay (in 2001) depending on how many years you have worked for the employer.

➤ As an after-tax contribution, with the total contribution subject to the same maximum amount of $13,500.

Your account is allowed to compound tax-deferred, so the same rules apply here as with other qualified retirement plans. A 10 percent penalty is usually levied if you take your money out before age $59^1/_2$. If you change jobs, you should be able to roll the taxable portion of your 403(b) into another 403(b) or into an IRA, but check the fine print. Some annuities have a back-end surrender charge, so even if the IRS regulations allow a rollover, the insurance company may not permit it or exact a penalty from your account. Withdrawals usually must begin at age $70^1/_2$, unless the money contributed is pre-1987. Then you have until age 75 to begin withdrawals on those funds.

The contribution limit for the employee is the lesser of 20 percent or $10,500. The $10,500 limit will be indexed to the cost of living. The employee and employer total combined contributions cannot exceed the lesser of 25 percent or $35,000.

You Do Have Choices

Originally, 403(b) plans could be accessed only in the form of annuities. Today, you can find good mutual fund choices as well. And you should be looking for the mutual fund choices! School districts and hospitals make it difficult or even impossible for employees to use a source other than the one they recommend. Petition your employer to make mutual funds available. Sometimes it takes only 10 employees who want a new provider for your employer to include it on their list.

You should be able to invest your 403(b) anywhere that will accept your account. The IRS ruled in 1990 that participants in a 403(b) can transfer out

From the Hammock

For more information on 401(k) plans pick up a copy of *The Complete Idiot's Guide to 401(k) Plans*, co-authored by Dee. Almost every mutual fund company has a 401(k) site that offers help and calculators. Also check out what else is available on the Web. Start with Quicken's 401k adviser Web site at www.teamvest.com/quick, and then head to www.401kafe.com and www.401kdoctor.com.

A Nugget of Gold

TSAs are more confusing than 401(k)s and IRAs because each plan may have its own wrinkles and rules. You should review the details of your particular plan to find out which, if any, of the options we discuss are provided. Ask questions until you are clear on them. You should also get IRS Publication 571 on Tax-Sheltered Annuities and Publication 575, "Pension and Annuity Income."

of their plan into mutual funds of their choice using a 403(b)(7). You don't have to change jobs to change your plan. Only the accumulated savings can be transferred, not the contributions. There may be surrender charges if you transfer out of an annuity.

Potholes

Annuities have a "penalty-free withdrawal" clause that allows you to move 10 percent of the balance each year without incurring surrender charges. But some companies make it difficult to move your money. Read that very small print in the contract before you sign on, and ask questions until you get clear answers, preferably in writing.

Consider a 403(b)(7) if you're looking for better investment choices for your account. Your payroll department or plan administrator may not know or understand 403(b)(7) plans. Transferring your account may not be easy, but it will be worth the effort if the 403(b)(7) offers better choices.

403(b) plans have a catch-up election, allowing participants who did not take advantage of earlier contribution levels to "catch up" and put away extra money. The IRS rules on this (and everything else) are complicated, so you'll need to get some help from the plan provider. We suggest checking out the IRS Publication 571, "Tax-Sheltered Annuity Programs for Employees of Public Schools and Certain Tax-exempt Organizations." You can contact the IRS at 1-800-829-3676 or online at www.irs.ustreas.gov.

Here's a Web site that can help you with your 403(b): www.403bwise.com. Also check out the 403(b) forum at www.morningstar.com. More mutual fund companies are responding to the needs of 403(b) participants and offer good material on their sites as well.

Getting the Money Out

Getting your money out of a 403(b) plan can be difficult. You want to check the fine print of the contract. Although IRS regulations allow you to roll your account into an IRA, your 403(b) provider may not allow rollovers. Your only option may be a fixed annuity. If you can do a rollover, check out Chapter 21, "The IRA: Your Personal Tax Shelter," for information on getting your money out of an IRA.

To get at your 403(b) money before age $59^{1}/_{2}$, you can use Rule 72t. This rule allows you to take the money out of your account in substantially equal periodic payments. Under this rule, you can avoid the 10 percent penalty by taking withdrawals in substantially equal annual payments based on your life expectancy (or joint life, with owner and beneficiary). You use IRS tables to figure out what percentage of your account you could access each year.

Once you've made this election, you must continue for five years or until you reach age $59^{1}/_{2}$, whichever is later. The younger you are, the smaller the payout will be. Check IRS Publication 590, "Individual Retirement Arrangements," for more information, and get professional tax advice before you do it.

457 Retirement Plans

457 deferred compensation plans are available for state, county, and city employees. An employee may elect to annually defer the lesser of $8,500 or 25 percent of compensation. There is a "catch-up" provision here, as well, that allows participants who have not utilized the 457 plan to the max each year to put away more money in the years before retirement.

Mandatory withdrawals must begin by age $70^{1}/_{2}$, and withdrawals are taxed as ordinary income. Plan assets compound tax-deferred, but employees can get at their money without a penalty before age $59^{1}/_{2}$ if they terminate service or retire. Upon termination, you have 60 days to make a decision on when to start distributions.

This privilege is costly because the 457 plan is considered a nonqualified deferred compensation plan by the IRS. This means that the IRS doesn't allow you to use an IRA rollover when you leave your job. If you take a job with another employer that has a 457 plan, you may be able to transfer your account to your new employer's plan, but that's it, folks!

A Nugget of Gold

Even as we write this, Congress is planning to make some changes in 401(k), 403(b), and 457 plans. Congress wants to increase the contribution levels and allow transfers between the different plans when you change jobs. This isn't allowed at present. Stay tuned.

Self-Employment Retirement Plans

If you're self-employed, even if it's only a part-time sideline in addition to your day job to make extra money, you may be able to set up your own retirement plan. Although they're as good or even better than the preceding employer-sponsored plans, you are the one who must set it up and administer it. That means paperwork, legal and tax hoops to jump through on time, and money. You'll want an experienced small business tax adviser to help you with the issues, choices, and paperwork.

SIMPLE IRAs

The Savings Incentive Match Plan for Employees (SIMPLE) IRA was designed for the small employer with fewer than 100 employees and no other qualified retirement plan. With the SIMPLE IRA, each employee has her own IRA. She can make elective contributions up to the lesser of $6,500 or 100 percent of her compensation. The $6,500 limit will be indexed in the future.

The employer must put some money in a SIMPLE IRA for the employees, too. Employers have the option to match the employees' contributions dollar for dollar up to 3 percent of compensation. Or, they can use an alternative matching contribution method by making a flat 2 percent contribution of the employee's compensation.

The employer's contribution is vested immediately, which means that it belongs to the employee. Because this is basically an IRA, all of the IRS rules pertaining to IRAs apply here. But there is one exception that you need to know about: Withdrawals made before age $59^1/_2$ and within the first two years that an employee is enrolled in the plan are not subject to that 10 percent penalty we keep mentioning. "Yay," you say. Wrong! They're subject to a 25 percent penalty. Ouch! Congress does not want you messing with your retirement dollars.

SIMPLE IRA plans are easy to set up, but they must be set up by October 1 of the first year you start the plan. Most large mutual fund companies have standard plans that they can offer you, and they function as both the administrator and the trustee.

SEP-IRAs

An SEP-IRA is a Simplified Employee Pension plan that uses an IRA format. A SEP is by far the easiest self-employment plan to set up and use. A call to your favorite mutual fund company will get you an application as well as help in calculating how much you can contribute.

The employer's maximum annual contribution rate is the lesser of 15 percent of the employee's compensation or $25,500. The maximum amount of compensation that can be used in determining contributions is $170,000. The contributions are deductible for the tax year for which they are made, and they can be made when you file your tax return.

Say What?

You're a **sole proprietor** if you own and operate an unincorporated business with no partner as a co-owner. Your part-time business buying second-hand lamps at flea markets and selling them as antiques on the Internet is a sole proprietorship. You file a Schedule C with your Form 1040 detailing your income and expenses relating to your business.

If you're a *sole proprietor,* your compensation is the net earnings that you report on a Schedule C of Form 1040 after deducting your SEP-IRA contribution. There's a formula to help you calculate this in Publication 590, "Individual Retirement Arrangements."

If you have employees, they must be included in the plan. They receive the same contribution percentage of compensation that you choose for yourself. You, as the employer, contribute directly into their self-directed IRA accounts, and they make the investment choices. If you're having a poor year, you are not required to contribute to the SEP for you or your employees.

An employee is anyone who meets all the following criteria:

➤ Is at least 21 years of age

➤ Has performed services for you

➤ Has received at least $400 in compensation

Plan assets compound tax-deferred, and you can't take the money out before you reach 59$^1/_2$. Yup, there's a 10 percent penalty here also. Distributions from the SEP-IRA are treated like distributions from a regular IRA, which we'll look closely at in Chapter 21.

Keogh Plans

Keogh plans come in two types: defined contribution and defined benefit. Defined-contribution plans set aside a specific percent of income/profit each year for the participants. A defined benefit plan sets aside enough money to meet a particular retirement income goal in the future. Defined benefit plans are more expensive to maintain, but they benefit the older owner. You can put away a lot more money to reach your financial goals for retirement. You need a prototype plan that has been approved by the IRS. The large mutual fund companies have prototype plans available and are happy to help set up a Keogh plan.

Defined-benefit Keogh plans allow the self-employed individual to contribute the lesser of 15 percent of earned income (from your Schedule C) or $35,000 into a profit-sharing plan. A money purchase Keogh plan allows you to contribute a set percent of earned income, up to 25 percent or $35,000 per year, whichever is less. But the percent is fixed when you set up the plan and must be contributed each year. That includes any eligible employees that you may have. The profit-sharing plan allows you to change the percentage each year or skip it, if necessary.

If a profit-sharing plan is combined with a money purchase plan, you now can contribute up to 25 percent of earned income or $35,000, whichever is less, but you must split the contributions between the plans. Sound complicated? It is. You will definitely need some help setting these up. But among the plans available to the self-employed, Keoghs offer you the ability to put away the most money for your retirement.

Your employees must be included as well. You can require that they be 21, have worked for you for one year, and be working full-time, if you choose. These plans do have reporting requirements. You must file Form 5500EZ annually with the IRS if you have an employee who isn't your spouse or if the plan has total assets of $100,000.

A Keogh plan behaves like other qualified retirement plans. The assets grow tax-deferred, and if you take the money out before 59$^1/_2$, there will be that ubiquitous 10 percent penalty due—plus ordinary taxes. If you shut down the plan, assets can be rolled into an IRA or left in the Keogh. You can draw down your Keogh after age 59$^1/_2$ just as you would an IRA. In some states, a Keogh account has legal protection from creditors and legal judgments against you.

The Company Pension

The company pension is beginning to resemble the Panda—it's getting close to extinction. A company pension is a plan set up by your employer and, usually, only the employer contributes to it. But in the public sector, such as state governments, the employees also contribute dollars to the pension plan.

The pension is a promise from the company of a future benefit and is referred to as a defined-benefit plan. Pensions have been around since 1900 but became more popular in the 1940s and 1950s when workers were joining unions to get better working conditions and better benefits.

You may have to work for the company or government entity at least five years or more to be eligible for a pension in retirement. Once you have met that requirement, you will be vested. Vested means that you are now eligible to collect the pension benefit sometime in the future, usually when you reach a certain age such as 62. And the longer you work, the larger your future pension will be.

A pension plan is expensive for the employer to provide and plan for. Nobody really knows how long you will live in retirement. They hire well-paid actuaries to make educated estimates of how long the participants will live and how much money the employer must put away each year on behalf of each employee.

What's It Really Worth?

Employers use many different formulas to calculate your pension benefit in retirement. It could be a percentage of your earnings or a fixed amount, such as $20 a month, for each year of service. The formulas get complicated, and you often need a calculator to figure out what you're going to get. Your company benefits office can help you make projections for your financial plan.

Most pensions don't come with a cost-of-living adjustment (COLA). So, if you're going to receive a $30,000 pension in retirement, you need to plan for the ravages of inflation. Thirty grand may sound like a great pension until you factor in inflation. With an average inflation rate of 4 percent, in 10 years your $30,000 pension will have the buying power of only $20,000. Although you may have worked somewhere long enough to receive a pension, it may not be enough in future dollars to live on. The public sector is more likely to have an adjustment for inflation than the private sector.

> **It's Been Said**
>
> "A nickel ain't worth a dime anymore."
>
> —Yogi Berra

What Can Happen to It

There's no law that states that a company has to keep a pension plan. More companies are dissolving their pension plans because of the expense. In some instances, they drop the defined-benefit plan in favor of a 401(k) plan. Other companies have converted the defined-benefit plan to a hybrid plan that exhibits qualities of both a defined-benefit plan and a defined-contribution plan.

The most common of these is called the cash balance plan. The cash balance plan defines a future benefit by using either a percentage of pay formula or a flat dollar formula. The plan guarantees a specified interest rate that the account will earn. Each employee has an individual account. If you leave that employer, the account goes with you and can be rolled over into an IRA. This is a much cheaper plan for the employer to use because the employer has to contribute much less money annually per employee than it would for a defined benefit plan.

The problem comes during the transition period when there is a conversion. The older employees have the ability to stick with the old plan or go with the new one. For them, it's a no-brainer: Stay with the old plan. The younger employees like the cash balance plan because it's portable, and at least it gives them something if they work for a company for only several years. The employee that has 20 or more years of service gets the short end of the stick in these plan conversions.

Take the Money and Run

So how do you get your money out of the company pension plan? Most pension plans do not offer a lump-sum distribution yet. If the company allows a lump-sum distribution, consider taking it and rolling it over into an IRA. You can control how it is invested and take it only when you need it (subject to IRS minimum distribution requirements at age $70^1/_2$).

To set up a rollover IRA account, contact a reputable brokerage or mutual fund company and request the proper forms. You will want your company to do a direct transfer to your new IRA account. Otherwise, your employer will have to withhold 20 percent for taxes. That amount becomes a taxable distribution unless you make it up out of your pocket. Put the money in a money market fund until you have a new investment plan for it.

If your company doesn't offer a lump-sum distribution option, you'll get a monthly check when you reach a certain age and are retired from the company. If you are married, by law you're required to have your spouse as the beneficiary of your pension plan. That said, we'll tell you the ways you are eligible to get at your pension money. Usually you can choose from at least three payment options:

Potholes

The Pension Benefit Guarantee Company (PBGC) is a federal agency that was created to handle pension plans from bankrupt companies. Many pension plans are underfunded based on actuarial projections of how much they should have to cover their obligations in the future. The PBGC is funded by a small, per-employee annual fee. In practice, it's another paper tiger. Congress spends the annual cash flow and writes an IOU.

The government—we the taxpayers—will bail out the agency if too many bankrupt companies dump underfunded pension plans on it. The pressure has been on companies to convert pension plans to something else like the cash balance plan to avert any such problem in the future.

➤ **Life only:** Provides you with a 100 percent benefit of your pension payout. If you're married, your spouse must sign off that he or she understands that when you die, the pension will stop.

➤ **Joint life:** Provides you and your spouse a reduced pension payout, but guarantees that, upon your death, the pension payout will continue for the life of your spouse.

➤ **Period certain:** Provides you a guaranteed number of payments. If you die before receiving them all, the remainder will go to your spouse.

The days when employees worked for 45 years with one employer have gone, for the most part. During the course of your working career, you're likely to have the option to participate in more than one type of retirement plan. A married couple could accumulate quite a few different plans.

Keep track of the ones you're in, and learn your options before you leave for a new job or retire. If you want to move the money to a rollover IRA or a series of rollover IRAs as you take new jobs, you can. This will enable you to keep track of the money more easily and will give you maximum flexibility and options in retirement.

It's not all you need to retire early; you'll also need taxable savings to pay your expenses until you're 70. Then the retirement plan can take over and carry you into your 90s or beyond. The tax-deferred compounding over many years makes a financially comfortable retirement a lot easier. Unless you have a couple million dollars in your retirement plan when you retire, don't plan on tapping it early. You may not have enough left later.

The Least You Need to Know

➤ Any tax-sheltered retirement plan is a gift that you need to use to help you save enough to retire early.

➤ Every plan has its tricks and treats. It's worth understanding them so that you know your options. Ask questions until you know; it's your money.

➤ When you retire, if you can roll over your plan money to an IRA, it's usually a good idea. This way, you can control the investment choices and manage the money better.

➤ Take company stock out of the 401(k) plan when you roll it over. Pay the taxes (and penalty, if you're under $59^1/_2$), and the rest of the profit will be taxed later when you sell shares at the lower capital gains tax rates.

Aaah....

Chapter 21

The IRA: Your Personal Tax Shelter

In This Chapter

➤ Which IRAs you can use

➤ Why and how to convert to a Roth IRA

➤ When to take distributions

➤ How to take early distributions

➤ New rules for minimum distributions

When the IRA was introduced in 1975, it was hailed as a great way for people with no other formal retirement plan or pension to save for retirement. The tax-deferred feature allowed money to compound, untouched by taxes. Because tax rates were much higher back then, that was a very big deal.

The $1,500 allowed per worker was a healthy sum, too. If it was indexed to inflation, it would be $4,850 for 2001, instead of $2,000. But even $2,000 ($4,000 per couple) adds up, especially if you start early and invest it in the stock market. If we're fortunate enough to return to long-term annual returns in the market of 10 percent, serious money can accumulate. Those years of 20 percent-plus returns year after year that we saw in the 1990s are likely to be only a pleasant memory.

There have been major changes in the eligibility rules over the years that limit participation in traditional IRAs. The rules governing distributions before age 59$\frac{1}{2}$ were loosened slightly in 1986. Nondeductible IRAs were introduced for those who didn't qualify for the original IRA because of participation in a plan at work.

From the Hammock

When Individual Retirement Arrangements (the real name) were created, Jim was lucky to find a bank that had set up a program for them. Many banks weren't interested. One banker told him that there wouldn't be enough demand to justify the trouble to set up and administer it. Over the next 10 years, CD rates as high as 15.65 percent gave annual contributions a big boost in dollars, although inflation rapidly eroded the value of those dollars. It was several years before mutual fund companies got in the game.

Say What?

The IRS requires you to begin taking **required minimum distributions** (RMDs) from your IRA and most other retirement accounts by April 1 of the year after you turn 70$^1/_2$. The new rules, issued in January 2001 and effective in 2002, come with a chart specifying how you calculate the amount each year from age 70 to 115 and older. You take the total of the assets in your retirement accounts on December 31 of the previous year and divide that by the distribution period factor for your age. At age 70, this factor is 26.2 years.

In 1998, the Roth IRA debuted. It, too, is a nondeductible contribution of $2,000 per person, but qualified distributions are free of federal tax. In this chapter, we'll look at rules for making contributions and taking distributions from the different plans, and we'll try to help you decide what to do.

Income Limits for Contributions

Rules to determine who is allowed to contribute to which plans, and how much, are somewhat complex. You might expect as much from Congress and the IRS. Different sets of rules often apply for each type of IRA. You should also know that the rules can change, as can the interpretation of the rules at a later date.

There are many ifs, ands, and buts in the rules for the various IRAs. We can't cover them all here. IRS Publication 590, "Individual Retirement Arrangements," covers IRAs, Roth IRAs, SIMPLE IRAs, SEP IRAs, and the Education IRA (which isn't an IRA at all) in only 80 pages, including sample forms and table.

A whole new set of rules (108 pages) covering *required minimum distributions* of traditional IRAs after age 70$^1/_2$ was released on January 11, 2001. It was then suspended by the Bush administration for 60 days on

January 24. It should be effective by the time you read this for 2002 and for people already taking distributions in 2001 if their plan sponsor adopts the rules immediately. But there's no guarantee that these rules won't change now or in the future. Eventually, a new Publication 590 will be available. We try to use the new rules as issued in January throughout the book.

Who Can Contribute?

The basic income qualification rules for traditional and Roth IRAs for 2001 are in the following chart. Except for the Spousal IRA, which we'll discuss in the following section, you must have earned income to qualify each year. That means income reported on a W-2 or a Schedule C (for self-employment income).

The phaseout levels for traditional IRAs are indexed to inflation, so they'll increase a bit each year. The contribution limit in all cases is $2,000 per person per year. With earnings of less than $2,000, the full earnings amount can be contributed as long as the other rules are met. Congress is again looking at increasing this limit. Someday, it will.

A Nugget of Gold

If you get taxable alimony, that counts as income for determining income limits and for calculating allowable contributions. However, alimony received under a written agreement that is not part of a divorce decree doesn't count toward either income or contribution limits.

The income levels are based on modified adjusted gross income (MAGI), not your paycheck. MAGI is usually your total income reported on a Form 1040 or 1040A before *any* deductions. Then you have to add the following:

➤ Any foreign earned income that you elected to exclude, and related deductions

➤ Qualified EE U.S. Savings Bond interest reported on Form 8815 for qualified education expenses

➤ Any employer-paid adoption expenses reported on Form 8839

Status	MAGI	
Traditional IRA—Under Age 70¹/₂		**Deduction Allowed**
Covered by plan at work		
Single	Under $33,000	Full deduction
	$33,000–$43,000	Partial deduction
Married, filing jointly (MFJ)	Under $53,000	Full deduction
	$53,000–$63,000	Partial deduction

continues

continued

Status	MAGI	
No plan at work		**Deduction Allowed**
Single	Any income	Full deduction
MFJ	Under $150,000	Full deduction
	$150,000–$160,000	Partial deduction
Roth IRA—Any Age		**Contribution**
Single	Under $95,000	$2,000
	$95,000–$110,000	Partial deduction
MFJ	Under $150,000	$2,000 each
	$150,000–$160,000	Partial deduction

Married persons filing separately are limited to an income of only $10,000 to qualify for either IRA. The only exception is if you didn't live with your spouse at any time during the year. If you file as the head of the household, the rules are the same as for singles.

Partial deductions or contributions in the phaseout ranges are calculated using a form for traditional IRAs in your IRS 1040 instructions. For Roth IRAs, or if you contribute to both types of IRA in the same year, you follow instructions in Publication 590 to determine the allowable amount that you may contribute. The Roth IRA is almost ignored in current 1040 instructions.

Spousal IRAs

A Spousal IRA may be funded up to $2,000 for a spouse with little or no earned income, subject to the rules in the preceding table. A Spousal IRA contribution is limited by the earned income of both spouses filing a joint return (MFJ), minus any IRA contribution on behalf of the first spouse. If a total of $4,000 or more of earned income is reported, contributions of $2,000 may be made for each spouse.

This is a great way to increase IRA contributions in any year that one spouse has little or no earned income. In all other cases, each spouse figures the contribution limit based on personal earned income and whether each is covered by a plan at work.

Traditional or Roth IRA?

If you're covered under a retirement plan at work (even if you're not vested yet) and your income exceeds the limits for a traditional IRA, you have no choice: Use a Roth IRA. If you're not covered at work—even if your spouse is—the total income limit is much higher, so you may have a choice.

Let's look at three couples, all age 35, saving for retirement. The Arthurs contribute $2,000 each every year for the next 20 years in traditional IRAs. The Benders do the same, but they use Roth IRAs. And the Cowleys didn't use either; they just socked away $4,000 a year in a taxable account.

Let's assume that they all use our basic investment strategy portfolio, putting 80 percent in an S&P Index fund and 20 percent in a U.S. Treasury bond fund. They all retire at age 55 and allow their contributions to keep growing, untouched, until age 70. We'll also assume that they're all in the 28 percent federal tax bracket until they retire. After that, they'll drop to the 15 percent bracket. (Your results will differ, depending on your tax brackets during these years.)

At age 70, the couples all switch allocation to 70 percent equity, and, at age 85, to 30 percent equity. Then they begin taking the money over 25 years. They all use a declining years method to calculate how much to withdraw each year ($1/25$ the first year, $1/24$ the second year, and so on). This keeps them ahead of the minimum distribution required (MDR) rules, but they have taken all the money after 25 years. How do they match up?

It's Been Said

"The safest way to double your money is to fold it over and put it back in your pocket."

—Kin Hubbard

	Arthurs	Benders	Cowleys
Contribution	80,000	80,000	80,000
After-tax cost	80,000	111,120	111,120
Value at age 55	229,100	229,100	214,020
Value at age 70	957,008	957,008	858,292
25 years of withdrawals	3,199,420	3,199,420	2,647,521
Tax rate on withdrawals	15%	0	8%
Tax paid on withdrawals	479,924	0	211,801
Net withdrawals	2,719,496	3,199,420	2,435,720
1st-year net withdrawals	32,538	38,280	31,585
25th-year net withdrawals	232,443	273,463	196,276

The Arthurs made tax-deductible contributions each year, saving $1,120 (at a 28 percent tax rate) in taxes. The other couples needed to earn $5,556 on which they paid $1,556 in taxes to save $4,000 each year. Over the 20 years, the Benders and the Cowleys had to devote 39 percent more of their incomes than the Arthurs to save the same $80,000. The difference is solely in federal taxes.

The Cowleys had to pay taxes on the dividends paid by their funds each year. Even though it's a fairly tax-efficient portfolio, the taxes cut the annual growth by 0.6 percent, from 10 percent to 9.4 percent. Consequently, they had accumulated less when they retired. And after 15 more years, the Cowleys, still paying taxes on the dividends (though at a lower rate of 15 percent), had $98,716 less.

Who Did Best?

After age 70, the Arthurs had to pay taxes on distributions at regular rates—in their case, 15 percent. The Benders took their distributions from their Roth IRAs tax-free. And the Cowleys cashed in shares at long-term capital gain rates of 8 percent (for those in the 15 percent tax bracket), while still paying taxes at 15 percent on their dividends.

Obviously, all made out well with their plan; that's what saving and compounding does for you over long periods. After tax, the Benders did best, with 17.7 percent more than the Arthurs and 31.3 percent more than the Cowleys. The Roth IRA gave them an average after-tax amount of $127,977 each year, compared to $108,780 for the Arthurs and $97,429 for the Cowleys.

This is one advantage of the Roth IRA, though not necessarily the biggest. Another advantage is that the Benders don't have to take any distribution if they don't need the money. It could keep growing, and they can pass it on to their kids or grandkids by naming them as beneficiaries of the Roth IRAs. Or, they could donate some or all of the money to their favorite charities after death. They have options.

The third advantage of the Roth IRA is the tax advantage. Regardless of their tax bracket in retirement, the money is tax-free to them. If the Arthurs and Cowleys were in higher tax brackets after they retired, their taxes jump to 28 percent (the Arthurs) and 18 percent (the Cowleys).

You don't even know for sure what your tax bracket may be next year. With Congress (as of this writing) in a tax-cutting mood, no one will know for the next few years. Other years, Congress decides to raise taxes. What will tax rates and brackets look like in 35 years? The Roth IRA is a way to make that a nonissue for you. Yes, Congress could decide to tax Roth IRA balances or distributions down the road. We wouldn't want to run for reelection to Congress after either move, though.

Here's one more way of looking at our three couples. Remember how the Arthurs made tax-deductible contributions? Their net cost of $80,000 grew 34 times after taxes by the time they finished taking 25 years of distributions. The Benders and the Cowleys had to pay taxes on $5,556 a year to save their $4,000. The Benders generated 28.8 times their total cost of $111,120, and the Cowleys harvested 21.9 times the same cost.

The traditional IRA is much more efficient than the Roth IRA. If the tax on the distribution is 28 percent, the actual dollars distributed are the same after tax. The Arthurs would still generate 28.8 times their contributions. What if the Arthurs put the $1,556 they saved each year in taxes into a taxable investment account? At age 70, there would be another $320,400 to fund their golden years.

What Should You Do?

The future is uncertain. The first answer, of course, is to do something, even if you have a retirement plan at work. You need to save more to reach financial freedom. If you can do a traditional IRA because your income is below the thresholds, and if you're under 35, do the Roth anyway. The tax deduction is nice but not worth the taxes you're likely to pay later.

Here's a table that can help you decide not only which type of IRA you can use, but which type we suggest is the most advantageous for you to use.

Are You Covered in a Plan at Work?	Filing Status	MAGI Income on Tax Return	Recommendation
Covered	Single	Less than $33,000	Roth IRA*
		$33,000–$43,000	Some in both
		$43,000–$95,000	Roth IRA
		$95,000–$110,000	Part Roth and save
	MFJ	Less than $63,000	Roth IRA*
		$63,000–$150,000	Roth IRA
		$150,000–$160,000	Part Roth and save
		Over $160,000	taxable savings
Not covered	Single	Less than $41,000	Roth IRA*
		$41,000–$110,000	Either or split
		Over $110,000	Traditional IRA
	MFJ	Less than $62,000	Roth IRA*
		$62,000–$160,000	Either or split
		Over $160,000	Taxable savings

Although you're allowed to take the traditional IRA in the lower income brackets, the tax deduction at 15 percent isn't worth the taxes you'll have to pay later. And, if you're in a plan at work, then you'll have both a taxable and a nontaxable plan to use in retirement.

Over the Limits

If you're single and not in a plan at work, there's no income limit for contributing to a traditional IRA. But, if you're married, either IRA is out of bounds when MAGI exceeds $160,000. Go figure. At this point, your only IRA option is the nondeductible traditional IRA. You have to file a Form 8606 each year that you contribute or withdraw money.

You'll pay taxes at ordinary tax rates on most of the distributions. You use a formula each year that exempts the portion of the IRA represented by your taxable contributions. The tax deferral on the growth of nondeductible contributions is beneficial. However, putting the money in a taxable account and investing it in a total market index fund is very tax-efficient.

When you sell your index fund shares in the taxable account many years from now, your gain may be taxed at a lower long-term capital gain rate, as it currently is (we can hope that continues). You're likely to come out ahead doing this, and you'll skip all that paperwork and the calculations. Of course, you're saving like crazy anyway in taxable accounts, right? So ignore the IRAs altogether, and don't feel too bad that you make too much money for an IRA.

A Nugget of Gold

A rollover, whether for a Roth conversion, to change trustees, or to roll over 401(k) plan money to an IRA, is dangerous. Once you get the money, the IRS is notified. If you don't get it into a qualified IRA within 60 days, you owe taxes and a 10 percent penalty.

But, even if you do it in time, there's still a "penalty" of sorts. The first trustee is required by the IRS to withhold 20 percent. You have to make up that 20 percent, or that 20 percent is considered a taxable distribution. You owe taxes on it plus the extra 10 percent tax for an early distribution if you're under 59$^1/_2$. Of course, you get a withholding credit on your 1040 for that money. The message? Don't do the rollover yourself; use one of the other methods.

To Rothify or Not: Converting Your Traditional IRA

If you've been saving in a traditional IRA (or a nondeductible IRA), you have the opportunity to convert to a Roth IRA. This will allow the money to grow tax-free, and you can take tax-free distributions in the future. There are three ways to convert:

➤ **Rollover:** Take a distribution from your traditional IRA and contribute it to a Roth IRA within 60 days.

➤ **Trustee-to-trustee transfer:** You instruct the trustee of your traditional IRA to transfer an amount to the trustee of the Roth IRA. The latter can provide you with the necessary forms when you set up the account.

➤ **Same-trustee transfer:** Keep the transfer in-house if the trustee offers both plans. Most do. In practice, if the entire account is converted at once, the trustee just redesignates the account as a Roth IRA.

For the last two options, you're allowed to convert your investments as they are—funds, stocks, bonds, and so forth—rather than selling them and repurchasing them in the Roth account. Both accounts need to be brokerage accounts for stocks and bonds. However, problems may crop up with trustee-to-trustee transfers if the Roth trustee doesn't offer the particular funds that you own. It could take a lot of phone calls and letters over many months to locate the transferred funds, even though it shouldn't be such a problem. Look closely before you transfer your account between trustees.

More Limits

You can convert to a Roth IRA only if you're single, or married and filing a joint return (MFJ). Your MAGI, not counting the conversion amount, must be less than $100,000 in the year you begin the conversion process. If you're married and filing separately, you may not convert at all for that year.

What happens if you convert and then you get a big end-of-year bonus that puts you over the $100,000? You have a failed conversion. You can recharacterize your Roth IRA back to a traditional IRA. Contact the trustee of the Roth IRA for instructions immediately. The recharacterization must be done before the due date of your tax return for the year in which the problem arose.

Taxes

When you convert to a Roth IRA, you owe taxes on all but the nondeductible contributions, if any, at your regular tax rates. The amount converted is reported on Form 8606. This form will help you figure the amount to report on your 1040 (usually all of it).

If the conversion amount is significant, it could put some of the money in a higher tax bracket. Therefore, you might convert a part of your traditional IRA each year in amounts that don't push you into a higher bracket. That takes some good tax planning toward the end of each year, however.

The financial key to justifying the conversion to a Roth IRA is that you can pay the additional tax from non-IRA funds. If you convert $30,000 and owe $8,400 in taxes on the conversion, pay that $8,400 out of your taxable account money. And don't sell anything to raise the cash if it creates a capital gain, either. If you can't use free cash, don't convert. It may not pay off, even in the long run.

There are other downsides to the conversion besides just paying the taxes. That tax money could be invested for the long term and grow to become serious money. The conversion amount also affects all tax limits and thresholds for medical expense

Potholes

A failed conversion that isn't recharacterized in a timely manner costs you a 10 percent penalty in addition to the regular tax. Plus, there's a 6 percent excise tax per year on any contribution not withdrawn from the Roth IRA. A tax professional should be consulted before you do a conversion to help you run the numbers and to make sure that the ifs, ands, and buts are all considered.

deductions (7.5 percent of AGI), miscellaneous deductions (2 percent of AGI), and any tax credits that you would otherwise be allowed.

Should You Convert?

You might consider a partial or full conversion under these circumstances:

➤ You know that you'll qualify that year.

➤ The conversion doesn't raise your tax bracket above 31 percent.

➤ You can pay the tax due from other funds.

➤ You don't need the money for 20 years or so.

This issue has no easy answers and has generated more heat than light among planners and others. Calculators on the Internet can help you, but they don't consider every detail. And most don't consider what you could do with the money that you use to pay the taxes, either. The biggest problem is that no one knows what tax bracket you'll be in when you take money out of a traditional IRA. Ultimately, that may make the biggest difference.

Look at the calculators at http://news.morningstar.com/news/ms/NumberCrunchers/calcs.html, www.rothira.com, www.fairmark.com, and others that you may find at your favorite financial sites. Your tax professional should have a way to help you evaluate the issue. Don't go for any quick and easy answers; you now know that it isn't an easy question. Our suggestion is to consider a partial conversion at some point, if you can meet the preceding requirements. That way, you'll have some money in each, and you'll have more options in retirement.

How to Get Money Out

We've said all along that the longer you can wait, the more money you'll have. The effect of compounding is incredible in the later years. Plan to live off your taxable savings, Social Security, and pension as long as you can. Sooner or later, however, most people need some money from a retirement plan.

Withdrawing Money from a Roth IRA

We'll take the "easy" one first, the Roth IRA. You never have to take distributions of this money while you're alive. And neither does your spouse as a sole beneficiary, if the spouse elects to treat it as his own Roth IRA. When you need to use the money, there can be a qualified distribution after the fifth tax year following the year for which you made the initial contribution and in one of the following circumstances:

➤ You're $59^1/_2$.

➤ You're disabled.

➤ You're deceased, and the beneficiary takes a distribution.

➤ You (and your spouse) qualify as "first-time" homebuyers.

For the last two circumstances, we refer you to Publication 590 or your tax adviser. If you convert to a Roth IRA, each conversion date begins its own five-year time frame before qualified distributions can be taken. The five tax years required begin the year for which you make the conversion or contribution, even though the money might not be received in the account until the following year.

If the distribution isn't qualified, or if it is premature (before the five years pass), you owe a 10 percent tax on the part of the distribution that represents your contribution or conversion amounts. You owe regular taxes plus the 10 percent penalty on any earnings in the Roth IRA that are prematurely distributed. Your contributions are counted first, followed by the conversion amounts and then the earnings. There are exceptions to avoid this tax, in addition to the four preceding circumstances:

➤ The distributions are part of a series of substantially equal payments.

➤ You have significant medical expenses that have not been reimbursed.

➤ You're paying medical insurance premiums after losing your job.

➤ The amount isn't more than any qualified education expenses that you pay that year.

➤ The amount is due to an IRS levy of the plan.

Potholes

For any distributions from traditional IRAs, the trustee is required to withhold 10 percent and send it to the IRS. You can file a form with the trustee requesting no withholding for each IRA you have. If you're a U.S. citizen or resident alien living outside the United States, you aren't allowed this option. The IRS wants to keep you on a leash.

If you begin a program to withdraw substantially equal amounts from your IRA, Roth or traditional, before age 59$^1/_2$, you must continue the program for at least five years *and* until you are 59$^1/_2$. No change is allowed, or the 10 percent penalty is retroactive to the first distribution. You will also owe the IRS interest on all previous withdrawals. There are three IRS-approved methods to calculate the amount that you're allowed to take, each with a different amount as a result.

In short, if you need money before age 59$^1/_2$ and the five years have passed, get the help of a qualified tax professional before you do anything. But, if you need to tap your retirement plans only because you retired early, you retired too soon. What will you live on in your old age?

Withdrawing Money from a Traditional IRA

You can take distributions from traditional IRAs before age 59$^1/_2$ without paying the 10 percent penalty if you meet the same conditions listed in the preceding section on Roth IRAs. Of course, you will owe taxes on the distributions at your ordinary income tax rates. You should also consult with a tax adviser first.

After age 59^1/$_2$, you can take any amount that you want without a penalty. Only your regular tax rates apply on everything except any nondeductible contributions that you made and filed on a Form 8606. By April 1 of the year after you turn 70^1/$_2$, you must take a required minimum distribution (RMD) each year. There's a 50 percent excise tax on the difference if you fall short of the RMD in any year.

We suggest that you plan on taking the first year's distribution in the year you turn 70^1/$_2$. Otherwise, you must take two RMDs the following year: one by April 1 and one by December 31. That may put some of the money in a higher tax bracket. There's no sense giving the IRS money that you don't have to. Take your first distribution three months early.

A Nugget of Gold

As these new rules are examined and tested, the whole area of beneficiaries and inheritors will become clearer. A variety of tricks and treats are involved that will take some time to be fully interpreted. Your estate planning process should take this into account, and you may need to periodically review your estate plan once it is set up under the new rules.

Be careful with your estate planning so that one person doesn't get the IRA and another person is required to pay the estate taxes on it. You should have a beneficiary at all times, however. Otherwise, the IRA becomes part of your estate and is subject to claims against it. And if you use trusts, IRAs and trusts don't always mix well. Be sure to get competent advice in this area before you commit your IRA to a trust.

New Distribution Rules

From this point on, the rules appear to have changed completely with the January 11, 2001, proposed required distribution rules issued by the Treasury Department. They're much simpler and are generally beneficial to you. The IRS stated on January 12 that the old withdrawal rules were "unreasonably restrictive" and "too complex." Evidently, even the IRS couldn't figure them all out to collect the money that it felt it was owed. It's worth noting that the old rules were proposed in 1987 but never officially adopted as final. Nevertheless, they were the only rules.

Under the proposed new rules, there's only one table to calculate your MDR every year, and it ensures that your money can last forever if you take only the minimum. The new rules automatically assume your beneficiary is 10 years younger. This stretches out the life expectancy number you use to calculate you RMD. If your spouse is the sole beneficiary and is more than 10 years younger, you may elect the old joint life expectancy table from Publication 590. This stretches out the distributions a bit more.

You also have more flexibility in naming beneficiaries. You can change your mind after you begin taking distributions. And the final decision on beneficiaries isn't made until the end of the year following your death. The beneficiaries that you named can sort things out among themselves for the most tax-efficient way to pass on the money.

Upon your death, each nonspousal beneficiary's life expectancy determines his RMD after that. In the absence of any beneficiaries, inheritors of the IRA from your estate may also be able to use their life expectancies to take distributions.

One new requirement of the proposed rules orders the custodian of your account (the fund, brokerage, bank, or trust) to report the RMD to you and the IRS each year after you turn $70^{1}/_{2}$. If you have more than one IRA, you can still take distributions from them in any way you want, as long as the total equals or exceeds your RMD for the year. The IRS will do the math to check that it all adds up properly.

Annuities

Many early IRAs were set up to make it easy to convert them to a *fixed annuity* that pays a guaranteed sum every year for life. We looked at annuities for retirement in Chapter 20, "Keep the Taxman Waiting While You Work." They didn't look so good then, and they don't look any better here.

You now know that a fixed income is slowly but surely destroyed by inflation. You can't depend on a fixed income to support you for 30 or 40 years in retirement. Perhaps at age 85 or so, you may want to consider this option with part of your money, but not all of it.

A variable annuity gives you options to invest in the stock market with mutual fund subaccounts. However, the price that you pay for this annuity, the fees to the insurance company and the mutual funds, and the insurance charge will reduce your growth considerably. All the insurance covers is a guarantee from the company to your beneficiary that, at your death, your account will be no less than what you contributed. And when you take money out of the annuity, the contributions are counted first.

The new distribution rules combined with our basic investment strategy in Chapter 12, "How to Pay for Your Goals," will serve you much better.

Say What?

A **fixed annuity** is a contract with an insurance company. In return for giving the company a sum of cash, the company agrees to pay you a fixed income for a set period, your lifetime, or your lifetime and your spouse's lifetime. The payments are guaranteed by the insurance company, so the financial health of the company is critical.

Potholes

We strongly recommend against using an annuity of any kind inside an IRA or other tax-sheltered retirement plan. An accumulation annuity is a financial product sold by insurance companies that allows money to grow tax-deferred. You already have a tax shelter. The extra fees for an annuity greatly reduce your long-term return. As of this writing, five insurance companies are being sued for selling annuities inside retirement plans. You can do much better with a low-cost index fund.

The MDR schedule increases payouts automatically, unless your IRA is temporarily reduced by a drop in the stock market. Then your fixed-income portion provides your distributions until the market recovers. And you can always take out more than the MDR because it's your money. You can't do that with a fixed annuity.

If your retirement plan is an annuity such as a 403(b) or 457 plan, you can roll part of your distributions into a traditional IRA. When you're eligible for distributions, you are allowed to roll over any amount that would otherwise be taxable to you. You have 60 days to do this.

You're better off instructing your plan administrator to make the rollover directly to an IRA and avoid any tax withholding. The company where you set up your IRA can help you, but your plan administrator is supposed to give you this option before your first distribution. You can control the money in your IRA and take distributions when you need them, subject to the MDR rules.

The Least You Need to Know

➤ There are often no clear answers on which IRA to use if you have a choice. The future is uncertain. You can choose both, making partial contributions or alternating years.

➤ If you don't have a choice on which IRA to use, take advantage of the one you can. And if you can't use a traditional IRA or a Roth IRA, save more in a tax-efficient index fund instead.

➤ Pay careful attention to income limits. If you make a mistake, you're allowed to correct it before your tax return for that year is due.

➤ Tax-wise, converting to a Roth IRA may be a good gamble on an unknown future.

➤ New rules in 2001 simplify the choices for taking minimum distributions after age $70\frac{1}{2}$ from a traditional IRA.

Social Insecurity and Mediscare

For most of you, when you retire early, Social Security will play a role at some point. Although you may begin collecting benefits at age 62, they'll be significantly reduced compared to those for someone who retires at full retirement age, or even someone who works until age 62. The benefits will make a difference to you, if only because they'll assist you in dealing with the effect of inflation on your expenses.

Social Security may also enable you to keep your hands off your tax-sheltered retirement plan money for up to eight more years. This will allow it to continue compounding, tax-deferred, until age 70. How Social Security will work and how much you'll actually receive in benefits many decades in the future is unknown. Some form of the program will exist, and you will receive some benefits. But, as an early retiree, we don't think that Social Security should play a big role in your retirement planning.

What Social Security Really Is

The Social Security program is neither an investment program nor an insurance program, strictly speaking. There's no guarantee that you'll get anything in return for your contributions today. Most of the money collected each year goes right back out to pay current benefits. Future benefits are at the mercy of each Congress. This was made clear when the program began. We quote from the notice from Social Security that was posted at workplaces at the inception of the program: "There's no guarantee that the fund thus collected will ever be returned to you. What happens to the money is up to each congress."

Congress has always been eager to raise benefits but unwilling to raise taxes to support the benefits until an emergency arises. Despite the brave talk in Washington, there's no reason that this will change. Whenever it is determined that something must be done to save the system, something will be done. What that is, know one knows. And only time will tell whether it will work.

The History

The Social Security Act was passed by Congress and signed by President Roosevelt on August 14, 1937. It was designed to pay a small benefit to retired workers age 65 and older beginning in 1942. The life expectancy of Americans was about 63 at the time. Few people anticipated that life expectancies would continue to increase as much as they have since then.

Congress added survivor benefits in 1939 for the worker's spouse and children, and added disability benefits in 1956. Benefit levels and calculation formulas to increase benefits were enacted several times. One of the goals was to reduce poverty among our older citizens, especially women. Today, women comprise about 72 percent of beneficiaries over age 85. Social Security represents 90 percent of income for 41 percent of older women, and it is the total income for 25 percent of them.

The average monthly benefits paid in 2001 are as follows:

> All retired workers: $845
>
> Retired couples: $1,410
>
> Aged widow(er): $811
>
> Widowed mother with two children: $1696
>
> Disabled worker: $786
>
> Disabled worker, spouse, and one or more children: $1,310

More than 44 million people collect Social Security benefits, 7.5 million collect survivor benefits, and more than 6 million get disability benefits. Beginning in 2008, 76 million baby boomers will start turning 62. The strain on the system that this causes will be the catalyst for changes between now and 2015.

The Future

The problem isn't so much that the baby boomers are going to be retiring and collecting benefits; that's been known for some time. They've been paying into the system at higher and higher rates of taxation to try to prepare for that. The problem is two-fold, aside from the political one in Washington.

First, the next generation after the baby boomers was originally labeled the baby bust generation because they were far fewer in number than the boomers. The number of workers supporting a retiree was 16 in 1950. Today it's only four, and by 2025 it's expected that there'll be only two workers per retiree. Do you know two kids who will want to pay all of your Social Security out of their paychecks after 2025?

From the Hammock

No one likes paying the Social Security and Medicare tax out of each paycheck, and for many people it's a larger amount than their income tax withholding each paycheck. We try to remember two groups who are collecting the money whenever we start grumbling about it. First, many families who have lost a breadwinning parent receive survivor benefits which often make a big difference in how the children grow up. The second group is millions of elderly women who outlived their husbands and their savings. This is the only income they have, and it usually isn't very much. Thinking about these people allows us to move on in a better frame of mind.

The second problem is the fact that we're living so much longer, collectively. We may or may not see an extension of human life through medical science much beyond age 100, but more of us will make it to our 90s. And we'll still be collecting Social Security. That no one has a good idea of how many of us will see our 90s prevents firm Social Security financial planning today. They know it's coming; the fastest-growing age group now is people in their 80s.

Without any significant changes, the combined Social Security, Medicare, Medicaid, and Federal Employees Retirement System will consume the entire federal budget by 2030. That's according to the 1994 Interim Report to the President by The Bipartisan Commission of Entitlement and Tax Reform. This assumes that the federal tax take maintains its historical 20 percent or so of the country's gross domestic product (GDP). Something's gotta give before then.

What You Should Expect

We're not going to try to sugarcoat this. Based on the preceding information, either taxes of all kinds will get raised, big time, or the retirement payouts will be reduced in some fashion. Probably some combination of both will happen. These actions represent two of the three possibilities that our elected representatives hate most. The third is losing elections, which the first two have a tendency to cause. Whatever happens isn't likely to be pretty.

A Nugget of Gold

The Social Security Administration has begun mailing out Social Security statements on an annual basis, shortly before your birthday. If you didn't get one, call 1–800–772–1213, or visit www.ssa.gov to request one. This will give you a better idea of what you may look forward to at age 62. More important, whenever you receive a statement, check the earnings record for the past several years for accuracy. If you aren't getting credit for earnings, call 1–800–772–1213 with your W–2s or tax returns in hand.

As a wealthy early retiree, you should look forward to these pleasantries:

➤ Not collecting much from Social Security

➤ Paying federal income tax on what you do get

➤ Paying more taxes on your unearned income

As we suggested in Chapter 8, "Estimating Your Retirement Costs," through Chapter 10, "Achieving Your Retirement Goals," your Social Security benefit may be enough to cover your out-of-pocket healthcare expenses, including premiums for Medigap Insurance (more on Medicare in a bit). Or maybe not. Healthcare expenses are likely to be one of biggest expenses (if not *the* biggest expense) you'll face throughout your retirement. It's as difficult to project those expenses as it is to project your Social Security benefit.

You may have received a Social Security statement projecting your benefits at various ages in the future. It also shows the benefits that you or your family would qualify for if you die this year or become severely disabled. The projections for retirement benefits assume that your current earnings will increase at a projected wage inflation rate until the specified ages at which you can collect. When you retire before age 62, you won't receive even the lowest benefit cited on the statement.

How Your Benefit Is Reduced

By 2022, under current rules, the amount for someone who begins to collect benefits at age 62 will be 70 percent of full retirement benefits. By then, the age for full retirement benefits will be approaching 67 at the rate of two months for each year you were born after 1954. You can find your full retirement age in the following chart.

Retirement Age for Full Benefits

Birth	Year Age
Before	
1938	65 and 2 months
1939	65 and 4 months
1940	65 and 6 months
1941	65 and 8 months
1942	65 and 10 months
1943–1954	66
1955	66 and 2 months
1956	66 and 4 months
1957	66 and 6 months
1958	66 and 8 months
1959	66 and 10 months
After	
1959	67

The formula that the Social Security Administration uses to calculate benefits now works like this:

1. They take the number of years you worked, up to 35. If you worked more than 35 years, they use the 35 years with the highest income.

2. They adjust the earnings year by year to current dollars for wage inflation.

3. They determine your average adjusted monthly earnings based on the number of years in step 1.

4. They apply a complex formula to the average monthly earnings in step 3 to determine a percentage of those earnings as your full retirement benefit.

5. This full retirement benefit amount is then reduced based on how long before your full retirement age you apply to collect your benefit.

You can see how your benefit is reduced when you voluntarily give up your high earning years by retiring early. If you retire so early that you don't have 35 years of earnings, the Social Security Administration uses zeros for those years, further reducing your average.

In Chapter 9, "How to Pay Your Expenses in Retirement," we made a ballpark estimate of retirement benefits based on a percentage of benefits at age 62. For a person retiring at age 55, we used 80 percent; at age 50, perhaps 75 percent; and at age 45, maybe 70 percent. The resulting earnings estimates may appear high, and they may be. But your average monthly earnings are depressed by retiring early. The Social

Security system is skewed to provide a higher percent of benefits to lower-income workers. So, it's not a flat-percent reduction in benefits as a result of retiring early.

It's Been Said

"I don't know how much money I have in the bank. I haven't shaken it lately."

—Milton Berle

A Nugget of Gold

There's a lot of useful information at the Social Security Web site. You can see what your projected life expectancy is at www.ssa.gov/search/index.htm. Enter "life expectancy," and click on the Life Expectancy for Social Security button. You can also play with projected benefits at various ages at www.ssa.gov/ retire/calculators.htm. Remember that the projections assume that you'll work at your current income, increased by inflation annually, until the age that you enter for applying for benefits. If you retire early, you'll have to discount the numbers given.

You can choose to delay applying for benefits beyond age 62, if you want. After 2022, each month you wait beyond 62, your benefit increases by half of 1 percent until your full retirement age. You come out ahead by around age 74 if you wait until your full retirement age to apply. If you need the money before age 66 or 67, there's no reason to wait.

The biggest cloud in our crystal ball, of course, is the nature of the changes that Congress will make over the next 30 years. Your guess is as good as ours. For these reasons, you might decide to plan your retirement finances without any Social Security. Then anything that you receive, after taxes, will be a bonus.

Spousal Benefits

If you were married for at least 10 years, you are entitled to collect benefits based on your own earnings, or based on half of your spouse's benefit, whichever is greater. If you begin collecting at age 62 on your spouse's earnings, your benefit will be reduced accordingly compared to the potential full retirement benefit. Your spouse also must be collecting for you to file this way.

You can file under your own earnings at age 62 if your spouse is still working. Later, when your spouse also retires and begins collecting, you can switch and collect half of your spouse's benefit if it would be higher than yours. You may also collect on a former spouse's Social Security record if the ex-spouse is receiving benefits or is deceased. You must meet these qualification:

➤ Be presently unmarried

➤ Have been married to that spouse at least 10 years

➤ Be at least age 62 if the spouse is alive (60, if the spouse is deceased)

If you remarried before age 60, you cannot receive a widow's benefit as long as you're married. But, if you remarry after age 60, you may continue to receive benefits based on your deceased spouse's record. If you have been divorced at least two years and your ex-spouse is 62, you can apply at age 62 for spousal benefits even if the ex-spouse is still working. You must still meet the preceding requirements, however.

When to Take It

Our first suggestion is to take it when you need it after you turn 62. If you don't need it because you can live comfortably on your taxable savings until later, it may pay to wait a few years. If you can wait until your full retirement age, you'll lock in the higher benefit level for the rest of your life.

"The rest of your life" is the important phrase. If you're in good health and your parents lived long and healthy lives, the odds are pretty good that you will, too. At age 90, the higher benefit level from waiting a few years to begin collecting may come in handy. That's a call that you'll have to make when you're in your 60s. Then you can see how your retirement finances are shaping up.

As the program changes in coming years, all kinds of advice will be available on what you can do. That's just one reason why you should revisit your financial plan every few years to update it. If the program changes as much as some are calling for, you can make any necessary changes to your plan to account for them.

Potholes

If you continue to work while collecting Social Security benefits before you reach your "full retirement age," the cost can be very high. On your earned income, you will owe your regular federal and state taxes plus payroll taxes for Social Security and Medicare. If you're making a good income and it puts you in the 28 percent federal bracket, this tax rate total could exceed 40 percent.

Then your Social Security is reduced by $1 for every $2 that you earn over the limit. In effect, you pay a 50 percent tax on your benefit. Finally, 85 percent of the remainder of the benefit is taxed at 28 percent, too. It's not worth collecting under those circum-stances. Wait until you stop working or are working less before you file for your benefit. Your benefit will also be higher because you waited.

Taxing Your Benefit

If you're working part-time and you begin to collect Social Security before your "full retirement age" (65 to 67, depending on the year you were born), your benefit may be reduced. In 2001, when your earned income exceeds $890 in a month, you lose $1 of your benefit for every $2 that you earn over that limit. The annual earnings limit is $10,680, but the calculation is done monthly. Your monthly benefit is reduced following any month in which you earn more than $890. This calculation is per person, so you may collect benefits without a penalty while your spouse works full-time.

For purposes of income taxes on Social Security, your tax filing status and your *provisional income* determine and how much of your Social Security benefit is taxed.

Current laws tax Social Security payments based on the amount of your provisional income as shown in the following table.

Filing Status	Provisional Income	Amount Subject to Federal Tax
Single or head of household	Under $25,000 $25,000–$34,000 over $34,000	None 50% Up to 85%
Married, filing jointly (MFJ)	Under $32,000 $32,000–$44,000 Over $44,000	None 50% Up to 85%
Married, filing separately	Any income*	Up to 85%

Unless you lived apart from your spouse for the entire year—in this case, the single limits apply.

These income limits are not indexed to inflation. Congress periodically thinks about eliminating the 85 percent tax level and just taxing 50 percent of the benefit. That might happen, but our guess is that Congress will decide to raise the income limits instead. Means-testing is how the government can afford to increase benefits to lower-income and poor people. Remember, Social Security benefits are up to each Congress to pay or not pay as they wish.

Medicare

Medicare was created in 1965 to provide a basic level of health insurance to people over 65. It also includes persons with kidney failure and certain disabled persons.

Medicare is run by the Health Care Financing Administration, not the Social Security Administration.

Review the section on Medicare in Chapter 4, "Life in the Slow Lane," to refresh yourself on the basics. Even with Medicare, you still have a significant cost burden to cover all of your healthcare expenses. You can take the risk of paying for everything not covered by Medicare out of your pocket. Or, you can opt to purchase a Medigap insurance plan. Either way, we're talking big bucks.

Many of the breakthroughs in healthcare that increase our longevity and improve the quality of life today are in the form of prescription drugs. They're often expensive and may have to be taken for the rest of your life. Medicare doesn't cover them. The better Medigap policies usually do. That's why the premiums are high and rising.

Even if Congress decides to include some drug coverage under Medicare in the future, it will be a low level. It will also have to be funded out of general revenues, not the Medicare portion of the payroll tax (1.45 percent of your gross pay). If the level is increased enough to cover a significant amount, you can be sure that it will be subject to means-testing. Thus, middle-income retirees will still need to pay for most of their prescription drugs on their own or through Medigap insurance.

Medicare will likely be redesigned before Social Security because its emergency condition is approaching much sooner. The debate will be loud, and the lobbying will be heavy, as the various constituencies (all of us) seek to be heard. We can hope that what comes out will be good in the long run for the people of the country. It won't be directly beneficial to wealthy retirees, early or not.

From the Hammock

Just thinking about our potential health care needs and wants in the future from the perspective of middle age is often enough motivation to stick to a financial plan all by itself. If you've watched elderly parents or grandparents lose their health care options because they ran out of money that would allow them to make choices, it's painful. And if the state of our health care system doesn't improve, it will be totally overwhelmed by aging baby boomers. Whether you agree with it or not, those who can afford to pay have a better chance of getting good care.

The Trust Funds

The *trust funds* that we hear debated in Congress and in the media are merely special Treasury bonds. Whatever cash surplus results from these programs each year is loaned to the government by the trust funds. The trust fund gets an IOU from the government, with interest, and the government spends the cash. In effect, the government owes itself the money. And we are the government; we'll pay this IOU to ourselves later by raising taxes or by issuing Treasury bonds.

Some of Part B of the Medicare expenses are already paid from the general budget. Thus, much of the money in the Medicare trust fund may be there only because of this budget maneuver. It, too, will quickly become exhausted as medical costs rise, as more people retire and live longer, and as the tax rate remains flat. So perhaps we should consider any discussion of a Medicare trust fund as an accounting fiction on the government's books.

The Disability Trust Fund has been bankrupt for years and has been "borrowing" from the Social Security Trust Fund. If other programs draw on the "big daddy" fund, it, too, will be reduced sooner.

Say What?

In any year that Social Security, Medicare, and other government retirement programs take in more money than they send out, the balance goes in what Congress calls a **"trust fund."** It's really only an accounting gimmick; the actual cash is spent through the budget process. We have to trust Congress to increase our taxes to pay this money out of the trust fund at a later date.

It's Been Said

"Lack of money is the root of all evil."

—George Bernard Shaw

As long as the cash flow for each program is positive and the government pays part of Medicare from the general budget, the books look to be in balance. However, when money is needed from any of the funds, the government swaps its "private" accounting debt to itself for real, public debt. It has to borrow through the Treasury to get the actual cash. When the trust fund balances read 0, the government will keep on borrowing, increasing the public debt. Eventually, taxes will be increased, if only to pay the interest and principal on the increased debt.

Long-Term Care Insurance

One option that you should consider when you're in your late 50s is long-term care insurance. The odds that you will require a couple years in a nursing home, or the permanent services of a home health aide, are not great. But, if you do find yourself in that situation, the expenses are very high. Medicare doesn't cover that level of care. Medicaid does, but only when you're essentially broke.

Depending on your location, costs for long-term care facilities run from $150 to $300 a day, or more for the fancy homes. That's $55,000 to $110,000 a year. In 30 years, you may be looking at $250,000 to $500,000 a year. If that devastates your nest egg before you die, what will remain for your spouse or heirs?

Long-term care insurance is fairly new and still evolving. Companies aren't sure whether they're charging enough because there's no solid experience to draw upon, and who can predict how we'll age in the future? Nevertheless, the federal government doesn't want your business (through Medicaid). Qualified long-term care insurance premiums may be tax-deductible for you. That's subject to a ceiling based on your age (the ceiling rises with age and premiums charged) and the 7¹/₂ percent Adjusted Gross Income floor for medical deductions on Schedule B of your Form 1040.

If you decide that you want a policy (you can usually get a 20 percent discount for a husband-and-wife policy), make sure that it has these characteristics:

➤ Has a 90-day waiting period (much lower premiums)

➤ Has a three- to five-year benefit period

➤ Includes home care

➤ Has a realistic per diem rate (at least $150 today)

➤ Has a compound annual inflation clause

Premiums are relatively cheap at age 50 ($400–$500 a year), but you'll likely be paying for years. They escalate rapidly if you wait until after age 60 to begin, and you do need to be in relatively good health to qualify. Sixty may be a good time to look into signing up. Your financial situation in retirement will be much clearer then. You can get quotes at www.quicken.com, and price guidelines are available at the American Health Care Association Web site, www.ahca.org.

Your other option is to self-insure. Find out the costs for a year's stay in a facility in your area, and put three years' costs in an S&P or total market index fund and let it grow. Don't touch it for anything else. It should keep ahead of the growth in the cost over the years. If you never use it, your heirs will be doubly grateful.

From the Hammock

The Health Insurance Association of America has a good policy checklist at www.hiaa.org for you to use in reviewing policies. AARP, formerly known as the American Association of Retired Persons, provides free guides on the whole subject, including "Before You Buy: A Guide to Long-Term Care Insurance." Write to AARP Fulfillment, 601 E St., NW, Washington DC 20059, and visit the Web site at www. aarp.org.

You're on Your Own

It's safe to say that both Social Security and Medicare will continue well into the future. The only question is what form they will take. If you are financially successful, whether you retire early or not, we suspect that these programs will not help you very much. You may see a small benefit, or you may not. You may also wake up one fine day and discover a new tax on wealthy, retired people to cover the government's expenses for these programs.

The money will come from somewhere, and you know that's "from thems that has it." There's a lot of speculation that many, perhaps the majority, of those 76 million baby boomers will not have enough money to retire. Yet, they *will* retire, sooner or later. The government will fulfill the role of providing the safety net, a minimal level of Social Security benefits and health benefits, to this huge number of aging boomers.

Your goal of financial freedom includes maintaining your options for this uncertain future. You will need to provide yourself with a comfortable income from your savings and investing. You will want to be able to afford good healthcare and have the option of what, where, and how you get it. That, too, will cost money.

Finally, if you find that you need to enter an assisted-living community, a continuing care facility, or a comfortable nursing home, or if you need to hire the necessary home healthcare, you want to have the money to make those choices. Those options already cost a lot today. They won't get cheaper in the future. The government, through Medicare, doesn't pay for them today, and the government won't pay for them in the future.

The Least You Need to Know

➤ When you retire early, Social Security and Medicare won't help at all, initially. Later, they may assist you in covering some expenses.

➤ As a wealthy retiree, your Social Security benefit will be taxed, and your Medicare benefit will be limited. Don't build your retirement plan around these programs.

➤ If you continue working part-time before your full retirement age, it probably isn't worth filing for Social Security. The penalty and taxes will eat up most of the benefit.

➤ Take your plan for financial freedom seriously. It's how you'll support yourself in retirement and how you'll preserve your options to get the healthcare you want.

Chapter 23

Your Estate Needs a Plan, Too

In This Chapter

➤ What a will can do

➤ Ways to hold property jointly

➤ The estate tax and what you can do

➤ Trusts can do more

➤ Powers of attorney can aid and protect you

Estate planning may be the final chapter in the book, but that's not because you should put it off until the end. You need to think of it as a vital part of your financial plan. You're not done until the estate plan is complete. On the other hand, when you're *really* done, you can no longer change your estate plan. If you put off doing your estate plan, you jeopardize your entire lifetime of planning and work.

You go through life working hard, planning well, and executing your plan to reach financial goals for you and your family. But it can all fall apart without a proper estate plan. When you die or are incapacitated, you want certain things to occur:

➤ You want to be sure that you are properly cared for.

➤ You want your spouse to know that protections are in place to ensure his welfare.

➤ You want your kids and grandkids to share in whatever is left.

➤ You may want to recognize other relatives and friends for their support, encouragement, and friendship.

➤ You may want a special charity or two to receive a gift from your estate.

The only way that you can be sure of these things occurring is through an estate plan. An estate plan protects your wealth so that it continues to serve you and your family as you intended when you are no longer available.

Wills and Won'ts

Sooner or later, as Shakespeare put it, we'll "shuffle off this mortal coil." Not knowing when you're going to die means that you need to be prepared in advance.

From the Hammock

We're paying close attention to the current debates in Congress over changing or eliminating the estate tax. We're sure something will change, but we have no idea what or when. Don't use this as an excuse to put off making a will—you'll still need that. But, if you're under 65, wealthy, and healthy, hold off on making any major estate plans until Congress manages to hammer out a new program in the next year or two.

It's Been Said

"In this world nothing is certain but death and taxes."

—Benjamin Franklin

A will is the critical first step in your estate plan. It's a written and properly witnessed document that directs your named executor in just how you want your assets distributed. Be sure that the executor, or co-executors, that you name are aware of the responsibility and are willing to perform this role.

You should also name a guardian or guardians for your minor children in your will. Be sure to discuss this with the guardian in advance. The court approves the guardian(s) following your death. In the absence of a named guardian, the judge will appoint someone.

You can change or rewrite your will at any time, as long as you are competent. A pair of witnesses who are not interested parties (heirs, for instance) to your will, or changes in your will, are important in the determination of your competence. If your will is challenged on the basis of your competency at a later date, a judge will prefer objective witnesses.

You should review your will every five years or so, or when there are major changes in your life. These changes include, of course, changing your mind. Other reasons to make changes or write a new will include these:

➤ A move to a different state

➤ Marriage, divorce, children, and remarriage

➤ Significant growth or shrinkage of your estate

➤ Changes to federal or state estate laws

Whenever you hear about changes in the estate laws at the federal or state level (and they can occur regularly), you should automatically contact your attorney for a review. And when you move, schedule an appointment with an attorney in your new state to see whether you need to adjust your will to conform to that state's laws. If you own property in two states, you need to have your attorney check for any applicable laws in the other state. That property is subject to the laws of the state it is situated in, and it will be probated there upon your death.

Probate and Lawyers

Probate is the processing of a will and your estate after your untimely demise (it's almost always untimely, isn't it?). When you die, all your assets and debts are under control of a special court, known as a probate court. The state probate court oversees the management and disposal of your property and affairs. Your executor finds and inventories all of your assets, pays all of your debts, and settles the remainder of your estate in accordance with your will and the laws of the state. State laws govern the entire procedure, and each state has a different set of laws and taxes.

Your executor does all the work under the watchful eye of the court. Lots of paperwork and forms, and the approval of the court for any actions, keeps an executor busy. You don't need to appoint an attorney as your executor, but your executor may want to have one to help steer through the maze. Co-executors, including your estate attorney, may be a good move, especially if your estate is large or complex.

With all the legal hoops and mumbo jumbo, it's advisable to have an attorney who specializes in estate law at least review your will. Better yet, take your best shot at writing down your desires, and then take that to the attorney. A thorough discussion will clarify what you want and conform those wishes to state law. Then let the attorney draw up the final draft for your approval. Have two people who aren't connected to the will witness your signature.

In the absence of a will, or a properly drawn will, the laws of your state will direct the probate judge on all the necessary decisions. The probate court

Say What?

Probate is the legal process to settle your estate. Your appointed executor notifies beneficiaries and heirs, and advertises for creditors to present their bills. The executor also files your personal and estate tax returns. Eventually, when all appears to be complete to the probate court, an Order of Distribution is granted, and your estate is distributed.

A Nugget of Gold

You may name more than one guardian per child, if you want. The first should be a guardian to take physical care of any children, to house and raise them on your behalf. The other guardian is designated to manage the child's property, the assets that you leave for support. The assets are usually left in a trust through the will. You may, of course, make one person the guardian and the trustee of the trust if you believe that the person can handle both jobs responsibly.

will appoint an administrator. Each state's laws determine who gets a piece of your pie.

'Til Death Do Us Part

Assets owned jointly with your spouse should have a "right of survivorship" provision. This is often designated on account names and documents as JTWROS— "joint tenants with rights of survivorship." In some states, married couples hold their property in "tenancy by the entirety, with rights of survivorship." In either case, the property passes directly to the surviving spouse without going through probate.

The nine states in the following list are governed by community property laws. All property acquired after the marriage (except by gift or inheritance by one spouse) is legally community property. This property is half-owned by each spouse. A will can dispose of the half-ownership only of the deceased, and only half is included in the estate. That half must go through probate. This could tie up disposal of the asset, such as a house, by the surviving spouse while the estate is probated.

From the Hammock

The probate process has acquired a bad reputation and one which it largely deserved. However, many states have reformed their probate process in recent years to reduce delays and the potential for abuse. When you set up your estate plan, take care in selecting an experienced estate attorney. Take equal care in selecting an executor. Together, these choices will go a long way in determining how difficult or easy the probate process is for your heirs.

Community Property States

Arizona	Idaho
California	Texas
Louisiana	Washington
Nevada	Wisconsin
New Mexico	

Under the laws of most states, the doctrine of "spousal election" may override a will. If your will fails to adequately provide for your spouse in the eyes of the law, the surviving spouse has the option to "elect against the will." Each state's law of election guarantees that a surviving spouse gets a reasonable inheritance. The amount is defined by law and is generally a third of the assets in probate.

How Should Spouses Own Property?

It usually feels right and proper that most assets are held jointly by a husband and wife, with rights of survivorship. It certainly makes life a little easier for the surviving spouse under otherwise difficult circumstances following your death. When your assets are relatively low, there's no reason not to do this.

Potholes

When property is jointly held, but without the right of survivorship provision, the undivided ownership share of the deceased is tied up in probate proceedings. Joint owners need not be married. Then the assets are usually held as "tenants in common." Until the deceased's share is distributed at the close of probate, the asset is effectively frozen. The living joint owner(s) cannot sell or otherwise dispose of the shares because the ownership is undivided.

Where ownership shares are specified, say, by percentage, each owner is free to dispose of his own interest in accord with the provisions of the ownership document. This is an instance of divided ownership. Spouses usually don't hold assets this way, but your will may specify divided ownership for your heirs.

There may be circumstances in which joint ownership is not the best idea. Take the case of a second marriage, with children from a first marriage on either or both sides. That's usually time to rewrite your will to make sure that all parties are taken care of as you wish.

A second issue to consider is the estate tax.

The Estate Tax

Under federal law, jointly owned property with right of survivorship automatically passes to the survivor upon the death of the first spouse, free of any tax. This is called the unlimited marital deduction. However, when the second spouse dies, a tax is levied on the full estate. This is the estate tax, and it could increase Uncle Sam's take beyond what is necessary unless you plan in advance of your death.

The Unified Federal Estate and Gift Tax is assessed on assets that you give to others during your life or after your death, through your will. It's a transfer tax on large estates. The two taxes are unified because they charge the same tax rates and have the same deductions.

Say What?

The **unified credit equivalent** is the total amount that you're permitted to give away in amounts over $10,000 per person per year without paying gift taxes (while you're alive) or estate taxes (after you die).

In 2001, the federal estate tax kicks in on amounts over $675,000. This amount is called the *unified credit equivalent*. It is scheduled to rise, in increments, to $1 million in 2006. However, there's activity in Congress to phase out the estate tax altogether. At the least, we expect the effective limit to be increased, over time, to $5 million or even $10 million. If so, this may not be an issue for any but the extremely wealthy.

A Nugget of Gold

A popular way to move part of your wealth (when you have some) out of your estate is through gifting. A married couple can give $10,000 each to any number of individuals per year without triggering the gift tax. Older couples use this technique each year to give money to their children or grandchildren. By using gifts, they can maintain the full amount of their exemptions to apply against the remainder of their estate.

The tax rates on amounts over the unified credit equivalent of $675,000 for 2001 begin at 37 percent. The rate rises to 60 percent on amounts from $10,000,000 to $17,184,000, and then drops to 55 percent over that. Clearly, the larger your estate is, the bigger the bite the taxman takes. And that's just the federal tax.

Except for Nevada, every state also wants a piece of your estate. Only a few states have a direct estate tax. Many states use what is called a credit estate tax. This means that they impose a tax on federally taxable estates (over $675,000 in 2001) that equals the rebate, or credit, allowed for a state estate tax. The estate may deduct the amount paid the state from what is due to the federal government. The overall tax doesn't increase; it just gets divided.

The 18 states listed in the following table impose an inheritance tax rather than a tax on the estate. The heir is taxed based on the value received and the relationship to the deceased. Close relatives pay the tax at lower rates than others. All rates rise as the value inherited increases. Inheritance taxes are imposed on very low levels of inherited value in most states.

States with Inheritance Taxes

Connecticut	Louisiana	New Jersey
Delaware	Maryland	North Carolina
Indiana	Michigan	Pennsylvania
Iowa	Montana	South Dakota
Kansas	Nebraska	Tennessee
Kentucky	New Hampshire	Wisconsin

Both spouses have a credit equivalent. However, when jointly owned property passes through the marital deduction at the death of the first spouse, the first-to-die spouse's credit isn't used. Upon the death of the second spouse, the estate tax applies to the entire estate after the surviving spouse's credit.

If you expect your combined estate (husband and wife) to be over the $2 million level in the foreseeable future, there are ways to use both of your unified credit equivalents. This can maximize the amount that you pass on to your heirs by minimizing the estate tax. The first step is to divide jointly owned property in more or less equal amounts. You'll need to do some paperwork to retitle property and accounts in individual names and to place them in proper trusts. Let's look at how trusts work.

Trusts

Two kinds of trusts exist. The first is a living trust, which operates while you're alive. You fund it by retitling some of your assets in your trust name. The second, called a testamentary trust, is created in your will and comes into existence when you die.

With a properly drawn trust, you can avoid losing your unified credit equivalent. Instead of passing to the surviving spouse, your assets in the amount of your credit are held in trust for the next generation. Your spouse can get the income from the trust and can apply for amounts of money for necessary expenses to maintain a standard of living and health. Your trustee should be understanding in these matters. But those assets are out of your spouse's estate and, therefore, are not subject to the estate tax upon death.

Living Trusts

A living trust, legally called an *inter vivos* trust, may be either revocable or irrevocable. With a revocable trust, you can change your mind, move assets in or out of the trust, or cancel it altogether. An irrevocable trust cannot be changed or canceled. If you and your spouse set up your living trusts properly, you can both take full advantage of the unified credit equivalent.

The revocable trust legally holds the assets, but because you control the trust, any income is taxed as if it were yours. The assets are part of your estate but generally avoid the probate process. An irrevocable trust over which you have no control of the assets or income is taxed separately. The trustee files the tax returns, but the tax rates escalate quickly to 39.6 percent. Most of these trusts are set up to allow enough control by the grantor (more than 5 percent of the income will do it) to get taxed at the grantor's personal tax rate.

Testamentary Trusts

Testamentary trusts take advantage of the unified credit, but because this trust is created through

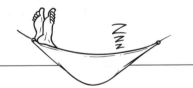

From the Hammock

Trusts are not a way to escape paying income or estate taxes. The trust is part of your estate. These tricky issues are what you pay the trust attorney to sort through when you set up a trust. No matter what kind of trust you use, you will require the services of an attorney who specializes in trusts and estate planning.

your will, the assets must go through probate. You will name a trustee—it can be you or your spouse, both of you, someone else, or a bank trust department—and a successor trustee, if you name yourself as sole trustee. The successor trustee manages the trust after your death for the trust beneficiaries as specified in your trust document.

You still need a will for any remaining assets not in a trust. This is called a "pourover will." The assets in your pourover will are subject to probate while the trust assets are distributed or managed by the trustee based on your trust document.

Finally, there are a number of other types of trusts that you may have a use for. Each serves specific purposes to manage and distribute your assets in simple and complex ways, as you specify. When you know what you want to do in a general way, the estate attorney that you select can explain how one or more might suit your purpose.

Charitable Trusts

You can use versions of trusts called Charitable Remainder Trusts (CRTs) to serve a variety of functions at the same time. With CRTs, you can do the following:

➤ Make a charitable contribution

➤ Remove assets from your estate

➤ Take an income tax deduction

➤ Get a stream of income for yourself or someone else, beginning now or later

At some future date, the charity gets the remainder of the money in the trust. A Charitable Remainder UniTrust (CRUT) allows you to make more than one contribution over time. The Charitable Remainder Annuity Trust is for a one-time-only contribution. Within these two formats of CRTs, there are variations and options that you can select to suit your needs.

A Charitable Lead Trust enables you to contribute an asset to the trust for a specified period. The income from the trust goes to the charity during that time. At the end, the ownership reverts to you or to a beneficiary that you chose. There's no tax deduction for the asset because you will regain ownership, but the income is a deduction and is not taxable to you.

With CRTs, your tax deduction is less than your contribution because of the income that you control. Some of that income is taxable. Both the amount of the deduction and the amount of income subject to tax are based on IRS formulas. The other big advantage to CRTs comes from donating highly appreciated securities. You owe no capital gains tax, but the full current value is your donated amount, and the income is based on that amount.

Many charities have established programs to take advantage of CRTs. You can pick the one that most closely fits your needs and desires. A few mutual fund companies, including Fidelity and Vanguard, have charitable gift funds. You make donations and take the full tax deduction when you make them. You can allow the money to grow in the fund, and you can advise the fund when to distribute the money, and how much to distribute, to the charities of your choice.

Other Options You Should Use

In addition to wills and trusts, you can arrange to manage your affairs in the future in two other ways: powers of attorney and healthcare directives. They can take effect when you become incapacitated and unable to make financial/legal decisions, or when you're unable to make healthcare decisions for yourself.

The Powers of Attorney

The powers of attorney that you may use are listed here:

➤ **A limited power of attorney:** This legal document authorizes someone to act for you in specified circumstances and for a limited time. If you die or become incapacitated, it ceases automatically. Therefore, it isn't useful in estate planning.

➤ **A springing power of attorney:** This document "springs" into effect only when you become disabled. You authorize someone to act on your behalf in defined ways.

➤ **A general power of attorney:** This one authorizes someone to conduct all your legal and financial affairs for you, but it ceases if you become incapacitated.

➤ **A durable power of attorney:** This is a general power of attorney with a durable clause stating that the power is not affected by your incapacity.

➤ **A healthcare power of attorney:** Called a healthcare proxy in many states, it specifies who may make medical decisions for you if you are unable to make them yourself.

From the Hammock

Make sure that the person you appoint as the decision-maker for your medical needs understands the nature and depth of your beliefs and feelings in these difficult areas. It is wise to name an alternate in case the first person is unable to serve as your agent, if the occasion arises.

In the absence of the proper power of attorney document, if you become incapacitated and unable to conduct your affairs, a probate court will appoint someone as your conservator and the guardian of your property. This may be someone other than your spouse. In such a case, your spouse may not sell, mortgage, or transfer jointly owned assets without express, written permission of the court-appointed person. If you'd rather have this power reside with your spouse or a trusted friend or other relative, a springing power of attorney should be executed as part of your estate-planning process.

Healthcare Directives

Most of the powers of attorney are intended to manage your legal and financial matters on your behalf. Advance directives, including the healthcare proxy or healthcare power of attorney, are designed to allow someone to make medical decisions for you if you become incapacitated. What specific directive you use is determined by the laws of your state. Under federal law, healthcare facilities that accept federal money, including Medicare and Medicaid, must advise you what medical directives are available.

A healthcare proxy specifies who may make medical decisions for you. Doctors consult with your designated decision-maker about your care and treatment options. This person is empowered to sign any medical consent forms relating to your treatment on your behalf if you are incapable. Of course, if an emergency occurs, treatment decisions are usually made by medical personnel on the scene without the necessary permission to attempt to save your life.

Potholes

What happens in cases of severe accident or illness while you're traveling out of state or out of the country? Even if you have a copy of your medical directive or living will available, it may not be valid in that jurisdiction. Emergency care will be given, and if your family can be reached back at home, the existence of a medical directive may be able to provide guidance to the doctors. It doesn't hurt to pack whatever documents you have when you take a long trip away from home.

A medical directive, such as living will, provides specific instructions on whether, and to what degree, you want to receive life-sustaining medical care. This comes in to play if you are in a coma or have a terminal condition and are unable to make these decisions. In states where a living will or similar directive is not recognized, your living will may still provide guidance to medical personnel and your family.

Your living will should be known to your spouse or other close relatives. They should understand ahead of time what you want and why. This will make it easier for them to accept the difficult decisions that you made and what you have directed the doctors to do when you're in an extreme condition.

Each state has its own laws, so if you move, be sure to check whether your new state recognizes the validity of your medical directives. You can do this when you have your will and estate plan checked over. If your living will isn't recognized in your new state, you might want to inform those who were familiar with your earlier directive.

As with financial planning, estate planning is an ongoing process. Once you have a plan in place, you need to review it and make changes when necessary.

We control few things in life, and we should make sure that we take advantage of those that we can. Otherwise, someone else—a judge, or a stranger appointed by a judge—will make the decisions for you. You and your family deserve more than that.

The Least You Need to Know

➤ A will is the basic requirement for your estate plan. Without a will, you give up control over much of what you have to the probate court and the laws of your state.

➤ Take care how you own assets jointly with your spouse. The laws differ from state to state, so understand what happens to jointly owned property when one spouse dies.

➤ When you're wealthy, good estate planning preserves much of your wealth for your heirs rather than giving the government a big slice.

➤ There are trusts to help protect and manage your wealth while you're alive as well as after you die. You can design trusts of many kinds to meet your needs.

➤ Powers of attorney and healthcare directives are two other ways to manage not only your wealth but also your health when you are unable to do so.

Financial Worksheets

See Chapters 6 and 8–10 for guidelines on using the following forms to calculate your retirement costs.

NET WORTH

Date: _____

	TOTAL	SELF	SPOUSE
ASSETS (what you own)			
Cash or Equivalents			
Cash	$_____	$_____	$_____
Checking Accounts	$_____	$_____	$_____
Savings Accounts	$_____	$_____	$_____
Money Market Funds	$_____	$_____	$_____
Certificates of Deposit	$_____	$_____	$_____
Savings Bonds	$_____	$_____	$_____
Life Insurance (Cash Value)	$_____	$_____	$_____
TOTAL CASH EQUIVALENTS	$_____	$_____	$_____
INVESTED ASSETS			
Retirement Assets			
IRA Accounts	$_____	$_____	$_____
Pension/Profit Sharing Plans	$_____	$_____	$_____
401(k), 403b, 457 Plans	$_____	$_____	$_____
Keogh Accounts	$_____	$_____	$_____
Annuities (Surrender Value)	$_____	$_____	$_____
Other	$_____	$_____	$_____
Investments			
Stocks	$_____	$_____	$_____
Bonds	$_____	$_____	$_____
Mutual Funds	$_____	$_____	$_____
Government Securities	$_____	$_____	$_____
Royalties	$_____	$_____	$_____
Rental Property	$_____	$_____	$_____
Business Equity	$_____	$_____	$_____
Receivables (Money owed you)	$_____	$_____	$_____
Limited Partnerships	$_____	$_____	$_____
Patents, Copyrights	$_____	$_____	$_____
Trusts	$_____	$_____	$_____
Other	$_____	$_____	$_____
TOTAL INVESTED ASSETS	$_____	$_____	$_____

LIFESTYLE ASSETS
Personal Property

Home	$_____	$_____	$_____
Vacation Home	$_____	$_____	$_____
Automobiles	$_____	$_____	$_____
Household Furnishings	$_____	$_____	$_____
Clothes and Jewelry	$_____	$_____	$_____
Antiques, Collectibles	$_____	$_____	$_____
Boats, RVs, etc.	$_____	$_____	$_____
Other	$_____	$_____	$_____
TOTAL LIFESTYLE ASSETS	$_____	$_____	$_____
TOTAL ASSETS	$_____	$_____	$_____

LIABILITIES (what you owe)
Debts

Medical/Dental	$_____	$_____	$_____
Taxes Owed	$_____	$_____	$_____
Educational Loans	$_____	$_____	$_____
Alimony	$_____	$_____	$_____
Child Support	$_____	$_____	$_____
Mortgage	$_____	$_____	$_____
Business Loans	$_____	$_____	$_____
Personal Loans	$_____	$_____	$_____
Pledges	$_____	$_____	$_____
Contracts	$_____	$_____	$_____
Mortgage on Rental Property	$_____	$_____	$_____
Home Equity Loans	$_____	$_____	$_____
Credit Card Debt	$_____	$_____	$_____
Other	$_____	$_____	$_____
TOTAL LIABILITIES	$_____	$_____	$_____

SUMMARY

TOTAL ASSETS	$_____	$_____	$_____
MINUS TOTAL LIABILITIES	$_____	$_____	$_____
NET WORTH	$_____	$_____	$_____

305

CASH FLOW

Date: _____

INCOME IN TAXABLE ACCOUNTS	Monthly	Annually
Salary	$_____	$_____
Salary/Spouse	$_____	$_____
Self-Employment Income	$_____	$_____
Social Security	$_____	$_____
Interest-Taxable	$_____	$_____
Interest-Tax-Exempt	$_____	$_____
Dividends	$_____	$_____
Rental Income	$_____	$_____
Alimony Received	$_____	$_____
Child Support Received	$_____	$_____
Other	$_____	$_____
Other	$_____	$_____
TOTAL INCOME	$_____	$_____

EXPENSES

Basic Expenses

Mortgage/Rent	$_____	$_____
Real Estate Taxes	$_____	$_____
Utilities	$_____	$_____
Telephone	$_____	$_____
Food	$_____	$_____
Clothing	$_____	$_____
Health Care	$_____	$_____
Medical Insurance	$_____	$_____
Homeowner Insurance	$_____	$_____
Homeowner's Assoc. Fee	$_____	$_____
Condo Fees	$_____	$_____
Other Home Expenses	$_____	$_____
Life Insurance	$_____	$_____
Disability Insurance	$_____	$_____
Auto Insurance	$_____	$_____
Auto Expenses	$_____	$_____
Auto Loan	$_____	$_____
Transportation	$_____	$_____
Work-Related Expenses	$_____	$_____
Childcare	$_____	$_____
Taxes: Fed, State, Soc.Security, Medicare	$_____	$_____

Alimony	$_____	$_____
Child Support	$_____	$_____
Misc.	$_____	$_____
TOTAL BASIC EXPENSES	$_____	$_____
Elective Expenses		
Dining Out	$_____	$_____
Entertainment	$_____	$_____
Personal Care	$_____	$_____
Vacations/Travel	$_____	$_____
Child Expenses (lessons, camp, sports, etc.)	$_____	$_____
Gifts	$_____	$_____
Charitable Contrib.	$_____	$_____
Membership/Dues	$_____	$_____
Subscriptions	$_____	$_____
Pet Expenses	$_____	$_____
Hobbies	$_____	$_____
Hobbies	$_____	$_____
Credit Card Payments	$_____	$_____
Other Loan Payments	$_____	$_____
Miscellaneous	$_____	$_____
TOTAL ELECTIVE EXPENSES	$_____	$_____
Other Expenses		
Educational Expenses	$_____	$_____
Home Repair	$_____	$_____
Other	$_____	$_____
TOTAL OTHER EXPENSES	$_____	$_____
TOTAL EXPENSES	$_____	$_____

SUMMARY OF INCOMES AND EXPENSES

TOTAL INCOME	$_____	$_____
TOTAL EXPENSES	$_____	$_____
DIFFERENCE	$_____	$_____

If the "difference in the preceding worksheet"—Income minus Expenses—is negative, your first priority is to find ways to make it positive in the near future. You're living on borrowed money. A positive difference is otherwise known as savings. Without aggressive saving, you have no fuel to propel your financial plan and reach your goals.

You can use your cash flow form to find where to reduce expenses so you can increase your savings. You will also use it as a basis for projecting your expenses in your first year of retirement.

307

Expenses for Year One in Retirement

Projected year _____

Expense Category	Current Cost	Inflation Factor	Cost at Retirement
Mortgage/Rent	$_____		$_____
Real Estate Taxes	$_____		$_____
Utilities	$_____		$_____
Telephone	$_____		$_____
Maintenance	$_____		$_____
Homeowner's Insurance	$_____		$_____
Homeowner's Assoc. Fees	$_____		$_____
Condo Fees	$_____		$_____
Other Home Expenses	$_____		$_____
Groceries	$_____		$_____
Dining Out	$_____		$_____
Clothing	$_____		$_____
Personal Care	$_____		$_____
Auto Expenses	$_____		$_____
My Auto Fund*	$_____		$_____
Auto Insurance	$_____		$_____
Vacations/Travel	$_____		$_____
Entertainment	$_____		$_____
Gifts	$_____		$_____
Charitable Contrib.	$_____		$_____
Memberships/Dues	$_____		$_____
Subscriptions	$_____		$_____
Pet expenses	$_____		$_____
Hobbies	$_____		$_____
Miscellaneous Other	$_____		$_____
Health Care Expenses Out-of-Pocket	$_____		$_____
SUBTOTAL EXPENSES	$_____	×_____	$_____
Add:			
Health Insurance	$_____	×_____	$_____
TOTAL EXPENSES	$_____		$_____

*My Auto Fund. In Chapter 7 we explain how you make monthly payments to your auto fund after you pay off your car loan so you can pay cash for a car the next time. You'll keep replacing cars every six to ten years, so this fund is a regular expense.

Life Insurance Needs Analysis

For our worksheet example below, we assumed a family of four, the major wage earner was the father, and spouse worked part time. They want to send their kids to college and pay off the mortgage if something should happen to one of them. You will need to do this for each spouse separately. To be accurate you will need to find out from Social Security what your survivor benefits will be. Call 1-800-772-1213, visit www.ssa.gov, or look at your last Social Security Statement.

We used 18 years for the lifetime living expenses to cover the number of years until the second child finishes college. An older couple whose children are through, or nearly through college, might use the number of years until the surviving spouse is able to retire.

Invest the lump-sum insurance settlement, after paying immediate expenses, in the wealth maintenance portfolio (see Chapter 12)—that is, 70 percent in an index fund and 30 percent in a U.S. Treasury bond fund. When you're within five years of paying a college tuition, move a year's college costs from the index fund to the bond fund to ensure that it will be available in five years.

Insurance isn't an investment. When you have calculated your additional need, and figured out for how long you will need the coverage, shop around for term insurance. You can buy 10-, 15-, or 20-year policies with a guaranteed premium. This is the best way to cover the expenses of raising your family in the event of the death of either spouse.

Life Insurance Worksheet

Expenses	Example	You
Immediate		
Funeral	$6,000	_____
Final Expenses	$2,000	_____
Subtotal	$8,000	_____
First Nine Months		
Probate Expenses	$2,000	_____
Estate Taxes	$4,000	_____
Mortgage Pay-Off	$50,000	_____
Subtotal	$56,000	_____
After Nine Months		
Emergency Fund	$15,000	_____
College Funding	$200,000	_____
Subtotal	$215,000	_____

continues

continued

Lifetime Living Expenses

Annual Living Expenses (from cash flow worksheet)	$60,000	_____
Less Mortgage Payments (if you pay it off)	–$12,000	_____
Less Spouse's Take-Home Pay (if spouse will work)	–$20,000	_____
Less Social Security Benefits (children's)	–$6,000	_____
Subtotal	$22,000	_____
Multiplied by Number of Years Needed	× 18	×_____
Subtotal	$396,000	_____
TOTAL EXPENSES	**$675,000**	_____

ASSETS (available for support of dependents)

Cash	$10,000	_____
Investments	$50,000	_____
Retirement Plans	$50,000	_____
Life Insurance Owned	$150,000	_____
Mortgage Insurance	$50,000	_____
TOTAL ASSETS	**$310,000**	_____

INSURANCE NEEDS (Expenses minus Assets)

Total Expenses	$570,000	_____
Minus Total Assets	–$310,000	_____
TOTAL ADDITIONAL INSURANCE	**$365,000**	_____

Insurance Notes

We used 18 years for the lifetime living expenses to cover the number of years until the second child finishes college. An older couple whose children are through, or nearly through college, might use the number of years until the surviving spouse is able to retire.

Invest the lump-sum insurance settlement, after paying immediate expenses, in the wealth maintenance portfolio (see Chapter 12)—that is, 70 percent in an index fund and 30 percent in a U.S. Treasury bond fund. When you're within five years of paying a college tuition, move a year's college costs from the index fund to the bond fund to ensure that it will be available in five years.

Insurance isn't an investment. When you have calculated your additional need, and figured out for how long you will need the coverage, shop around for term insurance. You can buy 10-year, 15-year, or 20-year policies with a guaranteed premium. This is the best way to cover the expenses of raising your family in the event of the death of either spouse.

Glossary

8-K form   An 8-K form must be filed by companies with the SEC when there are "unscheduled material events or corporate changes which could be of importance to the shareholders or the SEC."

10-K report   A detailed financial report that must be filed by a firm after the close of its fiscal year with the SEC. It includes extensive financial statements and reports on the year's operations, as well as thorough discussion of the business and its operations.

10-Q report   A detailed financial report that must be filed by a firm after the close of each quarter of its fiscal year with the SEC. It includes extensive financial statements and reports on the previous quarter's operations, as well as a thorough discussion of the business and its operations.

12b-1 fee   An extra annual fee charged by some mutual funds to cover costs of promotion and marketing, including the compensation of brokers who sold the funds.

401(k) plan   An employer-sponsored retirement plan that permits employees to divert part of their pay into the plan and avoid current taxes on that income. Money directed to the plan may be partially matched by the employer, and investment earnings within the plan accumulate tax-deferred until they are withdrawn. The 401(k) is named for the section of the federal tax code that authorizes it.

403(b) plan   Section 403(b) of the Internal Revenue Code permits employees of certain nonprofit organizations such as schools and hospitals to set up tax-deferred retirement plans. The plans are designed to compensate for the absence of profit-sharing plans at these organizations. Many such plans permit investments in mutual funds or annuities.

457 plan   Named after the Internal Revenue Code section 457, this plan is a tax-deferred supplemental retirement program that allows public employees to defer the lesser of $8,000 or 25 percent of their salary before taxes to a retirement account. The amount saved is tax deferred until the participants' funds are distributed to them upon separation from service. There is no penalty for receiving a benefit before age $59^{1}/_{2}$.

adjusted gross income (AGI)   Taken from the individual's income tax return, this term means total annual income, minus tax-exempt income, minus other "adjustments to income" such as deductible IRA contributions and self-employed health insurance premiums.

administrator   The person appointed by a court to administer and settle the estate of a person dying without a will, or the estate of a person whose will appoints an executor who cannot serve.

American Depositary Receipt (ADR)   A negotiable certificate held in a U.S. bank that represents a specific number of shares of a foreign stock. The ADR is traded on the U.S. stock markets.

American Stock Exchange (AMEX)   A private, not-for-profit organization located in New York City that handles roughly one-fifth of all securities transactions in the United States.

annual report   A document issued yearly by a corporation or mutual fund showing its financial condition at the end of its business year. It includes the results of operations for that year and a letter from the chairman or chief executive officer discussing the past year and, usually, the year ahead.

annuity   A series of regular payments, usually from an insurance company, guaranteed to continue for a specific time, usually the annuitant's lifetime, in exchange for a single payment or a series of payments to the company. With a deferred annuity, payments begin sometime in the future. With an immediate annuity, the payments begin right away. A fixed annuity pays a fixed income stream for the life of the contract. With a variable annuity, the payments may change according to the relative investment success of the insurance company. Annuities offer the advantage of tax-deferred compounding.

appreciate   When an item or property increases in value over time, it is said to appreciate; items that lose value over time are said to depreciate.

ask price   The price at which a dealer in the security is willing to sell at a given moment.

asset   Something with a monetary value, such as stocks, real estate, and accounts payable. Net assets are assets minus liabilities.

asset allocation   A strategy for keeping investments diversified. Fixed asset allocation plans set specific amounts or percentages in different areas and adjust the portfolio to match them. Active asset-allocation plans vary the allocation depending on market conditions.

back-end load   A fee charged by some mutual funds to investors when they sell shares, perhaps only if it is before a specified amount of time has elapsed since the shares were purchased.

balance sheet   A financial statement issued by a company describing its current assets, liabilities, and owners' equity at a given point in time.

312

balanced fund A mutual fund that includes both equities (stocks or convertibles) and fixed-income securities (bonds) in its portfolio, thereby attempting to gain both capital appreciation and income in varying degrees.

bankruptcy Personal bankruptcy is a legal option, but it costs money just to file. Chapter 7 bankruptcy eliminates all unsecured debt. Secured creditors repossess what you bought with the debt. Chapter 13 bankruptcy allows you to create a plan to pay all your debts and attorney's fees. You'll have an extended period of time to do this through the court.

basis Your cost, used in figuring gain or loss, when you sell a house or other property, such as stocks, bonds, or mutual funds. On real estate, basis includes the price that you paid plus the cost of improvements.

basis point One one-hundredth of a percent (.01 percent). The yield, or interest rate, of a bond is often stated in basis points. A yield of 5.5 percent is 550 basis points.

bear market A declining trend in stock markets.

bearish A bear investor thinks that the market is going to go down. This makes bearish the opposite of bullish.

benchmark You measure the performance of a mutual fund against an index that matches that fund's particular style. The specific index is the benchmark that the fund manager tries to beat. If no index is appropriate, the benchmark is the average of all other funds managed in that style. If no specific benchmark can be identified, use the S&P 500.

beneficiary The person or organization entitled to receive income or principal under the terms of a trust or a will. The person designated to receive the benefits of an insurance policy or a retirement plan such as an IRA.

bequest A gift or property by will.

beta A statistical measure of how volatile a fund or stock is compared to the S&P 500, which has a beta of 1.0. A beta greater than 1.0 means the fund changed by a greater percent than the S&P 500.

bid price The price that a dealer in a security is willing to pay at a given moment.

blue-chip stock There is no set definition of a blue-chip stock, but most people agree that it has at least three characteristics: It is issued by a well-known, respected company; it has a good record of earnings and dividend payments; and it is widely held by investors. Blue chips can go down, but because they are unlikely to go bankrupt, they are generally considered more conservative than holding a stock in small companies. Blue-chip stocks are usually high-priced and low-yielding. The term "blue chip" comes from the game of poker in which the blue chip holds the highest value.

bond An interest-bearing security that obligates the issuer to pay a specified amount of interest for a specified time, usually several years, and then to repay the bondholder the face amount of the bond.

bond fund A mutual fund that invests primarily in bonds.

bond ladder   A set of four or more individual bonds bought with maturities roughly equally spaced from 1 to 10 years.

bond rating   A judgment about the ability of the bond issuer to fulfill its obligation to pay interest and repay the principal when due. The best-known bond-rating companies are Standard & Poors and Moody's. Their rating systems, although slightly different, both use a letter-grade system, with triple-A as the highest rating and C and D as the lowest ratings.

book value   The net asset value of a company determined by subtracting the total liabilities from the total assets on the balance sheet.

bull market   A rising trend in stock prices.

bullish   A bull investor is someone who thinks that the market is going up, which makes bullish the opposite of bearish.

bypass trust   A flexible trust that takes advantage of the unified credit equivalent under estate and gift tax laws by allowing you to pass the full amount of the unified credit to your beneficiaries free of estate taxes.

capital   Wealth in the form of money or property owned and used in the production of more wealth or available to pay your expenses.

capital gain   The profit made on the sale of property or securities. A short-term capital gain is made on holdings held for less than a year; a long-term capital gain on those held for more than a year.

capital gains distribution   Payments to mutual fund shareholders of gains realized on the sale of the fund's portfolio securities. These amounts are usually paid once a year and should be added to the basis of your investment.

capital loss   The loss taken on the sale of property or securities.

capitalization   The total of a corporation's long-term debt, stock, and retained earnings on the company's balance sheet.

cash   A holding of a relatively stable asset denominated in currency terms. A mutual fund holding "cash" does not have a pile of dollar bills somewhere; the money is invested in interest-bearing short-term securities.

cash flow   The amount of money that a company generates. The figure differs from income because the income calculation includes noncash expenses required by accounting rules.

certificate of deposit   Usually called a CD, a certificate of deposit is a short- to medium-term instrument (one month to five years) that is issued by a bank or savings and loan association to pay interest at a rate higher than that paid by a passbook account. CD rates move up and down with general market interest rates. There is usually a penalty for early withdrawal.

certified financial planner (CFP)   An individual trained in all areas of financial planning who has passed a rigorous national certifying exam, who abides by a professional code of ethics, and who meets the continuing educational requirements of the professional organization.

certified public accountant (CPA)   An individual trained in accounting and taxation who has passed a rigorous national certifying exam, who abides by a professional code of ethics, and who meets the continuing educational requirements of the professional organization.

Charitable Lead Trust (CLT)   A trust by which the income from a property or investment is donated to a charity while the grantor is living, with the property or investment passing to other designated beneficiaries upon the grantor's death.

Charitable Remainder Trust (CRT)   An arrangement with a charity under which the trust pays income to one or more persons for the lifetime of the persons named. At some future date—say, at your death, or 10, 20, or 25 years hence—the charity receives the trust's assets.

churning   Selling a customer a new insurance policy to replace an existing insurance policy just to generate a new commissions. It also refers to a registered broker's improper handling of a customer's account—the broker buys and sells securities for a customer while intent only on the amount of commissions generated.

closed fund   An open-end mutual fund that has temporarily or permanently stopped selling shares to new investors.

closed-end fund   A company that sells a fixed number of shares in its portfolio of securities. The securities are managed within the fund. Shares trade in the market at a price that may be above or below the net asset value of the securities in the fund based on the supply and demand for the fund shares in the market.

COBRA   The Consolidated Omnibus Budget Reconciliation Act of 1985, a federal law that requires an employer to maintain enrollment for former employees in the group health plan for 18 months after they leave the company. The employee pays 100 percent of the premium plus 2 percent for the administrative cost.

codicil   An amendment to a will that must be signed and witnessed with the same formality as a will.

common stock   A unit of equity ownership in a corporation. Owners of common stock exercise control over corporate affairs and enjoy any capital appreciation. They are paid dividends only after preferred stock. Their interest in the assets, in the event of liquidation, is junior to all others.

compounding   You earn a return on your initial investment, and then you earn a return on your return, and so on, year after year.

convertible security   A bond or preferred stock that can be converted at the holder's option to common stock in a company at a fixed rate within some stated period of time.

co-sign   To take on the responsibility for debt repayment along with the person assuming the primary responsibility for loan repayment. If the primary debtor defaults on the loan, full responsibility for repayment of the debt falls to the co-signer.

coupon   The stated interest rate paid on a bond when it is issued at face value.

315

CPI (Consumer Price Index)   The CPI measures changes in consumer prices (food, transportation, housing, entertainment, medical care, and so on). It is published monthly by the U.S. Bureau of Labor and is used as a gauge for measuring inflation. The CPI is also used as a cost-of-living index.

credit rating   A measure of a bond's risk of not paying its interest or principal at maturity, usually stated in a letter system by credit rating agencies such as Standard & Poors or Moody's.

credit shelter trust   Sometimes referred to as a "bypass trust" or a "family trust." In a two will/two trust estate plan, the trust that is subject to federal and state estate taxes but sheltered by the first spouse's federal estate tax exemption in the estate of the first spouse to die, and that escapes estate tax entirely upon the death of the surviving spouse. The federal exemption (unified credit equivalent) will be gradually increased to $1,000,000 and will be phased in through 2006.

custodial account   An account set up for a minor usually with a bank or brokerage firm. By law, children cannot own securities directly. The account is registered in the minor's name using his Social Security number and is managed by an adult, the custodian, until the child reaches the age of majority. For children under 14, unearned income over $1,200 in the account will be taxed at the parent's rate and, after age 14, will be taxed at the child's rate. The assets in the account become the child's after that child reaches the age of majority, which is 21 in most states. This is sometimes referred to as an UTMA (Uniform Transfer to Minors Act) account, which is a law adopted by most states that sets the rules for administration and distribution of these types of accounts.

death taxes   Taxes imposed on the property that is transferred to another upon the death of an individual. Death taxes include the federal estate tax and state inheritance and estate taxes.

default   When a government or any other issuer is in default, it is unable to pay interest and principal on its debt.

defined-benefit plan   A "qualified retirement plan" that is designed to provide a specified benefit to all participants upon retirement.

deflation   A decline in general price levels; the opposite of inflation.

disclaimer   A renunciation or refusal to accept a bequest under a will or distribution under a trust, usually for tax-planning purposes. For instance, if a husband's will leaves all of his property to his wife outright, or to his children if she fails to survive him, she may want to disclaim the unified credit amount in order to prevent taxation of this amount in her estate upon her death. The disclaimed amount would pass as if the wife predeceased her husband—to the children, in this example.

discount   A bond is trading at a discount when its market price is less than par, or full value at maturity.

discount rate   The interest rate that the Federal Reserve Board sets for overnight loans to member banks.

discretionary income   Income that you get to choose how you spend. It's what you have left after you pay the income taxes due on it.

disinflation   A drop in the rate of inflation, a reduction in the rate at which prices are rising.

diversification   A technique for reducing investment risk. An investor diversifies by investing in several different areas. Disaster in one area usually doesn't affect an investment in the others. To diversify effectively, the investor must be certain that the areas are genuinely independent. A broad-based growth mutual fund is diversified in one sense because it covers many different sectors, but not in another because its performance depends on that of the overall stock market.

dividend   A share of company earnings paid out to stockholders. Dividends are declared by the board of directors and are paid quarterly. Most are paid as cash, but they are sometimes paid in the form of additional shares of stock. Mutual fund dividends are paid from earnings or from net capital gains from selling securities in the fund's portfolio.

dollar-cost averaging   A disciplined investment strategy requiring investing the same amount of money on a regular basis.

donee   A person to whom a gift is made.

donor   An individual establishing a trust, whether by declaration or indenture. A person who makes a gift.

Dow Jones Industrial Average   A stock market index. Despite its popularity, this index is not very reflective of the market as a whole because it is calculated by adding up the prices of only 30 stocks, all very large companies.

duration   A measure of a bond or a bond fund's sensitivity to interest rate changes; the percent by which the price will move for a given percent change in market interest rates.

Education IRA   An IRA for use in educational planning, although it's not really an IRA. A maximum contribution of $500 a year per student under age 18 can be made. Contributions are not income tax-deductible, but earnings accumulate on a tax-deferred basis and are tax free if used for education, including tuition, books, and room and board. There are income limitations for tax-free withdrawals.

equity   Interest in a corporation represented by shares of common stock; the company's net worth on its balance sheet.

estate   The assets that you leave to your heirs.

estate plan   A formal set of documents to manage your property both before and after your death for the benefit of you and your heirs.

estate planning   The process of analyzing your assets and liabilities, managing them effectively during your lifetime, and disposing of them at your death through a will to best serve the needs of your beneficiaries.

estate tax   An excise tax assessed against property transferred upon death by a decedent. This applies to property in the decedent's name alone, property jointly owned by the decedent and another, life insurance policies, annuities, pensions and other retirement arrangements, and certain lifetime transfers. Federal estate taxes range from 37 to 55 percent and are subject to a $675,000 exemption for 2001, which will increase to $1 million by 2006.

executor   A person nominated by the individual who writes a will to carry out the directions and requests in a will. An executrix, if it's a woman.

expense ratio   The percentage of the total assets of a mutual fund that is spent on the management and operation of the fund over the preceding year.

federal funds   Excess reserves that banks lend each other for short periods, often overnight. The Federal Reserve Bank sets the interest rate, called the fed funds rate, on these loans.

fee-based planner   A financial planner who is compensated by fees paid for services rendered. Fees can be charged on an hourly basis, or a flat fee can be charged for services. In addition, fees can be charged for asset management and commission income received for product sales and support.

fee-only planner   A financial planner who is compensated only by fees paid for services rendered.

fixed annuity   A contract sold by an insurance company that makes a series of regular payments for a guaranteed period, usually the annuitant's lifetime, in exchange for a single payment or a series of payments to the company.

fixed income   A general term for investments in bonds, certificates of deposits, and other debt-based securities that pay a fixed amount of interest.

front-end load   The sales commission charged at the time of purchase of a mutual fund, an insurance policy, or another financial product.

gift   A voluntary transfer of property from one person to another. Gifts can be given while you are still living to your children, grandchildren, relatives, other people, or charities, or they can be given after your death through your will.

gift tax   A tax on lifetime gift transfers designed to complement the federal estate tax system. Lifetime gifts are applied first against the $675,000 federal estate and gift tax exemption; gifts in excess of this amount begin to generate gift tax at the same rates as are applicable under the federal estate tax. An exclusion from gift tax exists for gifts of up to $10,000 per person to any donee during a single calendar year. A couple giving a joint gift can give a total of $20,000 to each individual per year, which is tax-free to both donor and recipient.

group insurance   A contract made with an employer or an association that covers a group of persons related to that association.

growth and income fund   A mutual fund that seeks to make shareholders' capital grow and also provide income. There can be wide variations in the relative emphasis on these two objectives.

growth fund   A mutual fund that seeks capital appreciation—that is, to make its shareholders' capital grow over time by investing primarily in stocks that increase in value. Dividends are a minor consideration.

guardian   A person who has the responsibility to care for a minor or an incompetent adult, or to control the property of such an individual, or both.

heirs   Those who inherit your property.

index   A benchmark against which financial or economic performance is measured. An index fund is a portfolio of the stocks that make up the particular index, in proportion to their market caps.

Individual Retirement Account (IRA)   A tax-sheltered account ideal for retirement investing because it permits investment earnings to accumulate tax deferred until they are withdrawn. The contribution limit is $2,000 per year, and penalties usually apply for withdrawals before age $59^1/_2$.

inflation   The rate at which prices in general are going up (usually quoted on an annualized basis). The Consumer Price Index (CPI) tracks many consumer goods; the Producer Price Index (PPI) tracks many industrial goods and materials. Inflation is a decrease in the value of money and is thought generally to result from an increase in the supply of money (both actual dollar bills in circulation and readily spendable money such as checking accounts.)

***inter vivos* trust**   A trust created while you are "among the living" (the Latin meaning).

intestate   Having died without leaving a valid will.

IPO   Initial public offering, a company's first public offer of common stock.

irrevocable trust   A trust over which the donor retains no rights to amend the trust, withdraw trust assets, or control the administration or distribution of trust assets. Irrevocable trusts are normally used for gift transactions and allow protective management of gifted assets for trust beneficiaries. A trust that cannot be changed or canceled during your lifetime.

issue   A term referring to descendants of an individual by blood. For instance, the issue of the donor includes the donor's children, grandchildren, great-grandchildren, and so on, and does not include the spouses of any of these descendants.

joint tenants in common   An account in which the two or more people participating have fractional interests in its assets. The interest percentage of the assets becomes part of each person's estate upon death.

joint tenants with rights of survivorship (JTWROS)   An account in which two or more people have an ownership interest and whose assets are inherited by the survivors upon the death of a participant.

junk bond   A high-risk, high-yield bond rated BB or lower by Standard & Poors, or Ba or lower by Moody's. They're issued either by relatively unknown companies or financially weak companies. Sometimes investment-grade bonds are downgraded by the rating houses to junk status due to current financial problems.

319

Keogh plan   A tax-sheltered retirement plan into which self-employed individuals can deposit up to 20 percent of earnings and deduct the contributions from current income. Investments within the Keogh grow tax-deferred until they are withdrawn. Withdrawals from the plan are restricted before age 59$^{1}/_{2}$.

letter of instructions   A memorandum of personal details that should be attached to your will with a copy to your executor and one for you so that it may be kept up-to-date. The letter of instructions should include such information as location of the will, location of vital documents, location of assets, employment or business information, and funeral and burial instructions.

liability   All forms of indebtedness for which an individual, family, or a business is legally liable.

living trust   Created by an individual who is living, to be effective during the maker's lifetime. The property is placed in the hands of a trustee to be managed by the trustee for the benefit of one or more individuals. This may be irrevocable or revocable.

living will   A legal document stating the maker's intention that extraordinary life-saving measures not be implemented to prolong the maker's existence if there is no reasonable hope of recovery from a medical condition.

MAGI   Modified adjusted gross income. On an IRS Form 1040, your adjusted gross income plus certain deductions that you're allowed to take are added back to determine your MAGI.

marital deduction   The amount of property that can be left to a spouse tax-free. The Economic Recovery Act of 1981 permits an unlimited marital deduction.

marital trust   Sometimes referred to as a "trust," a "Q-TIP trust," or a "power of appointment trust." A trust qualifying as a bequest actually passing to the surviving spouse and therefore qualifying for the estate tax marital deduction. Examples of marital trusts are qualified terminable interest property trusts (Q-TIP) and general power of appointment trusts.

market cap   The market price of the entire company, calculated by multiplying the number of shares outstanding by the price per share; also called the market capitalization.

market maker   A brokerage or bank that maintains a firm bid and ask price for a particular security and that stands ready to buy or sell shares at its quoted prices.

means-testing   Government programs and IRS provisions that are designed to phase out benefits at or within certain income levels use means-testing; you qualify for the benefit only if your income is below the specified level.

money market fund   A mutual fund that invests in short-term corporate and government debt and that passes the interest payments on to shareholders. A key feature of money market funds is that their market value doesn't change, which makes them an ideal place to earn current market interest with a high degree of liquidity.

mutual fund   An open-end investment company. Its portfolio is managed—that is, it buys or sells securities according to changing conditions. It sells new shares on a continuous basis and buys back (redeems) outstanding shares. Buy and sell prices are equal to the fund's net asset value (plus sales and redemption charges, if any). This contrasts with a closed-end investment company.

NASDAQ   The computerized National Association of Securities Dealers Automated Quotation system that provides price quotations of securities traded over the counter.

net asset value (NAV)   A mutual fund's assets (securities and cash) minus its liabilities, divided by the number of shares outstanding. For a load fund, this is also called the bid price; the price at which new shares are sold is the ask price, which includes the cost of the load. For a no-load fund, the NAV is the price at which you can purchase and redeem shares.

net worth   What a person owns, minus what he or she owes.

par value   In bonds, the face value; in stocks, an arbitrary value assigned to a share, primarily for bookkeeping purposes.

portfolio   Your collection of stocks, bonds, mutual funds, and other investment securities.

power of attorney   A legal document authorizing an individual to conduct the financial affairs of the maker of the power of attorney.

premium   For bonds, the market value amount above face value.

price/earnings (PE)   The price of a stock divided by either its latest annual earnings per share or its predicted earnings per share over the next 12 months. How many years of earnings are investors willing to pay for a share of the stock.

prime rate   The loan rate that banks advertise as their best rate—that is, the rate available to their best customers.

private mortgage insurance (PMI)   Insurance required by a lender when you put less than a 20 percent downpayment on a house. You pay for the policy to insure the lender in case you default on the mortgage.

probate   The process of proving the validity of the will in court and executing the provisions of it under the guidance of the court.

property   Includes cash, securities, real estate, and any other possessions.

prospectus   The document that describes a securities offering or the operations of a mutual fund, limited partnership, or other investment. It includes information that the SEC has determined necessary for investors to make an informed decision.

provisional income   Provisional income includes all your taxable income reported on a Form 1040, plus any tax-exempt income, taxable IRA distributions, taxable pension and annuity income, and 50 percent of your Social Security benefit.

proxy   A document requesting shareholders of a company or a mutual fund to vote for members nominated to the board of directors and changes in fees or operations. The proxy card instructs management on how your shares are to be voted.

qualified terminable interest property (Q-TIP)   A type of trust that will qualify as either a marital or a credit shelter trust, depending on whether an election to qualify the trust as a marital trust is made by the decedent's executor. An arrangement by which the surviving spouse has a right to the income from the principal for life but has no access to the principal. On the death of the surviving spouse, the property goes to such person(s) or organizations(s), as determined by the spouse whose property it was and who was the first to die.

ratio analysis   Methods of valuing a company and measuring its operations using comparisons of two or more items in its financial statements, often used over time to detect changes in the health of the company.

registered investment adviser (RIA)   By law, an individual or business that receives compensation of any form for advice or services related to money, securities, or any financial product must register with the SEC. The SEC does not approve or disapprove of the registered investment adviser's professional knowledge or practice. This designation simply means that the person or business entity has complied with the law and has registered with the SEC.

required minimum distribution (RMD)   The IRS requires you to begin taking required minimum distributions from your IRA and most other retirement accounts by April 1 of the year after you turn $70\frac{1}{2}$. The new rules, issued in January 2001, come with a chart specifying how you calculate the amount each year from age 70 to 115 and older. You take the total of the assets in your retirement accounts on December 31 of the previous year and then divide that by the distribution period factor for your age. At age 70, this factor is 26.2 years.

revocable trust   A trust over which the donor has retained the right to revoke the trust, withdraw any assets, or amend the trust at any time. Revocable trusts are often funded while the donor is living, to avoid probate costs upon the death of the donor. A revocable trust can be changed or canceled during your lifetime.

S&P 500   Standard and Poors benchmark indicator of 500 stocks, which tracks 400 industrial stocks, 20 transportation stocks, 40 financial stocks, and 40 public utilities. It is a market capitalization–weighted index often used as an index against which money managers measure their performance.

sector fund   A mutual fund that identifies a particular industry or area of the economy in its name. It invests at least 80 percent of its money in that area.

Securities and Exchange Commission (SEC)   A government agency responsible for the supervision and regulation of the securities industry.

Securities Investor Protection Corporation (SIPC)   Formed by the Securities Investor Protection Act of 1970, a government-sponsored, private, nonprofit corporation that guarantees repayment of money and securities to customers in amounts up to $100,000 of cash or $500,000 of securities per customer in the event of a broker/dealer bankruptcy or theft.

security   A certificate (usually book entry now) used as evidence of debt or ownership of property, especially bond or stock certificates. In general terms, a security is a stock or bond.

specialist   A member of the stock exchange who serves as the market maker in a particular stock. A specialist maintains an inventory of shares and then buys and sells as necessary to maintain an orderly market for that stock.

spread   The difference between the bid price and the ask price for a security, also called the markup.

stock market   An organized marketplace where securities are bought and sold on behalf of investors.

successor trustee   An additional trustee listed in a will, who can assume the responsibilities of trustee in case your initial trustee dies or is otherwise unable to perform the functions.

testate   Having made and executed a valid will.

TIPS   Inflation-indexed U.S. Treasury bonds formally called Treasury Inflation Indexed Securities (TIIS), but commonly called TIPS. The principal amount is adjusted each year for the previous year's inflation. The stated interest rate is paid each year on the new principal amount.

trust   Property held and managed by a person (trustee) for the benefit of another (the beneficiary). The terms of the trust are generally governed by a formal legal arrangement that the grantor has prepared when establishing the trust.

trustee   Person or organization entrusted to manage, administer, and distribute the trust for the benefit of the trust beneficiaries, in strict compliance with the terms of the document. Trustees are held to a high fiduciary duty of loyalty to the beneficiaries, as well as to reasonableness in investing and making distribution to trust beneficiaries.

umbrella insurance   Personal liability insurance protection that provides insurance beyond the underlying coverage of an individual's auto and homeowners insurance policies.

unified credit equivalent   An estate tax credit available against the federal estate or gift tax to offset the first $220,550 of federal estate or gift taxes incurred on any transfer or services of transfers for 2001 up to $675,000 (will increase to $1 million by 2006). It may be transferred at death or during your lifetime, and the entire amount of the transfers will be sheltered from tax by the unified credit. Taxable gifts are gifts in excess of the annual $10,000 gift tax exclusion for gifts to any single beneficiary.

unified tax credit   The amount that can be deducted from the gross estate tax. This deduction is applied against both estate and gift taxes due the government, thus shielding both transfers from taxation.

Uniform Gift to Minors Act (UGMA)   A legislative act that allows for a gift of money or securities to be made to a minor and held in a custodial account that is managed by an adult for the child's benefit until the child reaches the age of majority.

Uniform Trust for Minors Act (UTMA)   A legislative act that has been enacted in some states that allows for a gift of money or securities to be made to a minor and held in a custodial account that is managed by an adult for the child's benefit until the child reaches a stated age, not necessarily the age of majority.

value fund   Value funds hold stocks of good companies with lower PE ratios than the market. They patiently wait for the market to recognize the potential or the real value of these companies.

volatility   The nature of the market to go up and down. A standard measure of volatility over periods of one month to three years is the beta coefficient (beta).

will   A legal document, normally in writing and properly executed, that describes how a person wants property distributed after death and that designates an executor, the person or institution that will carry out the terms of the will.

yield   Income from an investment in the form of dividends or interest, not including capital gain.

yield to call   Yield to first call date, including any amortization of premium or discount.

yield to maturity   The yield, including the premium or discount paid on a bond amortized annually to maturity.

zero-coupon bond   Bonds bought at a large discount to face value that pay no interest. At maturity, the face value paid represents the compounded interest that was accruing over the period. The annual accrued interest is taxable every year in taxable accounts except for certain municipal zeros.

Web Sites

We're quite sure that everything you want to know (and a whole lot more that you don't want to know) exists somewhere on the Internet. This appendix lists Web sites on topics covered in *The Complete Idiot's Guide to Retiring Early*. There's a lot more than out there than the sites listed, but these cover the subjects well. As you no doubt have discovered, Web sites come and go, so some of these may have disappeared, merged, or changed names when you read this. Finally, remember that just because it's on the Internet (or in a newspaper, in a magazine, or on TV) doesn't mean that it's true.

General Web Sites

These sites cover just about any subject related to financial planning, retirement planning, and investing, as well as many other topics. Check them out, if you haven't already, and spend some time exploring them for the information you want.

Unless otherwise noted, "www." is the prefix for all.

fool.com	morningstar.com
kiplingers.com	quicken.com
money.com	smartmoney.com
moneycentral.com	yahoo.com

College Research and Aid Information

collegeboard.org—Information on college costs.

collegesavings.org—529 college savings plan network.

campustours.com—Virtual tour of more than 900 campuses, a college finder, and aid information.

ed.gov and fafsa.ed.gov—U.S. Department of Education site with information on aid programs.

embark.com—College preferences questionnaire to help in choosing a college.

fastWeb.com—Information on more than 3,500 scholarships.

finAid.org—Links to financial aid applications and cost calculators.

financenter.com—Calculators to help project future costs of college.

petersons.com—Information on colleges and aid programs.

review.com—*Princeton Review* site with full SAT, GRE, and MCAT sample tests.

salliemae.com—Leading supplier of loans for higher education.

savingforcollege.com—Information on all state 529 plans.

wiredscholar.com—Information on aid and scholarships.

Estate Planning

cof.org—Council on Foundations site. Information on foundations and links to them.

estateplanninglinks.com—Many links to related sites.

nafep.com—National Association of Financial and Estate Planning site. Free information on both subjects.

nolo.com—State and legal information.

philanthropy.com—Chronicle of Philanthropy site. Information on giving to charities.

savewealth.com—Wide range of estate planning information.

Financial Planning

calculators-financial.com—Many different calculators to use.

dcs.org—Debt Counselors of America. Debt and credit management and help.

directadvice.com—Online customized financial plans.

estrong.com—Strong Funds site, with a suite of planning tools to use.

fidelity.com—Information on a wide variety of topics.

financenter.com—Wide range of information on financial planning topics.

ihatefinancialplanning.com—ING Barings site, characterized as planning information with attitude.

morningstar.com—Free and fee-based information and tools.

nfcc.org—National Foundation for Consumer Credit. Debt counseling.

personalwealth.com—Standard & Poors site. Information on creating a plan, with some free and some fee-based stuff.

troweprice.com—T. Rowe Price fund site, with many good tools and calculators.

Insurance

insurance.com—Fidelity site for quotes from many companies and applications online.

insure.com—Background information on companies and complaints against them.

insweb.com—Complete insurance marketplace.

quickeninsurance.com—Quotes on all kinds of insurance from many companies.

quotesmith.com—Quotes on all kinds of insurance from many companies.

reliaquote.com—Quotes on all kinds of insurance from many companies.

Houses and Locations

aptguides.com—Local apartment guides.

BestPlaces.net—Great retirement locations.

harmonhomes.com—Local real estate guides.

realestate.yahoo.com—Local real estate listings.

realtor.com—National Association of Realtors site, with more than 1.3 million homes.

retirementnet.net—Retirement housing information.

Investing

Many of these sites offer much more than just the topic they're listed under. These are marked with an asterisk.

Investment Links Sites

company.sleuth.com

cyberinvest.com

investorama.com

investorguide.com

wrsn.com

Stock Information and News

bigeasyinvestor.com

bloomberg.com

*cbsmarketwatch.com

*cnbc.com

*cnnfn.com

*finance.yahoo.com

forbes.com

investools.com

*investor.cnet.com

marketguide.com

*moneycentral.com

*morningstar.com

nasdaq.com

bondsonline.com

*quicken.com

*smartmoney.com

thestreet.com

*wallstreetcity.com

Company Information

10kwizard.com

bulldogresearch.com

edgar-online.com

forbes.com

freeedgar.com

holtvalue.com

hoovers.com

sec.gov

starmine.com

stockdetective.com

Bonds

bondsonline.com

bondmarkets.com

bondpage.com

bondresources.com

bondtalk.com

briefing.com

Stock Screens

*stockpoint.com

zacks.com

Mutual Funds

brill.com

fidelity.com

fundalarm.com

indexfunds.com

mfmag.com

*morningstar.com

socialfunds.com

vanguard.com

Company Web Casts

bestcalls.com

investinginbonds.com

publicdebt.treas.gov

savingsbonds.com

streetevents.com

treasurydirect.gov

vcall.com

yahoo.com

Regulatory Bodies and Agencies

aicpa.org—CPA–Personal Finance Specialist organization site.

cfp-board.org—Certified Financial Planner Board of Standards site.

naic.org—National Association of Insurance Commissioners site. Links to state insurance regulator sites.

nasaa.org—National of Securities Administrators Association site. Links to sites for state securities regulators to check brokers in your state.

nasdr.org—National Association of Securities Dealers site. Tools to check the history of planners and brokers.

nasire.org/StateSearch/—Links to state revenue departments.

sec.gov—Securities and Exchange Commission site, the top regulator.

Retirement Planning

aarp.org—Many retirement planning services and information.

americanriver.com—Good retirement calculator that you can download free.

fidelity.com—Extensive information and tools.

finance.americanexpress.com—Overview of issues and interactive features to play with.

financenter.com—Expenses after retirement and more.

financeware.com—Retirement planning information and a financial adviser directory.

financialengines.com—Planning information and Monte Carlo portfolio test by Professor Sharpe.

ihatefinancialplanning.com—Comprehensive information, tools and planning help with an attitude.

ncoa.org—National Council on Aging site.

ssa.gov/retire/calculators.htm—Social Security site.

thirdage.com—Information for the over-50 set.

troweprice.com—Retirement-planning tools and calculators.

How Long You'll Live

beeson.org/livingto100/quiz.html

northwesternmutual.com/games/longevity

retireweb.com/death/html

ssa.gov/search/index.htm

Retirement Plan Information

fairmark.com—Advice on IRAs and taxes.

financialengines.com—Information on 401(k) plans; free initial Monte Carlo portfolio analysis.

irahelp.com—Ed Slott's IRA tax center.

irajunction.com—IRA information.

morningstar.com—Information and paid analysis of 401(k) plans and portfolios.

quicken.com/401kadvisor/—retirement calculators and Monte Carlo analysis of portfolio.

rothira.com—Information on Roth IRAs and conversions.

Social Security and Medicare

HFCA.gov/medicare—Medicare site for information on how it works.

ssa.gov—Social Security site for everything you need to know.

Taxes

1040.com—Information, forms, news, and links to state tax sites and the IRS Web site.

aicpa.org—American Institute of CPAs tax information.

el.com/dir/cat_taxes.asp?tree=126—Links to every major tax site listed here, plus updates, publications, and more.

fairmark.com—Online tax guide.

irs.ustreas.gov—A site that's surprisingly easy to navigate.

taxplanet.com—Tax guides, updates, and news.

turbotax.com—Quicken's tax site for information and online preparation.

Index

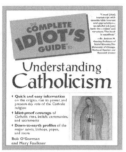

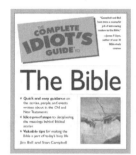

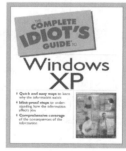